# Imaging in Corporate Environments

## McGraw-Hill Series on Computer Communications

# Imaging in Corporate Environments

## Technology and Communication

### Daniel Minoli

*Bell Communications Research, Inc.*
**and**
*New York University*

### McGraw-Hill, Inc.

New York   San Francisco   Washington, D.C.   Auckland   Bogotá
Caracas   Lisbon   London   Madrid   Mexico City   Milan
Montreal   New Delhi   San Juan   Singapore
Sydney   Tokyo   Toronto

651.5
M 666

**Library of Congress Cataloging-in-Publication Data**

Minoli, Daniel, date
   Imaging in corporate environments : technology and communication /
Daniel Minoli.
      p.    cm.
   Includes bibliographical references and index.
   ISBN 0-07-042588-4
   1. Document imaging systems.  2. Documents in optical storage.
 3. Information storage and retrieval systems—Business.  I. Title.
  HF5737.M56    1994
  651.5′0285—dc20
                                  93–46727
                                       CIP

1 2 3 4 5 6 7 8 9 0  DOC/DOC  9 0 9 8 7 6 5 4


ISBN 0-07-042588-4


*The sponsoring editor for this book was Marjorie Spencer, the editing
supervisor was Stephen M. Smith, and the production supervisor was
Donald F. Schmidt. It was set in Century Schoolbook by McGraw-Hill's
Professional Book Group composition unit.*

*Printed and bound by R. R. Donnelley & Sons Company.*

*For Gino, Angela,*
*Anna,*
*Emmanuelle, Emile, and Gabrielle*

*"...Musa, per l'imago del tuo bell core ..."*

# Contents

# Preface

Systems are now being deployed that permit the capture, retention, creation, manipulation, transmission, reception, and display of high-quality image material for both business and scientific applications. Such imaging applications have been implemented on a variety of computer systems, including, recently, desktop computers; these systems will soon be distributed and accessible across a local, regional, or nationwide distance.

Imaging is evolving rapidly in a number of fields, including medicine, banking, and insurance. This text provides an up-to-date assay of the imaging literature. It is directed at corporate managers who need to assess the potential business advantages of this technology but who do not wish to work through the heavy mathematics typically included in digital image processing textbooks. This book provides a mix of theory and practice, and just enough analytical methodology to understand the issues.

It is difficult to capture this dynamic field in a single book and it is not my intention to provide an exhaustive review of the subject. Rather, I have structured this text to:

1. Acquaint the reader with the technology, standards, and applications that will be the cornerstone of imaging in the 1990s.

2. Provide a foundation for understanding the trends and potential impact of image applications in business, education, healthcare, science, and related fields.

The word *Communication* in the subtitle emphasizes aspects of remote delivery of stored image information, whether across a local area network (LAN) in a building or campus, or a wide area network (WAN) covering a region, a state, or the nation.

Chapter 1 provides an overview of the field. Chapter 2 provides a discussion of how imaging systems fit in a corporate enterprise environment. Chapters 3 through 7 discuss the enabling technology required to support image applications spanning networks from desktop to wide area. The essential storage/compression standards that will be needed if image applications are to be adopted on a broad scale by businesses, government agencies, educational institutions, and libraries are also covered in these chapters. Chapters 8 and 9 cover aspects of image transmission and services that support distributed applications.

This material has been, in whole or in part, used for teaching imaging technology at New York University to students already familiar with communications. This text juxtaposes imaging technology and applications with supporting communications technology, thereby realizing a complete treatment of the field in one integrated text. In addition to its professional market target, I believe that this book can be used for an undergraduate or graduate course in applied imaging, particularly from an enterprise network perspective.

Tim Picraux, McGraw-Hill's technical reviewer, provided excellent and thorough feedback on the entire book and is hereby thanked for the much-appreciated support lent to this effort. The McGraw-Hill staff, in particular Stephen Smith, is acknowledged for its assistance and much-welcomed professionalism.

This book does not reflect any policy, position, or posture of any company. The writing of this book was not funded by any company or institution. All ideas expressed are strictly my own. Data pertaining to the public switched network are based on the open literature, and were not reviewed by the Bell Operating Companies or by the interexchange carriers. Vendor products, services, and equipment are mentioned solely to document the state of the art of a given technology, and the information has not been counterverified with vendors. No material contained in this book should be construed as a recommendation of any kind.

*Daniel Minoli*

# Imaging in
# Corporate
# Environments

# Introduction and Overview

## 1.1 An Overview of Imaging

*Imaging* (also known as *electronic imaging*) refers to the digitization of information embedded on a physical source such as paper, photographic film, or photographic print, or information generated in real time by way of TV programming, videocameras and other video sources, X-ray scans, CAT (computer-aided tomography) scans, MRI (magnetic resonance imaging) scans, PET (positron emission tomography) scans, and digital subtraction angiography scans, for computerized processing, access, display, storage, distribution, and archival.[1] Proponents claim that up to 50 percent of all office paper may be suitable for archiving through imaging methods. They call the 1990s the "age of image management integration."[2] There already is an extensive body of literature on imaging: for example, a 1992 bibliography showed over 1500 key papers while not even focusing on image analysis (e.g., pattern recognition), for which there is an equally extensive body of scientific research.[3]

This chapter surveys key facets of the imaging field in order to set the stage for the assessment of the industry and its potential for corporate applicability, which is undertaken in this text. Imaging can be defined as the combination of capture, compression, storage, transmission, and display functions. Issues pertaining to the compression of information, such as algorithms and related efficiencies, play an important role. At the hardware level an imaging system typically consists of (1) scanning station(s) for the capture of information, (2) the computer-based imaging system itself, and (3) local or remote output devices (e.g., a display station or printer). Imaging is the process of (1) obtaining or creating digital image data from a paper document, graphic, or video source; (2) performing optional compression of the data; and (3) storing the information in electronic or optical memory. The stored data can be accessed by a computer and directed to an output device for visualization. The size of uncompressed files for digital images ranges from about 1 MB for on-screen viewing only to 40 MB for magazine quality; compression plays a vital role, as discussed throughout this text.

Image communication (transfer) is rapidly emerging as an important business application of the 1990s in the insurance, banking, medical, publishing, and scientific communities, to list just a few areas.[4] Initially, communication capabilities have been targeted to a building or campus; requirements for wide area communication are now emerging. Businesses and governments are turning to imaging to improve the productivity and effectiveness of office workers. Document imaging is seen as a way to reduce the paper load in the office, as well as increasing the efficiency of the corporation in support of such 1990s goals as "expedited time-to-market," "just-in-time inventory," "customer service and customer focus," and "information-based marketing." Until recently, imaging was a niche technology; now there is increasing interest in this technology on the part of *Fortune* 1500 and *Fortune* Service 1500 companies. Just looking at LAN (local area network)–based imaging, U.S. sales are expected to grow from $0.9 billion in 1992 to $2.0 billion in 1995.[5] It is reported that most *Fortune* 500 companies have at least a pilot imaging program.[6] At the application level imaging includes document management, engineering document management systems, desktop publishing, medical applications, scientific visualization, and geographic information systems.

The financial services industry and the government are the largest market for business imaging at this time; other industries are in the process of introducing the technology, notably, legal, health care, and manufacturing. Actual applications include medical records, patient accounting, facility management, customer service, and regulatory compliance, to list just some of the key examples. Although small companies have not acquired this technology in any substantial manner thus far, they have shown interest for possible future deployment.[7] Potential corporate interest in the technology is demonstrated by the fact that over 33,000 individuals attended a recent show and conference of the Association for Information and Image Management, where over 350 suppliers exhibited products and services.

Microform (e.g., microfiche) now in place in many organizations is analog-based;* copying the document just a few times introduces

---

*Some vendors are upgrading micrographic systems with hybrid electronic tools such as computer output microfilm (COM) and computer-assisted retrieval (CAR); however, these are still based on analog techniques.

degradation. Digital imaging, on the other hand, allows the document to be copied as many times as needed. Some of the business advantages of electronic imaging systems compared to manual procedures are[8]

- Reduced storage costs.
- Increased productivity (including faster document delivery and electronic access to documents).
- Reduced cost of making quality copies for distribution.
- Reduced chance of document loss.

Besides governmental agencies, the banking industry and the insurance industry, in that order, are considered by experts to be the most paper-intensive industries in the services segment. Surveys show that the more paper an organization processes, the more likely it is to invest in imaging. Companies are looking for a technology that can solve both tactical and strategic objectives: imaging helps organizations downsize (now also called "rightsize") the office, eliminate paperwork, and reengineer work processes, while leveraging technology as a strategic tool to increase revenues and respond quickly to customer needs and business opportunities.[6]

According to proponents, office productivity is expected to soar as the capture, storage, manipulation, and retrieval of document images are computerized with imaging techniques.[9] Workflow will be streamlined, with significant reductions in paper and storage costs. The key question, however, is whether business imaging systems will allow industries, such as the banking and insurance industries, to benefit from image processing without having to sacrifice their previous software investment.[2] Others remain more cautious about automation: U.S. companies are spending more than $100 billion annually for office automation of all kinds, including, for example, $15,000 workstations ($25,000 per seat when including the server) used in some cases mostly to read text-based e-mail (electronic mail). These managers contend, according to a recent *Harvard Business Review* study, that high-tech innovations have not substantially improved office productivity, when productivity is measured using well-defined specific metrics (e.g., cost of clearing a check).[9]

At the technology level, much progress is being made in the imaging field. Imaging devices include flatbed scanners; optical character recognition (OCR) systems; facsimile machines; gray-scale* and color printers; medical X-ray scanners; X-ray film printers; digital video cameras; and red, green, blue (*RGB*) color monitors. Color and continuous-tone*

---

*These terms are defined in Chap. 3.

(gray-scale) scanning is possible at the desktop, supporting the corporate growth in desktop publishing.[10] The decreasing cost of scanners (including color scanning), the availability of high-density optical storage technology (in terms of both read-only disks and write-one read-many disks), efficient data compression/decompression hardware and software, and the emergence of high-speed communication systems at both the premises-campus level and the wide area level are fueling an expansion of this field and the rapid introduction of the technology in the corporate landscape. Observers now see imaging as a maturing technology; some degree of standardization is also beginning to appear, facilitating further integration and synergy.[11] Color-based creation and printing are beginning to enter the end-user market. Color is very common in the graphic arts and in magazine publishing. Observers expect rapid emergence of color imaging in the office environment in the next few years.

Optical storage media can store large amounts of information. CD-ROMs (compact-disk read-only memory) store 0.6 GB (about 16,000 compressed 40-kB business documents); 12-in WORM (write-one read-many) disks can store 6 GB (about 160,000 40-kB business documents). One way of appreciating this is that 16,000 documents are the equivalent of four file cabinets (160,000 documents equate to 40 file cabinets). A typical CD-ROM jukebox stores 25 disks (400,000 documents or 100 file cabinets, while the jukebox needs less space than a single file cabinet). A jukebox with fifty 12-in disks can store the equivalent of 8 million documents or about 2000 file cabinets. Jukeboxes storing as many as 250 disks are appearing on the market. Figure 1.1 compares the storage capacity of optical media. At the document level, scanning a document for storage in a WORM disk typically costs 10 to 30 cents per page, including quality checking and verification.[12] There were over 2 million CD-ROM drives attached to PCs, Macintosh systems, UNIX workstations, and PC networks at press time.

The cost of imaging systems with a write capability (scanner, CD-ROM drive, workstation with color monitor, and printer) ranges from $20,000 for an entry-level standalone unit, to $150,000 for LAN-based systems with a jukebox. A station with scan/retrieve capabilities for production-mode use (e.g., in a large law firm) costs in the $25,000–$80,000 range; a retrieval-only terminal for production-mode use, which is part of a larger system, costs in the $10,000 range. A full-blown high-production system can cost from $0.5 million to several million dollars.

Portable PC/CD-ROM systems (Diskman, Bookman, DynaVision/Scenario, etc.) have recently reached the market. Notebook computers now also come with CD-ROM components fitting the same footprint and adding a minimum of weight; 80386SX, 80486SX, 80486DX, and 80486DX2 notebook systems with CD-ROM drives can now be pur-

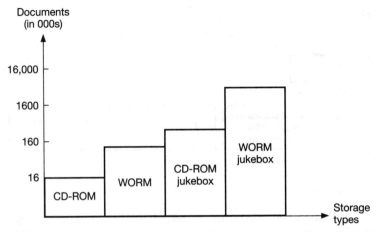

**Figure 1.1**  Comparison of storage capabilities for common storage arrangements.

chased for $2500 to $5000.[13] Notebooks can be outfitted with up to 130 MB of internal magnetic-disk memory and 20 MB random-access memory (RAM); some offer color liquid-crystal display (LCD) and/or can be connected to super-VGA (video graphics adapter) monitors. These notebook systems are used by a range of professionals needing CD-ROM databases and/or imaging on-the-go, including attorneys, stock brokers, physicians, emergency response teams, and field service engineers.[14]

Business documents today usually contain more than just text. Graphics, tables, company or other logos, and photographs may be present. Some are redefining documents to include multimedia "body parts," such as speech (voice annotations), music, and video clips. The assessment of the technology included in this book does not cover multimedia documents; the interested reader is referred to a recent text by the author.[15] Even without considering multimedia, documents can consist of highly complex mixtures in which not only the information content but also the format, layout, and appearance of the information are important.[16] This type of text is called *rich text,* and a document with rich text is also known as a *compound document.* To deal with rich text one must be concerned about type size, font, kerning, and proportional spacing.

## 1.2  Categories of Imaging Applications

At the application level, imaging can be classified as "low-end" business applications in the banking, insurance, and financial services sectors, among others, and "high-end" scientific and medical applications. Image processing was initially based on paper sources, but more

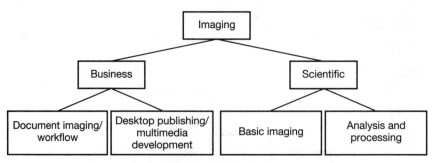

**Figure 1.2**  A simple taxonomy of imaging subdisciplines.

recently, as multimedia is beginning to experience more widespread deployment, image processing from video sources, such as TV programming, is also entering the field. Hence, in this text we look at two aspects of imaging technology, communications and applications (see Fig. 1.2):

- Business applications, typically involving low- to midrange resolution. Business applications of imaging are also known as *document image processing* (DIP). The typical size of a document in compressed image form is 40 kB. ITU-T Group IV encoding generates about 1 MB for a business document. Its compression scheme can reduce the document to 55 kB; if the document contains more than the "reference" amount of white space, as many business documents in fact do, it can actually be reduced to 30 to 40 kB. Note that if the content of a simple document could be interpreted (i.e., use optical character recognition technology), then it would be only about 3 to 4 kB.

- Scientific applications involving high resolution (e.g., medical imaging and engineering applications such as computer-aided design).

Business imaging can be further subdivided into (1) document imaging and (2) desktop publishing and multimedia development. There is a different emphasis in processes, goals, and tools between document imaging in workflow contexts versus imaging in desktop publishing and multimedia development. Scientific imaging can be further subdivided by considering (1) basic imaging aspects and (2) analysis and processing.

Pursuant this discussion, for the purpose of this text, we classify imaging systems as follows:

- BISs: business imaging systems
- DISs: desktop imaging systems

- EISs: engineering imaging systems
- SISs: scientific imaging systems

BISs typically convert paper documents to an electronic bitmap (raster format). Usually they support black-and-white (gray-scale) images, although some also deal with color images. EISs typically involve drawn (vector) images [say, from computer-aided design/computer-aided manufacturing (CAD/CAM) systems]. DISs support desktop publishing (DTP) functions. Medical imaging is considered here to be a SIS. EISs, DISs, and SISs usually support color images, although some also deal with black-and-white (gray-scale) images, for example, for some medical imaging systems. Specifically, some typical imaging systems that have actually been deployed commercially include[8]

1. Document transfer between branch banks and main office.
2. Medical X-ray transfer between hospitals.
3. Three-dimensional reconstruction of seismic data for scientific visualization.

Business imaging is relatively straightforward at the conceptual level; a document is scanned and stored in some kind of computerized media (typically, optical media). The document can then be retrieved from storage for display, printing, or transmission. This type of application is related to archiving functions. It is now possible to develop corporate databases of black-and-white as well as color images that can be accessed by every employee in the corporation.[10] Many companies are putting the technology to work to monitor and control the route a document takes through the corporation. This often leads to workflow reengineering and streamlining.

Organizations are now able to introduce imaging systems without having to redevelop existing information management systems; the imaging system can be integrated with these existing business applications. For example, many banks are looking at image management as a way to complete mortgage applications more quickly than the competition, and to allow existing staff to handle more work in less time, at the same or improved level of quality.

Some practical issues to be considered for BISs are

1. Scanning generates separate image pages in the case of a multipage report. Hence, a way to build folders encompassing the entire document is needed.
2. A supporting database (server) is needed to store retrieval information. Sophisticated retrieval algorithms also may need to be supported.

3. The issue of how to address the multitude of files that may be stored on a WORM jukebox must be resolved in a DOS environment where file names are only allowed to have eight characters.

Image transfer occurs when the image information is moved from one storage and/or display device to another. Typical image transfer applications include medical imaging, engineering product design, secure image analysis for military purposes, and insurance claims processing. Image transfers typically require large communication bandwidths for movement of files representing images of X rays, three-dimensional CAD/CAM graphic images, etc. Table 1.1 provides a synopsis of the functions of a full-blown business imaging system from a functional perspective.

According to proponents, CD-ROM technology in general, and CD-ROM-based imaging in particular, can result in cost reduction, revenue generation, and efficiency for the corporate user.[17] Some of the advantages of even a *basic business imaging system* include

- Improved access to records.
- Decreased physical storage space.
- Decreased document management responsibility (e.g., physical security from theft, fire, and flood; filing chores; off-site storage).
- Easy duplication, distribution, and utilization (e.g., inclusion into another document).

## 1.3    Imaging Platforms

The past few years have seen improvements in scanner technology, optical storage, and communication services, making imaging more amenable to introduction in the corporate environment. These technological improvements make document image processing cost-effective compared to other methods of handling the information.[16] A number of vendors offer imaging across a range of platforms. Imaging platforms include

- Desktop imaging systems.
- Departmental/LAN-based imaging systems (also known as *workflow implementations*).
- Mainframe-based imaging systems.

The most basic business imaging system is a personal computer with a scanner, a printer, and large storage, typically in the form of optical disks. The scanner digitizes the document by converting the reflected

**TABLE 1.1    Key Functions of an Imaging System**

| | |
|---|---|
| Scanning station | Converts document into compressed data files and transmits them (typically over a LAN) to a shared-image database |
| Premises connectivity | Enables access to information; well-tuned LANs (e.g., LANs with small segments, because of capacity requirements—a process known as *microsegmentation*), can be used to support connectivity between the scanning station and the imaging system or archive |
| Data storage | Information repository: large data files generated by scanning the document or other source are archived in storage devices such as redundant arrays of inexpensive disks (RAIDs) or optical jukeboxes |
| Optical character recognition | The process of analyzing images of text and converting the image data into text data |
| Application services | Imaging and nonimaging applications are required to capture, compress, store, manipulate, display, transmit, and share imaging data |
| Full text services | Image information can be converted to a text file, indexed by keywords, and stored; it can be searched either by index, image, or text methods |
| Display station | A station of adequate resolution for the task at hand is required; this may be a PC or a workstation |
| Printing | Standard (300-dpi) or high-resolution (600-, 1200-, 2400-dpi) printers are usually needed |
| Workflow services | Imaged documents are delivered over a LAN using workflow software that tracks the documents over preprogrammed function-based paths |
| Telecommunication services | Existing and/or evolving communication services are required to support distributed imaging; the telecommunications service selection depends on the type of material being transmitted, the desired resolution, the transmission time, and the expense that can be sustained |

light into a digital stream. Software- or hardware-based compression occurs next, in order to reduce the amount of memory needed to store the document. An operator may enter information into an index in order to be able to identify and retrieve the image at a future date. Following this step the image can be reviewed, and if needed, printed, edited, and transmitted.

In practical business terms, most systems in use today are on small LANs and are yet to be used for true workgroup applications.[5] These systems are used principally for archival and retrieval functions. According to some observers, this is because the supporting network technology is not yet developed to the point where the bandwidths required to transmit (high-resolution) images can be obtained in a cost-effective manner. Compression algorithms and support hardware are critical to the viability of imaging technology at both the storage level and communication levels, since image objects are large; while a business document is around 40 kB (0.04 MB), a digitized color picture at 35-mm resolution requires about 10 MB. It follows that compression schemes are the only hope for widespread deployment of digital video in general, and image technology in particular.

Workflow imaging implementations are multiuser systems that include storage and retrieval functions, as well as the capability to control document routing, and monitor system activities and performance. These systems can be deployed in a LAN or departmental (minicomputer) environment. They can also be found in mainframe-based environments. These systems were first available in the late 1980s. Workflow-based document routing has the advantage of reducing or even eliminating processing delay; for example, several employees can review and act on the same document simultaneously. In some corporations, a given document is handled manually up to a dozen times before the transaction (e.g., an insurance claim) is completed. In addition to the labor involved, the flow through such a company process can require weeks.

Fully automated imaging platforms enable users to combine client-server applications with access to information residing on multiple platforms, obviating the need to manually retrieve and process stored images. Imaging systems can interoperate and/or interface with existing business applications and databases. Many vendors support hybrid environments in which microfilm can coexist with electronic imaging. Many systems include a fax (facsimile) gateway that converts incoming faxes into images and outgoing images into faxes; this enables users without fancy scanning and display stations to have access to imaging services. Typical business systems use ITU-T Group IV fax compression, not (yet) the Joint Photographic Expert Group (JPEG) standard. Scanning speed of about 10 pages per minute can be supported, but that is not the true "shelf to shelf" speed, as many documents need preprocessing and preparation. Also, there are scanners that can scan both sides of the page simultaneously.

Well-known commercial document imaging systems that have been deployed in the past few years include the following:

- Digital Equipment Corporation's Image Express
- Eastman Kodak's KIMS 4000

- FileNet Corporation's document imaging systems: WorkFlow Business System and FolderView
- Hewlett Packard's Advanced Image Management System (AIMS)*
- IBM's ImagePlus
- Image Business System's ImageSystem
- Unisys' InfoImage
- Wang† Open/Image and Wang Integrated Imaging System (WIIS)

A look at the document imaging market in terms of the monetary value of the installed equipment shows that IBM holds nearly 50 percent, Wang 14 percent, FileNet 10 percent, and all others (including DEC, HP, LaserData, Metafile Information Systems, Sigma Imaging Systems, TRW, and Unisys) the remaining 26 percent. As for the market in terms of the number of systems deployed, IBM holds about 40 percent, FileNet 29 percent, Wang 14 percent, and all others 17 percent. Table 1.2 provides some cost information on a number of products on the market at press time for illustrative purposes. It should be noted, however, that different products have substantially different features, making the comparison difficult without looking at the specifics. One generic observation is that multiuser document imaging systems range from $50,000 to several hundred thousand dollars, depending on the features and number of users.

Most LAN-based commercial image applications on the market today utilize Microsoft Windows Graphical User Interface (GUI). Commercial customers are demanding such support of the imaging systems vendors.[5] Today, imaging systems are mostly in support of local

---

*Now marketed by Plexus.
†Wang filed for Chapter 11 bankruptcy protection in 1992.

TABLE 1.2    Some Imaging Systems on the Market at Press Time (Partial List) to Document Typical Early 1990s Costs

| System | Users | Access | Cost, in $1000 | | |
|---|---|---|---|---|---|
| | | | Hardware | Software | Total |
| FileNet: FileNet | Multiple | LAN | 136 | 222 | 358 |
| LaserData: Laser View | Single | | 35 | 10 | 45 |
| LaserData: Laser View | Multiple | PC LAN | 104 | 22 | 126 |
| Micro Dynamics: MARS | Multiple | AppleTalk | 140 | 58 | 198 |
| Techknowlogy: TIOS | Multiple | PC LAN | 76 | 31 | 107 |
| Wang: Open/Image | Multiple | PC LAN | 102 | 57 | 159 |

applications. Remote distribution of information is done with "removable" media such as tape, CD-ROMs, and WORMs. With the advent of broadband networking services, more distributed (networked) systems will come into place. Users that actually have implemented business imaging systems in their companies note, however, that the cost of the technology is not trivial for the following reasons:[11]

- Scan volume can be high.
- Storage cost can be high (200 dpi vs. 300 dpi, halftone, color, etc.).
- The computing environment (servers, etc.) is not trivial.
- Workstation video and memory requirements are fairly high.
- Lack of true standards (multitude thereof?) locks the user in with a vendor or small set of vendors.
- Backing up optical disks is a significant task.
- Integration with other data systems is not always trivial.
- Workflow establishment (i.e., reenginering document flow) is not a simple effort.
- Direct electronic text capture is not as simple as it would seem at first (e.g., dealing with multiple word-processing systems).
- A system integrator may be needed.

By the early 1990s, high-resolution digital video and image techniques, as contrasted to simple document imaging, were still being utilized in specialized environments because of their relatively high cost. This followed from the fact that chips implementing accepted compression standard(s) were not yet being produced in quantities sufficient to achieve a price goal of $200 to $500 for a PC plug-in board, and software compression was not fast enough on most PCs or workstations. Additionally, high-speed premises networks are needed. Public switched networks supporting high-capacity services (1.544, 45, and 155 Mbps) in a cost-effective manner are also required.

## 1.4  Image Types

Images, or more specifically documents, are comprised of one or more of the following four elements:

- *Text.*  Images comprise text [including, in addition to normal characters, Greek, Hebrew, and Russian (Cyrillic) characters], or computer-stored text (such as e-mail).

- *Bitonal images.* Images consist of two levels of intensity. Examples include line artwork, schematics, blueprints, and engineering drawings.

- *Continuous-tone images.* Images exhibit "indivisible" transitions from dark to light (shades of gray, or the so-called gray scale). Examples include black-and-white photographs and black-and-white TV and videotape pictures.

- *Color images.* Images consisting of the three primary colors and shades of gray to register brightness. Examples include color photographs and color TV and videotape pictures.

(The bit rate increases as one goes from a pure text image to a color image.)

## 1.5   Imaging Market Size

"As is the case with most industries...in the high-tech sector, the imaging industry (has) had to modify its great expectations about meteoric growth."[7] In 1990, optimistic projections placed the 1992 market at $12 billion;[18] such expectations did not materialize.

The Association for Information and Image Management (founded in 1941) undertakes yearly surveys on the state of the industry. In 1992, the most recent year for which data is available, the electronic imaging market achieved 19 percent growth in revenues (compared to the previous year), to about $2 billion.[19] Although this is smaller than the growth rates achieved in the past, it is still a good increment. Worldwide imaging hardware sales were expected to reach $4.5 billion in 1992.[6] Imaging hardware is estimated to cover 66 percent of the market, software 26 percent, and the balance miscellaneous services. Initially, government agencies were the largest users of imaging systems. Some now see the financial market as becoming the largest imaging market. About 25 percent of all banks with more than $2 billion in assets have already deployed imaging technology.[9]

## 1.6   Communications Aspects

Locally, many BISs utilize LAN connectivity. Wide area networking remains a challenge for commercial imaging users. Higher speeds and new communication services are needed to make image communication a reality. In the meantime, a number of BISs use conversion to facsimile as the only practical way to ship documents remotely in real time, particularly for international distribution. For example, a 40-kB document would require 30 s on a line with a 9.6-kbps modem; 15 s on a line with a 19.2-kbps modem; 0.5 s on an ISDN line; 0.2 s on a switched T1 line. (For comparison, note that in a 4-Mbps LAN the document could in theory be moved in 0.1 s, and in 0.04 s in an Ethernet environment.)

Newer communications services are needed and are indeed appearing. These services support connectivity from a fraction of one million bits per second to several billion bits per second.

## 1.7 What You Will Find in This Book

The discussion of the preceding sections provided a macro view of the imaging field and identified some of the themes that are important to prospective users of this technology. These themes are expanded on in the rest of the book. This text is geared toward those corporate planners interested in using the digital imaging techniques and systems in their organizations that have evolved in the past few years. The text is directed at managers that need to assess the potential *business advantages* of this technology without having to work through the tough mathematics typically included in digital image processing textbooks; readers requiring such an in-depth engineering view of the field are referred, after reading this text, to the books listed in the Additional Reading section. This book aims at a balance between theory and practice.

Table 1.3 depicts course of investigation of this text. After the overview found in this chapter, Chap. 2 provides a discussion of how imaging systems fit in a corporate enterprise environment. The next four chapters (Chaps. 3 through 7) discuss the enabling technology required to support image applications. Chapter 3 focuses on color imaging, which, according to proponents, will experience major penetration in the future. Storage and compression standards that are needed if image applications are to be adopted on a broad scale by busi-

**TABLE 1.3    The Course of Investigation of This Text**

Chapter 1: Introduction and Overview

Chapter 2: Imaging Systems in Corporate Environments

Chapter 3: Technical Principles of Resolution and Color

Chapter 4: Image Entry/Capture Systems

Chapter 5: Output Systems

Chapter 6: Compression and Storage Techniques and Standards

Chapter 7: Storage Technology

Chapter 8: Local Area Networks: Imaging Platforms

Chapter 9: Wide Area and Networking Services and Technologies for Imaging Systems

TABLE 1.4    Areas Related to Imaging*

| Area | Reference |
|------|-----------|
| Computer vision | 20 |
| Computer animation | 21 |
| Image analysis | 22 |
| Image processing | 23 |
| Pattern recognition | |
| Pattern classification | |
| Image interpretation | 22 |

*Not covered in detail in this text.

nesses, government agencies, educational institutions and libraries, are also covered. Chapters 8 and 9 cover communication technologies and services supporting image transmission, to facilitate distributed applications.

Table 1.4 depicts areas related to imaging that are beyond the scope of this text; the table reinforces the extent of researcher interest and ongoing work in this widely encompassing field.

Even for the topics that are covered, the intention is not to be all-inclusive or encyclopedic. We have set out to cover the imaging field with a particular point of view, as it would be seen from the eyes of practitioners who are considering deploying this technology in their organizations.

## 1.8  Examples of Commercial Applications

This section provides *some* recent examples of imaging applications from the literature, to familiarize the reader with some of the opportunities afforded by this technology.[24] The objective is to give a sense of the scope and range of applicability.

The Defense Logistics Agency is installing a $150 million imaging system to assist archiving and on-line access to over 285,000,000 engineering drawings and 500,000 technical documents. This fully automated optical disk system is being delivered to the DOD by Xerox Corporation, Digital Equipment Corporation, Eastman Kodak, and FORMTEK.[25] The Navy's Publishing and Printing Office has converted 40 million pages of document to optical disks. Exxon will scan about 1 million documents in 1993, and 50,000 per year in the future. Technical (research) reports, correspondence documents, and even viewgraphs are captured for archival and reference purposes.[11]

Commonwealth Bancshares uses an imaging system to expedite loan processing. The IBM Mid America Employees Federal Credit Union has also introduced an imaging system to store records on over 50,000 members, replacing a microfiche system. Northland Insurance Company similarly replaced a microfiche system to handle entry and management of about 1000 new documents per day.[2] Macess, a developer of turnkey document-control systems for the managed health care industry, uses recordable CD-ROMs to store scanned images of claim forms. The disks reside on a battery of networked CD-ROM readers. The vendor's software juxtaposes CD-ROM-based images to "fielded" data in Btrieve databases on NetWare servers. A client scans over 10,000 forms a day. Twice a day, as the accumulated image information reaches 600 MB, it is written to a recordable CD.[26] The system was under expansion, to about 170 networked readers and an archive of 100 GB of document images.

The National Library of Medicine in Bethesda, Maryland, scans research articles onto a custom CD-ROM produced each month, which is placed on a networked CD-ROM reader, thereby giving researchers computerized on-line access to the information. The U.S. Geological Survey in Reston, Virginia, has used recordable CD-ROMs since the late 1980s.

Art curators are now using imaging techniques to catalog works of art. About 9000 compressed pictures stored in RGB digital format (as contrasted to analog videodisks) can be packed in a 1-GB storage system (a WORM system, for example, can store 5 GB). The California Museum of Photography is employing Kodak's Photo CD technology to store over 400,000 historical photographs.[27] Many of these are oversized and extremely fragile and cannot be handled with conventional scanners. The photos are rephotographed using controlled lighting, and the negatives are converted to Photo CD storage (discussed in more detail in Chap. 4). Two levels of resolution are possible; although the photos are stored in a high-resolution mode, lower resolution output is possible for specific purposes.

Implant Graphics is reported to be producing 50 digitized photos a day using digital cameras that generate pictures of 6 MB (see Chap. 4) with half the staff that would be used for a conventional studio.[28] Their production of a catalog with 500 picture-images for Eckerd Corp. (a drugstore chain) now takes only 6 weeks to produce when it used to take 13 weeks. Digital cameras eliminate the need to send out the film for development and reshoot objects at a later date if the picture did not come out right the first time.

A daily paper uses a video grabber board to capture images off videotape taken from a local TV station with which it has an agreement to share resources. The video is loaded into a PC, where the user can zoom into any object in the frame and capture it in a standard file format. Because of the zooming and editing, the readership of the paper does not recognize the picture as having been previously broadcast.[29]

*Fortune Magazine* now publishes *Fortune* 500 on Disk, a PC-based information tool that includes financial and other information on the *Fortune* 500 and *Fortune* Service 500 companies. The disk includes descriptions of key business activities; complete 2-year financial statements; and 5-year summaries of sales, net income, and annual financial ratios.

Other examples documented in the literature include the following.[6] At San Jose Medical Center, imaging is contributing to the organization's strategic objective of increasing productivity and enhancing revenues. Crowly Maritime Corporation is using imaging to reduce paper handling and improve the flow of information to its field operations. At Western Provident Association, a large U.K. health insurer, imaging is being leveraged toward the goal of improving customer satisfaction. Bicktel and Brewer, a large law firm with offices in several noncontiguous states, has installed imaging systems to increase productivity and quality of work. It has implemented an imaging system for integrated litigation support aimed at streamlining the process of assembling and analyzing evidence. Attorneys and paralegals can more rapidly search for the appropriate case documents. The Defense Finance and Accounting Service (DFAS) has eliminated paper by adding an imaging system to its mainframe-based pay processing system, to handle disbursements to over 630,000 Air Force retirees. The system supports scanning, indexing, and workflow processing, enabling conversion of all documents received by the mail room into electronic documents. Commonwealth Industrial Gases Limited has installed an imaging system to support customer service, credit control, and product location functions.

Additional examples for specific industries are provided in Chap. 2.

## 1.9  Examples of Imaging Applications with Communication Requirements

### 1.9.1  Medical X-ray transfer

Hospitals use imaging for improved patient care, reduced cost of delivering health care, and new revenue opportunities.[30,31] One way to deliver improved patient care is to rely on extensive consultation during diagnosis and treatment; this is accomplished through liberal use of patient information in general and imaging data in particular. Reduced cost of delivering health care is obtained by better record storage, rapid access to imaging information, rapid image distribution, and collaboration using shared resources and medical talent. New revenue opportunities result from teleradiology, increased referrals, and improved billing. Resolutions of at least $1000 \times 1000$ pixels are required.[32] For this application, digital images of patient X rays are stored in a picture archival and communication system (PACS) that is attached to a LAN within the hospital. Physicians at remote hospitals involved in consultation on a particular case can access and view the X-ray images stored on the PACS using LAN-to-LAN networking capabilities.

PACS in its simplest form offers the ability to store and display X-ray scans digitally instead of relying on traditional film-based methods.[33] While a typical PC display does not have the same resolution and brightness as X-ray scans mounted on a viewing box, there are other advantages. For example, even a clinic of moderate size can have an archive of 5 or 10 million X-ray scans; getting the right film to the right doctor for the right patient at the right time can be a logistical challenge given such a large inventory of film. A computer-based image can be easily retrieved, enhanced, and enlarged, and it can transmitted to specialists at another location for consultation purposes. PACSs will change not only the way radiographs are recorded and viewed but also how physicians, nurses, technicians, administrative personnel, and patients interact with radiology labs and with each other.[33] For example, the U.S. Army is building a large PACS known as a *medical display and imaging system* (MDIS). With this system, medical records for all troops will be stored in digital format at one of five U.S. locations. The ID code of any person who is brought to a field hospital anywhere in the world (in a tent, in a hospital, or on a ship) is entered on a PC and within seconds data is transmitted over satellite back to the filed location for display on a 21-in landscape or portrait monitor.

As another example, New England Telephone has set up a broadband network connecting Massachusetts General Hospital (MGH) and a variety of other locations and/or hospitals for real-time medical collaboration between remote sites (locations include MGH Film Library, Somerville; MGH Engineering, Cambridge; MGH White Building, Boston; MGH Remote MRI, Charleston; The Children's Hospital, Boston; Spaulding Rehabilitation Hospital, Boston; Christian Science Publishing Society, Boston; Brigham & Women's Hospital, Boston; Faulkner Hospital, Boston; New England Medical Center, Boston; and Harvard Community Health Plan, Burlington). Most sites are currently connected via 45-Mbps links, and some of the sites are connected with 1.544-Mbps links. The broadband network provides connections between image producers, such as MRI archival scanners, and image consumers, such as radiologists at the hospital. The system provides nearly instantaneous access to both medical records databases and image sources.[30]

Initially the Children's Hospital automated the electronic medical records system to a text-based system; eventually, an image-based sys-

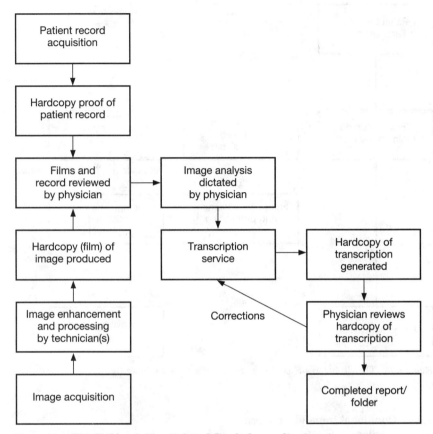

**Figure 1.3a**  The Children's Hospital workflow before on-line imaging.

tem was deployed to support medical workflow (see Fig. 1.3*a* and 1.3*b*). At the New England Medical Center, referring physicians did not have real-time access to catheterization results. Developers installed a telecardiology application allowing both remote private viewing and multiuser collaborative viewing of images of catheterization (full-motion images are available). This application is now slated to be used for collaboration throughout about 70 hospitals that are within the New England Medical Center consortium for catheterization studies. At the Brigham and Women's Hospital the nighttime on-call CAT specialist may need images that are in a remote geographic location. With the New England Telephone Broadband Network, radiologists, physicians, and surgeons are able to simultaneously review MRI and CAT images from their offices and/or homes.

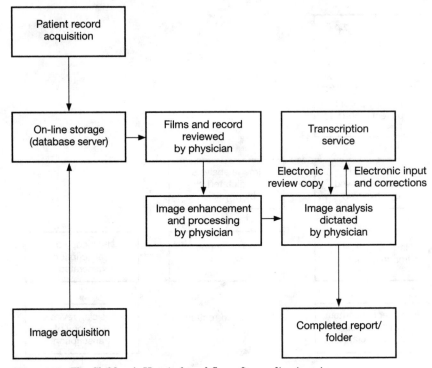

**Figure 1.3b**  The Children's Hospital workflow after on-line imaging.

### 1.9.2  Document transfer between banking offices

This application typically involves (1) scanning of documents at branch offices for transmission to a host computer at the main office or the central site or (2) document image retrieval from a central host by branch bank personnel. In the "back office," digital imaging is expected to create new opportunities for reducing noninterest expenditures and increasing noninterest income, while at the same time retaining and improving customer service. Digital technology is being positioned as enabling banks to do more work with improved quality while employing fewer workers.[9]

### 1.9.3  Engineering R&D application

This application uses distributed processing and diskless workstations to interconnect geographically dispersed engineers. Raw image data (i.e., image data obtained at the source under investigation) is stored on super computers or mainframes. Processed image data is electronically distributed to the engineering workgroup. Each engineer can access the data independently, annotate the image data, share the same image file with other team members, and save images locally.

## References

1. W. Saffady, *Electronic Imaging Systems: Design, Evaluation and Implementation,* Meckler, Westport, CT, 1992.
2. J. R. Vacca, "Metaview's Operational Image Management System," *Document Image Automation,* July–August 1991, pp. 196 ff.
3. *Optical Storage Technology, 1992,* Meckler, Westport, CT, 1992.
4. N. Muller, *Computerized Document Imaging Systems: Technology and Applications,* Artech House, Norwood, MA, 1993.
5. J. Schwartz, "Windows Corners LAN Imaging Market," *Communications Week,* April 6, 1992, pp. 39–40.
6. D. Goulden, "Imaging Adds Vision to Information," *Document Image Automation,* Fall 1992, Vol. 12, No. 3.
7. M. Thomas, "Electonic Imaging Posts Impressive Gains," *The Office,* January 1993.
8. *Frame Relay vs. SMDS vs. T1: The Best Technology / Service Fit for Networked Applications,* Probe Report, Cedar Knolls, NJ, 1992.
9. M. Gumaer, "Making the Business Case for Imaging," *Document Image Automation,* Fall 1992, Vol. 12, No. 3, pp. 30 ff.
10. G. S. Kimbal, "Color Fundamentals—Part 2: Color Scanning and Data Compression," *Document Image Automation,* May–June 1991, pp. 156 ff.
11. G. D. Lee, Exxon Research and Engineering Company, ASIS Workshop, February 25, 1993, Bridgewater, NJ.
12. H. Urrows and E. Urrows, "Optical Data Storage and Retrieval in the Legal Profession," *Document Image Automation,* November–December 1991.
13. H. Nabil, "CD-ROM Supports Multimedia Applications on the Notebook," *Computer Technology Review,* February 1993, pp. 91 ff.
14. D. Guenette, "Making the CD-ROM Scene with Scenario: Portable CD-ROM Computing Comes to the Notebook," *CD-ROM Professional,* March 1993, pp. 85 ff.
15. D. Minoli and B. Keinath, *Distributed Multimedia Through Broadband Communication Services,* Artech House, Norwood, MA, 1994.
16. B. Wiggins, "Document Image Processing—An Overview," *Document Image Automation,* Fall 1992, Vol. 12, No. 3.
17. Dataware Technologies Inc., "CD-R: The Next Stage in CD-ROM Evolution," *CD-ROM Professional,* March 1993, pp. 79 ff.
18. H. Urrows and E. Urrows, "Automated Imaging in Financial Services," *Document Image Automation,* September–October 1991, pp. 259 ff.
19. AIIM, *Information and Image Management: State of the Industry, 1992,* Silver Springs, MD.
20. A. P. Reeves, "Parallel Programming for Computer Vision," *IEEE Software,* November 1991, pp. 51 ff.
21. N. M. Thalmann and D. Thalmann, "Six-hundred Indexed References on Computer Animation," *The Journal of Visualization and Computer Animation,* July–September 1992, Vol. 3, pp. 147–174.
22. J. R. Jensen, *Introductory Digital Image Processing—A Remote Sensing Perspective,* Prentice-Hall, Englewood Cliffs, NJ, 1986.
23. B. Zavodovique et al., "Mechanism to Capture and Communicate Image-Processing Expertise," *IEEE Software,* November 1991, pp. 37 ff.
24. *Corporate Computing Magazine,* Premiere Issue, "Scanning Paper Is Just the Beginning," Ziff-Davis, Riverton, NJ.
25. W. Gnerre, "EDMICS—The Foundation for Future CALS Initiatives," *Document Image Automation,* November–December 1991, pp. 327 ff.
26. J. Udell, "Start the Presses," *Byte,* February 1993, pp. 116 ff.

27. M. Waltz, "Photo CD Brings Historic Images On-line and into Archives," *MACWEEK,* February 15, 1993, p. 37.
28. M. Waltz, "Studios Swear by Their Digitals," *MACWEEK,* February 15, 1993, pp. 38 ff.
29. L. Stevens, "Don't Abandon that Board Yet—Video Capturing Is Alive and Well," *MACWEEK,* February 15, 1993, p. 42.
30. H. Hindin, "Multimedia Communications: An Opportunity for Telecommunications Companies in Open Systems Environments: A Case Study," *Personal Communication,* March 1993.
31. L. Allen and O. Frieder, "Exploiting Database Technology in the Medical Arena," *IEEE Engineering in Medicine and Biology,* March 1992, pp. 42 ff.
32. M. Wiltgen et al., "An Integrated Picture Archiving and Communication System—Radiology Information System in a Radiological Department," *Journal of Digital Imaging,* February 1992, Vol. 6, No. 1, pp. 16–24.
33. D. Scheff, "Medical Displays: Challenge and Opportunity," *Information Display,* September 1992, pp. 14 ff.

# 2

# Imaging Systems in Corporate Environments

The purpose of this chapter is to describe typical BIS deployment and use in corporate environments. Typical premises installations that have been put in place in the recent past are discussed to give a basic sense of imaging networks and arrangements. A number of examples described in the literature are listed to illustrate the breadth of applications and cost/benefit issues associated with the technology. This chapter sets the stage for the technical treatment to follow in later chapters.

## 2.1  Architecture of Typical Systems

Figure 2.1 depicts a typical BIS from a functional point of view. Although this functional view is similar to the functions shown in Table 1.1 (Chap. 1), the emphasis here is on work functions, possibly associated with different organizations or workgroups. Typically, input documents are stored in an intermediary magnetic disk, so that the captured images can be reviewed for quality assurance purposes, editing, and indexing. Indexing is important for retrieval functions. Indexing is the coupling of the image database with a means for searching and retrieving desired information. One example might be to store image information on an ORACLE database; the database contains descriptive information about the image itself stored on the optical subsystem. If the information base includes image as well as textual information that is to be frequently cross-referenced, a labor-intensive effort may be required to develop the indexing infrastructure. A major component of the cost of indexing is the cost of the index building and retrieval software.[1] On completion of the indexing step, the information is migrated

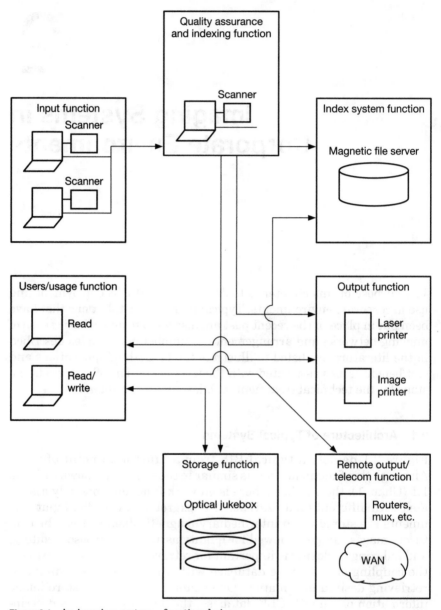

**Figure 2.1**   An imaging system—functional view.

to the optical data management system (e.g., Kodak jukeboxes). Systems now being deployed range from small desktop or departmental systems to very large customized systems. For example, EDMICS is a customized system now being put in place by the Defense Logistics Agency (DLA) to manage their accumulated inventory of 285,000,000 engineering drawings and 50,000 technical publications.[2] The overwhelming increase in drawing volume and in demand for document access in DLA has made the manual system obsolete.

## 2.2  Practical Requirements of a Business Imaging System

Table 2.1 enumerates some of the practical aspects of a BIS that users often find necessary to make an imaging system a cost-effective investment.

**TABLE 2.1    Typical Requirements for a Mid- to High-end BIS**

Must support input from scanners

Must support autofeed of single- or two-sided documents

Must support document scaling to 8.5 × 11

Must support upload from magnetic disk

Must support operator functions
   Monitor quality of scanned image
   Document maintenance (change document numbers, insert, delete, replace pages, change confidentiality status, etc.)

Must be able to perform sophisticated search algorithms, such as view, print, transfer, and/or fax identified documents

Must support viewing from any PC in the organization
   Hardware boards on PCs for decompression: fast; more expensive; limiting (cannot view documents unless PC has board)
   Software decompression on PC: slower; cheaper; ubiquitous access

Must support image manipulation (e.g., zoom-in, zoom-out)

Print on laser printers (but slow) or on image printers (faster, since optimized for image)

Must support hyperlinking ("hotspot" button allows user to jump to any other linked and/or navigable images, providing sophisticated entry points into a (long) document (e.g., interleaf)

Must support the ability to use cross-platforms for display (e.g., DOS, UNIX)

Must support "redlining": being able to overlay an image on top of an existing image to make modifications, etc.; CAD systems have had this capability for years; raster systems are now beginning to support this functionality

Must support document distribution in an effective manner; issue: how do workers that need to go into the field (engineers, installers, etc.) get access to documents?

## 2.3  System Configurations

This section provides an initial overview of system configurations that are typical of what corporate managers installing BISs have already put in place as of the early 1990s. This overview characterizes system configurations based on the communication topology used to interconnect the various subcomponents of the imaging system. Chapters 8 and 9 will focus more specifically on technical aspects of these and communication technologies.

### 2.3.1  The emergence of client-server systems

There has been a major shift from host-based networking in the past 5 years to peer-to-peer architectures utilizing cooperative processing.[3] Client-server systems are well suited to imaging applications. Client-server environments allow imaging systems to exploit local computing resources, while relying on the server only for tasks that require centralized capabilities, such as databases and communication gateways. This reduces the network traffic as well as the load on the server. The local workstation handles major image processing tasks, including decompression.

The client-server entities use a message-based protocol to undertake their tasks: clients make requests for service to the server, which acts as the service provider. Client-server systems have been widely deployed in workstation and PC networks. Even high-end workstations have limited storage capabilities, particularly in an imaging context, dictating the need for a server. A distinguished machine on the network, customized at the hardware level, software level, or both, provides a file service by accepting network messages from client machines containing open/close–read/write file requests and processing them, transmitting the requested information back across the network.[4] Note that a client-server paradigm is not a true distributed storage system where the files reside on storage on the remote workstations.

In commercial terms, BISs range from standalone systems to corporationwide systems, as already alluded to in Chap. 1. Four typical approaches are[5]

1. *Standalone systems.*  This approach aims at automating the local storage and retrieval functions (basically, a file cabinet replacement). A basic image application running on the PC is often all that is needed. Some libraries (including corporate libraries) now have CD-ROM versions of keyword-based research tools such as INSPEC. This entry-level approach can also be used for prototyping and/or validating a system that is ultimately slated to cover the entire corporation. This

approach, however, is not effective when data-processing information residing on a corporate network is also needed in support of the imaging function. A number of organizations have found that soon after they install a standalone system, users express the wish to consult the imaging database from their work locations and directly from their desks.[6]

2. *Document image processing through the central host.*    Figure 2.2 depicts this arrangement. *Host-based imaging* implies that the host must individually manage each window of data. Since the host looks at each window as a distinct terminal, the result is processing-intensive computing at the host, with possible performance degradation. Sometimes, but not always, this arrangement can result in better integration with other host-based data-processing applications. This approach was used in the late 1980s.

3. *Document processing through a high level of cooperative computing between host and PCs/workstations.*    This approach (see Fig. 2.3) is amenable to full integration, enabling data processing and document imaging to become part of a total information management system. Also,

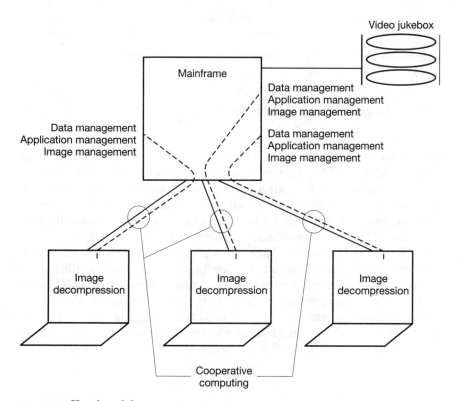

**Figure 2.2**  Host-based document imaging.

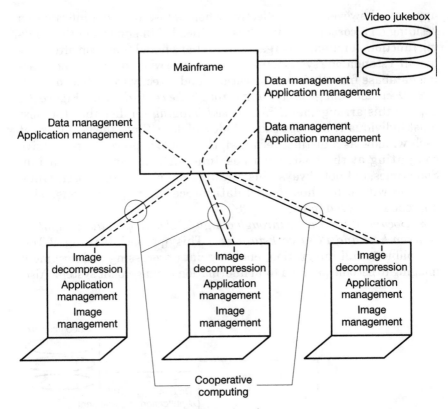

**Figure 2.3**  Distributed-computing document imaging.

this approach is often a cost-effective way to put to work the computing capacity of today's PCs and workstations [sometimes up to 60 MIPS (million instructions per second) and/or 70 SPECMarks*4]. Here the host handles the central data management and processing functions, while each workstation manages its instance of the application and the presentation of the image (and other ancillary data) at its monitor.

4. *Distributed systems based completely on LAN client-server arrangements.*  Here, the information as well as relevant applications reside in LAN-resident servers. In the most recent past, LANs have been employed in commercial settings to support imaging. Figure 2.4 shows a typical example. Current LAN technology is reasonable for BISs and DISs; EISs and SISs may be better off with emerging asynchronous transfer mode (ATM)–based LAN technologies described in

---

*A SPECMark is approximately the processing power of a single Digital Equipment Corporation VAX 11/780 on a particular benchmark.

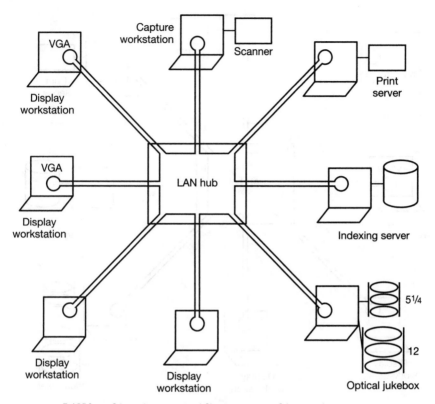

**Figure 2.4** LAN-based imaging system (client-server architecture).

Chap. 9. LANs can support workflow systems, but not all workflow systems are LAN-based.

BIS documents were quoted in Chap. 1 at 40 kB once compressed, as an average; some images result into smaller files; compound documents with some business graphics can be in the 100-kB range. A 4- or 16-Mbps token ring LAN or a 10-Mbps Ethernet LAN should be able to support a reasonable number of LAN-resident BIS users without many problems. Note, for example, that an Ethernet MAC frame can carry 1518 octets; hence 20 to 30 Ethernet frames should be enough to download an image—token ring and FDDI LANs can support even larger frames, simplifying or obviating the segmentation task.

Figure 2.5 shows an example of access to mainframe (e.g., IBM 3090) or departmental computer (e.g., IBM AS/400), for integration with other data-processing tasks or databases.

Figure 2.6 depicts a typical LAN-based imaging system at the hardware level. This figure provides a topological sense of an actual installation. Many BISs on the market support a variety of LAN platforms

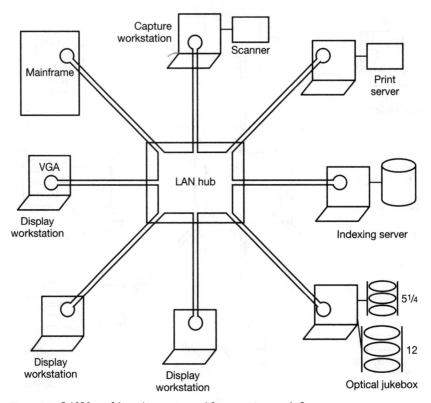

**Figure 2.5**   LAN-based imaging system with access to a mainframe.

including Novell's NetWare, Microsoft's OS/2 LAN Manager, Banyan's VINES, 3COM's 3+Open, AT&T's LAN Manager/X, and IBM's LAN Server. Many systems are independent of the physical LAN technology (e.g., token ring, Ethernet, FDDI).

An increasing number of vendors of groupware systems are including workflow automation capabilities in their offerings, although systems supporting imaging are less common. With workflow features, an organization can support forms routing and forms tracking, thus improving the efficiency of business processes. Workflow systems facilitate the coordination of human resources with the work that needs to be undertaken in an organization. In its simplest form, workflow automation is based on e-mail software; this allows the serial rotuing of electronic forms. More complex systems coordinate parallel processes and maintain the results in a database; this allows an organization to track work in progress. High-end workflow automation systems are complex transaction-processing systems, supporting, for example, airline reservations and claims processing.

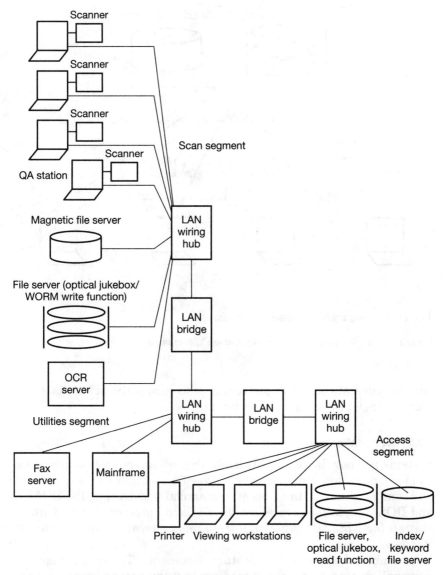

**Figure 2.6** A typical LAN-based imaging system at the hardware level. (*Note:* WORMs are created on equipment located on the scan segment. After they are "written," they are physically moved to the access segment servers.)

Figure 2.7 depicts a simplified logical view of a typical workflow management system. A workflow management system, such as Metafile Information System's Metaview, uses computers to manage the flow of folders of digitized information through several processing steps in an organization, analogously to manually routing a file of

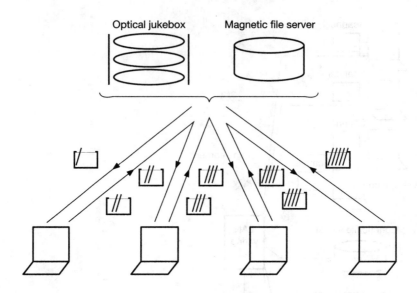

Optical jukebox        Magnetic file server

[///] Folder (aggregated/updated documents)

**Figure 2.7**  Simplified logical view of a typical workflow management system.

paper documents in the proper sequence to each of the individuals who
play a role in processing the document.[5]

### 2.3.2  Workstations and scanners

Systems are now becoming available that allow the user to employ a
single workstation station to capture, verify, edit, store, index, retrieve,
and compare images. In terms of commercial penetration, the IBM PC
and DOS compatibles represent the de facto industry standard workstation for BISs.[7] Many imaging systems operate under Microsoft
Windows.

A number of ways exist to capture documents. The capture mechanism will depend on the input medium (e.g., business document, computer-aided design, video programming, live scene), as well as the
desired quality. At the functional level, capture of documents* can be
accomplished as follows:

- Use of an appropriate scanner (this may entail different scanners for
  different documents)

---

*Video and photographic capture is discussed in Chap. 4.

- Retrieving documents already stored magnetically on optical disks or on microfilm

- Capturing CAD information by
  - Accepting CAD vectors natively
  - Converting CAD files to IGES (initial graphics exchange specification) and storing this format
  - IGES-to-raster conversion

Raster technology provides a means to capture documents in electronic format easily and effectively, modify them directly, and distribute them to remote locations.[2] The problem, however, is that bitmaps can be large, as already discussed (and further discussed in the next two chapters). Accepting CAD vectors natively can in theory result in more compact files.

### 2.3.3  Servers

Servers supporting an imaging system must have the capacity and speed to meet the performance requirements to support imaging applications. Many server systems utilize the UNIX operating system. It is to be noted that given current optical storage technology, which has an access time an order of magnitude longer than a magnetic drive, the bottleneck of a typical imaging system is in the video servers. However, ancillary processors, for example, for the keyword database, must be sufficiently fast in order not to compound the slow access time. A CD-ROM has a throughput at about 150 kbps (Chap. 4). For a typical BIS image of 40 kB, just the transfer time is 2 s. A document may comprise several images; an example of a multipage image is a technical report (this is the reason for needing hyperlinking discussed later). In some actual systems, the user has to wait for up to 20 s for the first image; other images within the same document can then be obtained within a 5-s interval.

There have been a number of instances where users have had to rework the architecture of major parts of the imaging system in order to obtain the power and flexibility to operate at current levels as well as enable anticipated growth.[7]

### 2.4  Networking Configurations

Transmission of imaging files can overwhelm a traditional network. Proper design is critical to achieve adequate performance. "Gigabit networks" are now emerging to support applications such as

- Motion video to the desktop
- Desktop videoconferencing

- Interactive manufacturing and test manuals
- CAD/CAM/CIM data transfers
- Database and file transfer in object-oriented systems
- Network image filing

(*Note:* This text focuses on the last three of these applications; see Ref. 8 for an up-to-date assessment of multimedia.) The introduction of ATM-based LAN and WAN (wide area network) technology will alleviate the bandwidth bottlenecks, particularly for DISs and SISs; however, organizations are already deploying imaging systems, and some observations pertaining to deployment options are in order.

### 2.4.1 LAN design considerations

Proper design applies to both the application and the communication infrastructure. For example, it may be desirable to develop a browsing application so that only a relatively small amount of information is sent to the user (say, a lower-resolution version of the image or a partial window), until the desired image is found and/or the user requests additional resolution, particularly for high-resolution large-size images used in SISs, DISs, and EISs. This approach can, in many cases, cut down the amount of data sent through the network by almost an order of magnitude. Some applications involve both a traditional textual part and an image part (casualty claims, credit card billing, medical records, etc.). Here the application could be designed to deliver only the text part automatically, while the image part is delivered on request. Applications dealing with image folders (files consisting of multiple images) could, for example, deliver only the first (or first and second) image, and deliver the rest of the file on demand. Hypertext methods could be used to facilitate delivery of only selected "pages" rather than the entire document. Applications where images may have to be reviewed (e.g., desktop publishing) should either print image catalogs or create "summary images" at low resolution for inspection purposes; higher-resolution images generating higher transfer rates should be used only for editing and/or final production.

Even after optimized application design, the network planner will find that imaging generates fairly high network traffic, even for BISs, particularly if there are numerous simultaneous users, as would be the case in a system used in "production mode." Some designers worry that client-server applications may overtax 4- and 16-Mbps LANs. One approach is to utilize evolving high-capacity LAN technologies [e.g., fiber distributed data interface (FDDI), local asynchronous transfer mode (LATM)] and WAN services [e.g., cell relay service (CRS), switched multimegabit data service (SMDS)], discussed later. Another approach is to make the best of existing LAN technology, at least as an interim solution, to meet existing needs.

Most, if not all, of the commercially available imaging applications are LAN-based, as implied by the discussion provided earlier. Therefore, network design for imaging systems utilizing existing communication technology (i.e., as contrasted to standalone systems) is intrinsically related to optimization of LAN resources. The design process should start with the core LAN and work outward to (1) any locally internetworked image delivery LANs, (2) WANs, and (3) remote-image-delivery LANs. The core LAN is the LAN on which the image servers reside; internetworked LANs include LANs for image delivery, i.e., where the users ("clients") reside, as well as off-premises LANs; refer again to Fig. 2.6. Users on different local segments are not as constrained as users on remote LANs; this arises from the fact that WAN connectivity at a reasonable price is still not a de facto situation. The WAN will normally constrain the operation of a distributed imaging system more that the remote LAN, because the cost of providing high bandwidth on the internet will usually prevent commercial customers, mindful of the bottom line, from using the evolving high-speed services.[9] There are a few options at $n \times 64$ kbps ($n = 2, 6, 12$) for both dedicated and switched services, and there are a few options at 1.544 Mbps for both dedicated and switched services (e.g., switched T1, frame relay service, ISDN, SMDS); however, there are fewer "inexpensive" options at 45 Mbps and higher speeds that are needed for DISs, EISs, and SISs applications.

One LAN design principle in support of imaging network design is "isolation" from other LAN applications, whenever possible. Existing LANs share the underlying bandwidth (4, 10, 16, or 100 Mbps) among all users of the LAN using a contention or token technique. Additionally, there is overhead from upper-layer protocols. Hence, a 10-Mbps LAN may support only, say, 6 Mbps (or less*). If 30 "production-mode" users are connected to such a network, each gets an average of only 200 kbps. As noted, a BIS document may be 40 kB or 320 kb

---

*Some claim that higher utilizations are possible. An analysis of the contention mechanism, for example, will show that as the number of users gets large, a sizable amount of the bandwidth is used up in managing the contention overhead (say, 25 percent). The throughput of an Ethernet LAN is $S = 1/[1 + 2a(1 - A)/A]$ with $A = NP(1 - P)^{N-1}$ and $a$ is the normalized propagation delay, that is, $a = $ (propagation time)/(transmission time).[10,11] A typical assumption is that $P = 1/N$, or $A = (1 - 1/N)^{N-1}$. As $N \to \infty$, $S \to 1/(1 + 3.44a)$. Any loading of the network results in reduced throughput; the higher utilization numbers quoted by some only come about when there are very few users on the network, and contention does not really exist. For example, for $a = 0.1$, the throughput with two users is 85 percent, while the utilization with 20 users is only 75 percent. For comparison, the utilization of a token ring network is close(r) to 100 percent. Here the utilization is $S = 1/(1 + a/N)$ (with $a < 1$); as $N \to \infty$, $S \to 1$.[10,11]

(images in DIS, EIS, and SIS environments may be much higher). This would imply that the utilization of the underlying media is more that 100 percent ($30 \times 320,000/200,000$), causing very long delays or even saturation.

In an environment where 10 to 40 LAN frames are needed to transmit a single (compressed) BIS image, the image traffic will severely load the shared network. This causes congestion, impacting the performance of not only the image application but also other applications on the LAN. It is desirable to segment the LAN, if possible, so that the production-mode image servers and the production-mode image clients are on the same segment, while keeping other users on a distinct segment. This implies that only the requests that need to cross the segment bridge (or router) will incur the additional delay (e.g., a nonimage user occasionally needing an image, or an image user occasionally needing data residing on a server connected on the backbone network). The result is that the backbone LAN will not have to carry a large fraction of the imaging traffic.

There are situations where isolation of image-based users is not possible, because of either the physical position where the users are located on the floor or the multitask nature of their job function. In this case the designer should try to create small LAN segments interconnected over a backbone LAN, thereby reducing the contention-induced overhead or the token waiting time within each segment. Also, the designer should deploy a backbone of adequate bandwidth to support the image servers which are now connected to it (e.g., a 16-Mbps token ring LAN in the presence of 4-Mbps access LANs, or a FDDI LAN in the presence of 10-Mbps access LANs; 100-Mbps Ethernet systems may also emerge in the near future, in addition to LATM systems).

Another approach is to employ switching hubs. The switching hub, in conjunction with point-to-point workstation wiring, enables traffic to be transmitted between the origination (server) and destination (client) while relying on the backplane of the hub as the only shared facility, in turn eliminating the other sources of delay and throughput bottlenecks. As a further optimization, it may be desirable to (re)wire the production-mode users of imaging applications to a specifically designated "image hub," as long as these users are within the reach of the wiring limits to such a hub.[9]

LAN interconnection also involves well-thought-out considerations. For example, in accessing a WAN service, the image traffic should not be cascaded through segments of a LAN that affects local users. Additionally, the image traffic should not be relayed over a WAN infrastructure that involves multiple hops and/or subnetworks.

A number of companies offer system-engineered imaging network systems, including Meridian Data (CD Net), Online Computer

Products (OPTINET), and CD-Plus (PlusNet). These systems are CD-ROM servers based on 286/386-DOS PCs that can be connected to the network with any NetWare-supported Ethernet interface, supporting multiple CD-ROM drives.[6]

### 2.4.2   Wide area considerations

Figure 2.8 depicts two WAN-access approaches. In the top case, all the imaging traffic destined for the WAN has to go through the LAN serving traditional users, affecting their performance; notice that a router is used for WAN access. In the bottom case, where the WAN router is directly positioned on the image segment, the traffic-intensive image transactions can reach the WAN directly, without impacting the nor-

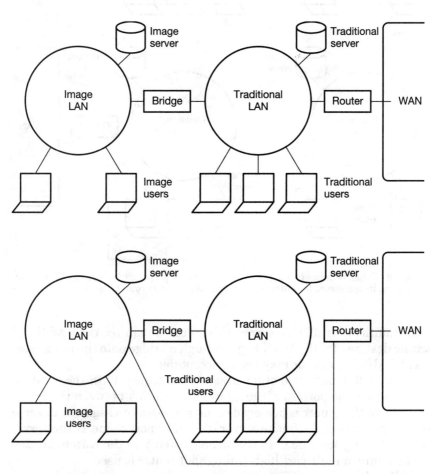

**Figure 2.8**  Connecting an imaging application over a WAN. Top: less desirable. Bottom: more desirable.

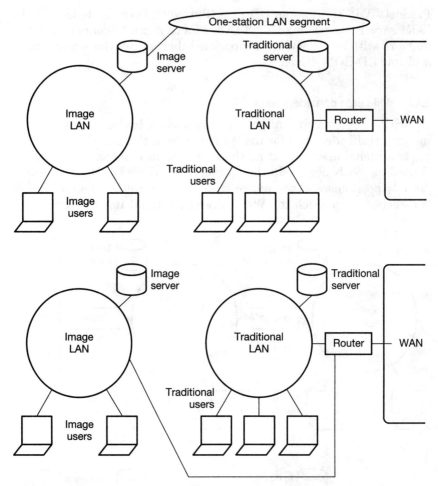

**Figure 2.9**  Other techniques for connecting an imaging application over a WAN. Top: connecting image server to router. Bottom: using multiport router.

mal traditional traffic. However, this solution requires the traditional traffic destined for the WAN to go through a bridge onto the image segment/LAN; this may or may not be acceptable.

Figure 2.9 depicts two other possible strategies. With the strategy shown in the top portion of the figure, a direct link between the image server and the router is achieved using a one-station segment to serve one of the ports of the image server (the other port connects the server to the imaging segment).[9] In the strategy shown in the bottom portion of the figure, a multiport high-throughput router is used.

Although traditional internetworking utilizes routers, as shown in Figs. 2.8 and 2.9, imaging interconnections may, in fact, be better

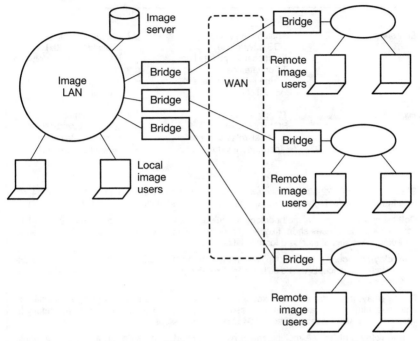

**Figure 2.10** Using bridges to establish an enterprisewide imaging network.

served, where possible, by bridges, as shown in Fig. 2.10. Bridges are (currently) faster than routers in terms of forwarded or filtered frames. As noted earlier, imaging traffic should not be sent over WANs using multiple hops, protocols, or subnetworks, because of performance considerations. Figure 2.10 shows a core LAN with the image server, with remote LANs connected directly to the central LAN.

### 2.4.3  WAN services in support of imaging

Better WAN services than dial-up facsimile are required to make imaging applications more distributed. A number of WAN services can be utilized: dedicated fractional T1 lines, dedicated T1 lines, dedicated T3 lines, ISDN (integrated services digital network) H0/H11 service, frame relay service, SMDS, and cell relay service. The higher speed (several times faster than the speed on a modem) required to facilitate image distribution is cited as the driver. X-ray scans, CAT scans, and other images are currently sent using Group 4 fax. Figure 2.11 provides a summary of some of the key WAN communication services that can be employed in support of distributed imaging in general and LAN interconnection in particular. High-speed digital services can be classified as *dedicated (nonswitched) services,* such as fractional T1 (FT1),

|  | Nonswitched | Switched |
|---|---|---|
| Low speed | Analog private line | Dial-up with modem |
|  | DDS private line | ISDN 2B+D, H0, H11 |
|  | Fractional T1 private line | Packet-switched network |
|  | T1 private line |  |
|  | Frame relay (permanent | Frame relay (switched |
|  | virtual circuit) | virtual circuit) |
| High speed | T3 private lines | Switched multimegabit |
|  | SONET private line | data service (SMDS) |
|  | ATM/cell relay service | ATM/cell relay service |
|  | (permanent virtual circuit) | (switched virtual circuit) |

*Terminology:*

**BISDN.**  155- or 622-Mbps public switched service commercially available in the 1994–95 time frame. Ideal for high-speed data, video, imaging, and multimedia applications.

**Cell relay/switching.**  A methodology to multiplex, switch, and transport a variety of high-capacity signals. It uses short, fixed-length packets. The asynchronous transfer mode is the accepted international standard for the cell layout.

**Cell relay service.**  A service, typically in the context of BISDN, but also possible over a private switch, that accepts user's cells (short, fixed-length packets) for high-speed delivery to a remote destination.

**Frame relay, private.**  A multiplexed service obtained over a private high-speed backbone equipped with appropriate nodal processors (fast packet switches). It is used principally to interconnect LANs. Access speeds of 64 kbps or 1.544 Mbps are supported.

**Frame relay, public.**  A multiplexed service provided by a carrier. The user has a single access line into the network and can deliver frames to remote users without having to provide dedicated communication links or switches. It is used principally to interconnect LANs. Access speeds of 64 kbps or 1.544 Mbps are supported. Provides logical connectivity.

**FT1.**  A point-to-point dedicated service supporting $N \times 64$ kbps connectivity (typically, $N =$ 2,4,6,12). This represents a "fraction" of the speed available with a T1 service.

**ISDN 2B+D.**  A switched service providing connectivity at $2 \times 64$ kbps, plus a 16-kbps channel that supports a packet service and the call setup mechanism.

**ISDN H0.**  A switched service providing connectivity at 384 kbps, using the ISDN call setup mechanism.

**ISDN H11.**  A switched service providing connectivity at 1536 kbps, using the ISDN call setup mechanism.

**SMDS.**  A public switched service supporting connectionless cell-based communication at 1.544- and 45-Mbps access speed. Positioned for LAN interconnection.

**SONET.**  A specification for digital hierarchy levels at multiples of 52 Mbps. A point-to-point dedicated service supporting $N \times 52$ Mbps connectivity over fiber-based facilities (typically $N =$ 1,3,12).

**ST1.**  A switched service providing physical connectivity at 1536 kbps, using a pre-ISDN call setup mechanism.

**T1 (DS1).**  A point-to-point dedicated service supporting 1.544-Mbps aggregate connectivity or twenty-four 64-kbps subchannels (these are also known as DS0).

**T3 (DS3).**  A point-to-point dedicated service supporting 44.736-Mbps aggregate connectivity or 28 DS1 subchannels.

**Figure 2.11**  Communications options to support distributed imaging.

T1, and T3, and *switched services,* such as switched T1, frame relay service (public or private), SMDS, and cell relay. Some products have already appeared that make use of ISDN services to transmit medical images such as photo IDs, signatures, and photos of treatment procedures that "follow the patient."[12–14]

Client-server applications generate bursty traffic. As imaging applications extend from a LAN/campus environment, where the traffic pattern does not greatly affect the economies of communication, to WANs, services that support burstiness in a (cost-)effective manner become critical. Switched services are better than dedicated services in this situation, since expensive dedicated links are not required (or justified). WAN services will be treated in more detail in Chap. 8.

### 2.4.4 Bandwidth considerations

Observers expect to see the growth in applications such as image storage and retrieval and graphics computer-aided design, both of which involve frequent transmission of large amounts of information, and the introduction of real-time high-resolution multimedia and visualization. As seen in Fig. 2.11 (and in Chaps. 8 and 9), new local and wide area networking services and architectures are being developed to support services such as imaging and other visually based services including multimedia and visualization. This section provides some background data in terms of bandwidth requirements for these applications as a motivation for the need to develop new high-end communications systems (additional information on bandwidth will also be found in the intervening chapters).

Table 2.2, based partially on Ref. 15, provides one assessment of the bandwidth needs to support these new applications; of course, the focus of this discussion is imaging.

### 2.4.5 Integrating facsimile

In standard facsimile operations a document, possibly in electronic form (e.g., a letter or a PC memo), is converted to paper, then to an image (with Group 3 or 4 encoding), then to paper (and possibly even rekeyed to electronic form). The paper facsimile may be photocopied for distribution and/or filed (faxes sent to individuals may be "thrown away" after they are read by the individual for whom they were intended, but faxes sent to a business—say, for ordering some goods—often have durable interest and have to be filed).

Many businesses are interested in being able to receive, send, store, and route images over a premises network (such as a LAN) or even to an outside recipient, without having to rely on paper. Many imaging

TABLE 2.2     **Bandwidth Requirements for a Number of Visually Based Applications**

| Application | Transaction length, s | Message length, octets | Throughput, bps/user |
|---|---|---|---|
| Traditional database read | 30 | 1,200 | 320 |
| Traditional database retrieval | 9 | 1,200 | 1,060 |
| Traditional database browse | 3 | 1,200 | 3,200 |
| PC server (client-server) | 20 | 12,000 | 4,800 |
| (Evolving applications) | | | |
| database retrieval | 4 | 4,300 | 8,600 |
| Image database retrieval, BIS | 50 | 60,000 | 9,600 |
| Image database retrieval, BIS | | | |
| (evolving applications) | 12 | 120,000 | 80,000 |
| EIS | 3 | 36,000 | 96,000 |
| Multimedia: voice-annotated text | —* | — | 33,000 |
| Multimedia: voice-annotated image | | | |
| (business image quality) | —* | — | 38,000 |
| Multimedia: voice-annotated image | | | |
| (high-quality image) | —* | — | 86,000 |
| Teleconference | —† | — | 128,000 |
| Higher-quality teleconference | —† | — | 768,000 |
| Video distribution (entertainment) | —‡ | — | 6,000,000 |
| Visualization: chemistry | 1 | 80,000 | 640,000 |
| Visualization: genetics | 3 | 1,000,000 | 2,670,000 |
| Visualization: biology | 1 | 800,000 | 6,400,000 |
| Visualization: fluid dynamics | 1 | 2,000,000 | 16,000,000 |
| Visualization: weather forecasting | 0.2 | 1,000,000 | 40,000,000 |
| Visualization: particle physics | 0.03 | 3,000,000 | 800,000,000 |

*Assumes ADPCM encoding.
†Assumes ITU-T H.261 encoding.
‡Assumes MPEG–2 encoding.

systems support this type of function. Documents created on a PC, on a desktop publishing system, or on form generators can be automatically injected into a workflow process, or sent off-net. Figure 2.12 depicts an example of incoming and outgoing document images (note, however, that a workflow system does not have to be LAN-based—it could equally well be mainframe-based).

In addition to encoding in Group 3 and/or 4 format, some commercial products (e.g., IBM's Image Plus banking system) use the adaptive bilevel image compression (ABIC) algorithm. The algorithm and chip implementation were developed by IBM; the algorithm is being proposed as a U.S. ANSI standard for banking.

## 2.5   OCR-enhanced Imaging

Electronic imaging systems can be extended to incorporate optical character recognition, to further increase the productivity and flexibil-

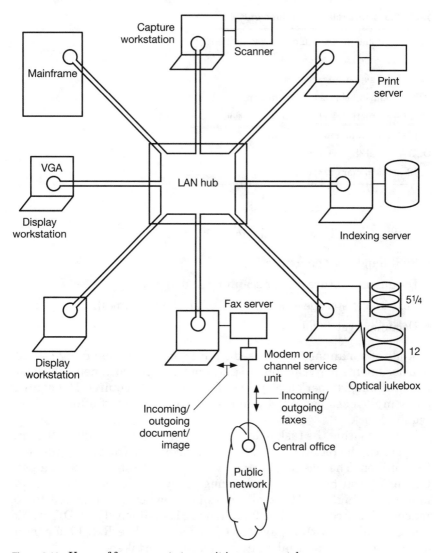

**Figure 2.12** Usage of fax servers to transmit images remotely.

ity of document-based transaction-driven data capture and storage (see Ref. 16 and Chap. 1). These systems are called by some *optical digital imaging text* (ODIT) systems. Proponents cite economic payback in 3 years or less.[17] Table 2.3 depicts some of the recognition technologies that can be employed. (These can also be interpreted as requirements that have to be supported by an ODIT.)

TABLE 2.3  ODIT-related Requirements

AN/HP—alphanumeric handprint recognition

BCR—bar code recognition

LSR—light signature recognition

ICR—intelligent character recognition

MICR—magnetic ink character recognition

NHP—numeric handprint recognition

OCR—optical character recognition

OMS—optical mark sense

ODITs typically support the following functions:[17]

- Mail handling and extraction
- Document capture and/or scanning and digitizing
- Text image storage [optical, DAT (digital audio tape)]
- Document retrieval

A study of a manual paper-based transaction system handling 1.4 million documents per year showed a cost of $2.08 per document (the labor cost was $29,248 per employee).[17] The operation required 100 equivalent-employees. Table 2.4 depicts the percentage of effort in each required task.

By automating the task using an imaging system the 100 staff-years per year can be reduced to 70, reducing labor costs from $2.9 million to $2.1 million. The imaging system would cost $2.4 million, with a payback of 36 months. Further enhancing the system to an ODIT for automatic indexing, the 100 staff-years per year can be reduced to 50, reducing labor costs from $2.9 million to $1.4 million. The ODIT would cost $3 million, with a payback of 24 months. See Ref. 17 for more details on how a financial analysis can be undertaken.

TABLE 2.4  Typical Document Handling Tasks and Costs

| | |
|---|---|
| Mail handling and preparation | 9.3% |
| Computer batch and data preparation | 11.7% |
| Data capture | 60.6% |
| Data processing and customer service relations | 11.7% |
| Other (storage, auditing, quality assurance, etc.) | 6.7% |
| Total | 100% |

## 2.6   Software Issues

The imaging platform must support a flexible and comprehensive application development environment, if the organization is to obtain the maximum benefits from the imaging system. Typical tools that are desirable include[7]

1. Tools for managing the lifecycle of the imaging system, beginning with prototyping (if any), development, maintenance, backup and disaster recovery, and documentation.

2. System administration tools for managing the imaging system in "production mode." This includes normal fault, performance, configuration, accounting, and security management functions.

3. Administrative tools to manage workgroup and workflow functions, to manage case and workfolder issues, to enable definition of new forms, and to track work in progress.

In addition, given the volume of information typically supported by an imaging system, as well as the need or desire to track and maintain images and folders, a relational database is usually required. Relational databases have been integrated in imaging systems as follows:[7]

- Imaging application data resides on the database with external references to image location tables.

- Imaging application data and image location tables are included directly in the database.

Structured query language (SQL) is the standard mechanism in support of image-related relational databases (as well as for other relational databases).

## 2.7   Storage Cost Considerations

Making an exact cost assessment between various document storage systems is not straightforward. Studies have shown that at the system (hardware) level, microfilm is the least expensive, followed by magnetic disk, and then followed by optical storage for small imaging systems; for large systems the order is microfilm, optical storage, and then magnetic disk storage.

Consideration of the cost of media depends on the compression rate. For microfilm, the cost per document is $0.001 ($16 per film, storing 16,000 documents at 300 dpi). The cost of optical storage media depends on the size of the document, the resolution (scanning density), and the compression algorithm. As an example, a 14-in optical disk can store 200,000 letter-size documents at 200 dpi and a compression ratio of 1:10. If the compression algorithm achieves a compression of 1:25, then 400,000 documents at 200 dpi can be stored. A document scanned at 300 dpi would result in storage capacities of 90,000 documents at 1:10 compression and 175,000 documents at 1:25 compression. The cost per document would then range from $0.002 to $0.008, given a media cost of $750. Note the two- to eightfold increase compared to microfilm. However, on-line computerized imaging provides ready access to the information, whether locally or remotely.

## 2.8  Legal Issues

At least for banks, paper and microfilm-microfiche storage are legally acceptable.[18] The issue is whether optically stored information is admissible in a court of law. Besides data integrity considerations, the issue is complicated by the fact that it involves several evidentiary laws, over 50 jurisdictions, and more than 100 regulatory agencies. Reference 19 provides a starting point for addressing this issue. In capsule form, the situation is as follows: There are laws in all 50 states as a legal foundation for admitting optically stored records in court. The specific legal basis is found in the Rules of Evidence and in the statutory laws. Specifically, the Rules of Evidence provide for the admissibility of "data compilations." This term was included in the 1974 revision of the Uniform Rules of Evidence and the 1975 revision of the Federal Rules of Evidence. Since that time, "data compilations" have been used as the basis for admitting magnetically stored information. Mead Data Central, owner of Lexis and Nexis, has a revenue stream of close to $500 million a year by processing court documents from over 2000 federal and state jurisdictions and making them available to 250,000 subscribers. This type of record keeping is a prime target for imaging. Imaging is now applicable to optically stored records.

## 2.9  Examples of Imaging Usage in Various Industries

Table 2.5 depicts some "horizontal" applications of CD-ROM technology in general and imaging in particular.[20] This section examines a number of "vertical" applications of imaging. It should be noted, as the discussion proceeds, that if the input materials, such as medical books, law books, and directories, are available in text form (i.e., ASCII), then they could easily be stored in a few $3\frac{1}{2}$-in floppy diskettes; however, when these books, directories, etc., are not available in ASCII form, they need to be scanned in as images, which, even discounting figures,

**TABLE 2.5   "Horizontal" Applications of CD-ROM Technology in General and Imaging in Particular**

| | |
|---|---|
| Accounting information | Manuscripts |
| Advertising information | Maps |
| Airline data | Marketing statistics |
| Architectural information | Medical books |
| Archives | Medical records |
| Armed forces data | Microfiche replacement |
| Artwork | Microfilm replacement |
| Banking records | Multimedia |
| Bibliographies | Navigation information |
| Billing information | Network backup |
| Birth records | Newspapers |
| Book lists | Numeric data |
| Bookkeeping | On-line services |
| Bulletin boards | Parts catalogs |
| Business documents | Parts manuals |
| Case reports | Patents |
| Catalogs | Personnel information |
| City, state, and federal information | Phone books |
| Company archives | Photographs |
| Computer images | Police records |
| Correspondence | Presentations |
| Credit card information | Pricing schedules |
| Data distribution | Product directory |
| Databases | Product training |
| Document storage | Profiles |
| Document distribution | Publishing |
| Drawings | Real estate records and images |
| Educational information | Records |
| Engineering | Sales records |
| File cabinet replacement | Samples |
| Financial information | Schematics |
| Geologic data | Shareware |
| Graphics | Sheet music |
| Hard-disk copy | Shipping information |
| Health records | Software backup |
| Historical information | Space exploration data |
| Insurance policies | Specifications and standards |
| Insurance records | Spreadsheets |
| Invoices | State laws |
| Legal briefs | Stock information |
| Library reference | Stock photographs |
| Magazines | Test reports |
| Mailing lists | Textbooks |
| Manifests | Town records |
| Manuals | Transportation data |
| Manufacturing information | User manuals |

diagrams, and photos, already require an order of magnitude more data.

Optical storage technology offers major benefits for the legal profession according to observers; according to these observers "CD-ROM is revolutionizing legal research."[21] It increases task effectiveness and cost control in at least three areas:

1. *Litigation.*   Allows lawyers to control information more effectively, helping them to win cases or obtain advantageous settlements.

2. *Administration.*   Allows firms to control costs and bill clients more promptly while adding new billable document-processing services.

3. *Preparatory research.*   CD-ROM libraries make research more effective as well as more economical.

Reference 21 provides a summary of known usage of imaging in the legal profession. A short survey follows.

Simon and Kelly introduced an imaging system based on the WIIS in the late 1980s. More than 30,000 records were put on line, with more being added as time went by. In 1990, Bickel & Brenner announced to be the first law firm to install a multisite electronic computer imaging system for capturing, storing, retrieving, displaying, editing, managing, and distributing documents. They implemented a system using WIIS, with the goal of eliminating costly and time-consuming processes in support of research, filing, and retrieval. At present, 850,000 pages are on image servers. Automation enhances the speed of research aiding litigation and cuts millions of dollars from legal proceedings. Portable terminals and printers have also been used to make access in the courtroom possible. A litigation firm, Wyman, Bautzer, Kuchel, Dworkin, represented Lincoln Saving and Loan in its bankruptcy proceedings. Over 1.8 million documents (1200 boxes) were involved. It was estimated that dozens of paralegal clerks would be required to process the paper, working around the clock for 6 months. Instead, the documents were scanned to WORM media in 30 days, using ODIT-like technology with character-keyword recognition.

Many of the legal references are now available on CD-ROM. Table 2.6 provides a partial list.

There has been press coverage of usage of imaging in the financial industry. Many of the major financial services institutions have incorporated imaging capabilities in their organization's information processing flow. The 1992 imaging penetration in this market was estimated to be $0.5 billion. However, some observers note that the majority of the 13,000 U.S. commercial banks and 5000 insurance companies "lag in taking advantage of the demonstrably effective ways to

**TABLE 2.6    Legal References Available on CD-ROM, Partial List***

| | |
|---|---|
| New Mexico Law on Disk (Michie, 1990) | CD-ROM(s) contain 15 text volumes of New Mexico statutes, annotated; state rules of the Court; state Supreme Court decisions; decisions of the Courts of Appeal since 1966; and other documents |
| California Practice Library (M. Bender, 1989) | CD-ROM(s) contain 103 text volumes, including *California Forms of Pleading and Practice*; *California Legal Forms*; *California Points and Authority*; *Penal Code* |
| Tax Library (M. Bender, 1989) | CD-ROM(s) contain 55 text volumes, including *Bender's Federal Tax Service, New York Tax Code*; *California Taxation*; *Florida Tax Service*; *Texas Tax Service* |
| Federal Practice Library (M. Bender, 1990) | CD-ROM(s) contain 104 text volumes, including *Moore's Federal Practice, Bender's Forms of Discovery*; *Disposition Strategy*; *Weinstein's Evidence*; *U.S. Rules*; *Modern Federal Jury Instructions* |
| Collier's Bankruptcy Library (M. Bender, 1990) | CD-ROM(s) contain 55 text volumes, including *Bankruptcy Cases*; *On Bankruptcy*; *Bankruptcy Practice Guide*; *Handbook of Creditors' Committees*; *Bankruptcy Compensation Guide* |
| Intellectual Property | *World Patent Law and Practice*; *Patents*; *Trademark Protection and Practice*; *Patent Litigation* |

*Some of these are in machine-readable form rather than in image form.

upgrade long-prevalent, relatively cumbersome, labor intensive and inefficient practices."[22] Some optimistic assessments claim that a fifth of the larger banks use or plan to use imaging; others say that 27 percent of the banks with more than $2 billion in deposits have imaging systems in place, while only about 3 to 10 percent of those with less than $1 billion had the technology at press time.[22]

Introduction of imaging is estimated by proponents to save back-office staffing by 10 to 20 percent.[22] Some of the applications of imaging in banks include new accounts processing, signature verification, microfiche replacement, loan applications and associated volume of documentation, and check processing. Examples of usage in the financial services area include credit card applications, charge card receipts, and credit reports.

About 15 percent of the U.S. insurance companies had incorporated imaging by early 1992, with about 50 percent having some kind of pilot. Some of the applications include policies, claim forms, photographs in support of damage reports, and medical invoices and reports.

Reference 23 provides a summary of known usage of imaging in the financial services industry. A short survey follows.

Gateway Bank saved $100,000 a year with a PC-based optical disk to manage microfiche (a single 5 1/4 WORM can store one month's worth of information). JCPenney has adopted an image-processing system to handle remittance processing. Worldwide Consumer Banking Group (Chemical Bank) uses Sony optical jukeboxes to store information on accounts outside the United States. American Express has replaced microfilm with imaging technology; they mail out 100,000 billing statements per hour. MasterCard International uses an imaging system to automate the exchange of charge slip information and other documentation between member banks for the resolution of disputed charges. Western Bank replaced microfiche for checking and saving account statements. Norwegian Bank's Clearinghouse uses a TRW imaging processing system for capturing images of checks and mailing the images, as proofs of receipt, to payees. Financial Systems and Equipment Corporation has installed approximately 100 optically based systems for signature imaging, document storage, and retrieval for banks in Texas and Oklahoma.

### 2.10   Some Technological Directions

This section provides a synopsis of some possible transitions over the next few years (these as well as other trends are discussed elsewhere in this text).

- *Workstations.*   Migrating from DOS and Microsoft Windows to The X Window System and Motif, or perhaps to Windows NT.
- *Image compression.*   Migrating from ITU-T Groups 3 and 4 to JPEG (see Chap. 6).
- *Image file format.*   Migrating from TIFF to ODA (TIFF is introduced in Chap. 5).

Database technology will migrate from a relational paradigm to an object-oriented paradigm. LAN technology will migrate from Ethernet and token ring to ATM-based LANs. Wide area connectivity will migrate from dial-up facsimile methods to cell relay, particularly for scientific and engineering applications.

### 2.11   A Balanced View

In this section, another view is presented for the sake of balance. The following quote, taken verbatim from Ref. 23, is worth considering:

> During the golden age of Hollywood, the movie mogul Samuel Goldwyn looked to purchase the film rights to George Bernard Shaw's plays. After

protracted haggling and negotiations over rights fees, Shaw declined to sell. "The trouble is, Mr. Goldwyn" said Shaw, "You are only interested in art and I am only interested in money." Today many manufacturers attempt to interest their markets in their particular "art" or technology, instead of focusing on customers' interest in making money. When it comes to imaging [or technology X] and the ways in which banks capture information, the question must be asked—is today's imaging technology [or technology X] something the industry really needs? Can banks afford to get involved in digital imaging right now? Can they afford not to? Is all the excitement really warranted? These questions are particularly relevant at a time when productivity, head count reduction, and profit enhancement issues command the attention of senior bank management. Many industry analysts have been heaping enormous praise on the technology, concluding that the question is not whether to buy the first piece of digital equipment, but when to make the purchase.

In today's business environment in general, and in the banking segment in particular, managers are reluctant to allocate additional resources into technology, since past investments have not resulted in measurable productivity gains or additional force reduction, according to industry observers. As a result, the acquisition of new technology is being scrutinized more closely than ever before; gone are the days of managers aspiring to be the first on the block to acquire new technology, just for the sake of it.[23] Of over 600 imaging programs looked at to assess the success rate of imaging technology introduction, 500 never passed the pilot stage, and only 100 went on to be fully implemented.

Financial considerations will ultimately be the gating factor for the introduction of the technology in the business environment. A specific metric used by an industry such as the banking industry is if the new technology can reduce check processing time and errors, while increasing the income by reducing float. Introduction in the scientific and/or medical environment is less tied to cost and productivity gains.

## References

1. T. J. Thiel, "Costs of CD-ROM Production—What They Are and How to Overcome Them," *CD-ROM Professional,* March 1993, pp. 43 ff.
2. W. Gnerre, "EDMICS—the Foundation for Future CALS Initiatives," *Document Image Automation,* November–December 1991, pp. 337 ff.
3. D. Minoli, "APPI or APPN," *Network Computing,* February 1993, Vol. 4, No. 2, pp. 126 ff.
4. R. H. Katz, "High-Performance Network and Channel Based Storage," *Proceedings of the IEEE,* August 1992, Vol. 80, No. 8, pp. 1238 ff.
5. J. R. Vacca, "Metaview's Operational Image Management System," *Document Image Automation,* July–August 1991, pp. 196 ff.
6. J. H. Bovenlander, "The Experiences of Erasmus University Rotterdam," *CD-ROM Professional,* March 1993, p. 30.
7. N. D. Natraj, "Architectures and Standards: Considerations in Document Imaging Systems," *Document Image Automation,* November–December 1991, pp. 333 ff.

8. D. Minoli and B. Keinath, *Distributed Multimedia Through Broadband Communication Services,* Artech House, Norwood, MA, 1994.
9. *NETWATCHER,* February 1993, Vol. 11, No. 2, pp. 11 ff.
10. D. Minoli, *Broadband Network Analysis and Design,* Artech House, Norwood, MA, 1993.
11. W. Stallings, *Data and Computer Communication,* 2d ed., Macmillan, New York, 1988.
12. "First ISDN Medical Document Imaging Shown," *Imaging News,* December 16, 1992.
13. E. Heatwole, "Processing Document Images on the Telco Network," *IEEE Communications Magazine,* January 1993, pp. 40 ff.
14. S. Akselsen, "Telemedicine and ISDN," *IEEE Communications Magazine,* January 1993, pp. 46 ff.
15. J. D. Russell, "ATM Applications Analysis," ATM Forum Contribution 93–651, May 19–21, 1993.
16. R. Kasturi and M. M. Trivedi, *Image Analysis Applications,* Marcel Dekker, New York, 1990.
17. H. F. Schantz, "OCR-Enhanced Electronic Image Management Systems Minimize Operations Costs," *Document Image Automation,* Fall 1992, Vol. 12, No. 3.
18. C. Tapper and K. Tombs, *The Legal Admissibility of Document Imaging Systems,* Meckler, Westport, CT, 1992.
19. R. F. Williams, "Is It Legal? The Second Most Frequently Asked Question in Optical Storage," *Document Image Automation,* Fall 1992, Vol. 12, No. 3, pp. 10 ff.
20. *CD-ROM Professional,* March 1993, p. 78.
21. H. Urrows and E. Urrows, "Optical Data Storage and Retrieval in the Legal Profession," *Document Image Automation,* November–December 1991.
22. H. Urrows and E. Urrows, "Automated Imaging in Financial Services," *Document Image Automation,* September–October 1991.
23. M. Gumaer, "Making the Business Case for Imaging," *Document Image Automation,* Fall 1992, Vol. 12, No. 3, pp. 30 ff.

# 3

# Technical Principles of Resolution and Color

This chapter examines some of the fundamental imaging concepts in terms of required resolution and color representation. Section 3.1, on resolution issues, provides information that is the basis for the rest of the book. Color and aspects of colorimetry play an important role in DISs, EISs, and SISs; they also play a role in some BISs. Hence, these issues are covered in some detail. However, it is not necessary to read Secs. 3.2 and 3.3 in order to understand the rest of the book, unless a more in-depth appreciation of the issues involved is desired; therefore, the novice reader or the corporate planner may choose to skip these sections on first reading. As indicated in Chap. 1, this book aims at a balance between theory and practice. The previous two chapters covered some aspects of practice—this chapter covers some theory.

## 3.1  Image Resolution Issues

This section provides an overview of the capture requirements in terms of resolution for a variety of input materials. These requirements will be revisited at the practical level in Chap. 4 in the context of scanners. Considering a certain image and imposing a cartesian coordinate system, one can represent the perceived light energy (or intensity) at point $(x,y)$ by a function $B(x,y)$. That is, $B(x,y)$ represents the monochrome visual information contained in the image. Individual image elements are variously called *samples, picture elements, pels,* or *pixels.* The term *pixel* is used in this text. Pixel may be used to refer to fixed samples in the image plane (e.g., in the phrase "the $2 \times 2$ block of pixels in the right-end corner of the image..."), or it may refer to samples of an object scene (e.g., in the phrase "the pixels of a boat moving left to right...").

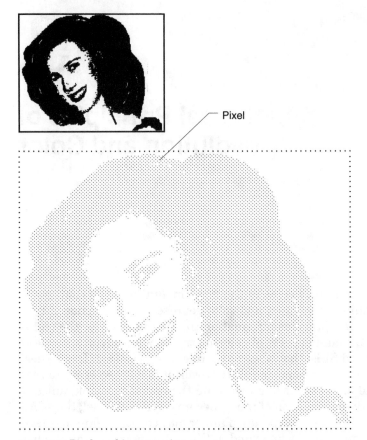

**Figure 3.1**   Pixels making up an image.

The terms *pixel at (x,y)* [or pixel @ (x,y)] and B(x,y) are often used interchangeably, even though the two concepts are not exactly identical. Figure 3.1 illustrates the concept of pixels contained in an image.

Multiple planes of pixels fill three-dimensional space. Voxels (volume elements) are cubic elements used for processing and measurements of three-dimensional images. Three-dimensional images are not considered in this book. See Ref. 1 for a discussion and other references.

At the high end of the resolution scale, one can start with the limits on normal human vision. The term *20/20 vision,* as measured by the Snellen eye chart used by optometrists, implies a degree of detail that can be resolved on the basis of distinguishability of line pairs if they are separated by *one minute of arc* or more. (More recent studies have shown a slightly better resolution, but the number just listed remains the point of reference.) At a viewing distance of 25 cm this equates with 13.5 line pairs per millimeter (343 line pairs per inch). For a 10 × 13-in viewing area corresponding (approximately) to a 19-in monitor, this implies a (steady) optical display of 4400h × 3500v (horizontal × vertical) pixels (line-pairs). This equates to about 15 million pixels of information. A 35-mm slide is estimated to have a resolution in the 20 million–pixel range (however, as noted in Chap. 1, an uncompressed digitized version of a 35-mm photo is typically coded with only about 10 MB—4 million pixels and 24-bit color, with $2000 \times 2000 \times 24/8 = 12$ MB, or 10 MB as an approximation).[2]

High-end professional imaging systems can exceed the 13.5 line pairs per millimeter resolution. For example, Eastman Kodak's T-Max 100 Professional black-and-white system can resolve 200 line pairs per millimeter (about 5000 line pairs per inch). High-quality photographic optics can also exceed the 13.5 line pairs per millimeter requirement, but by a smaller margin.[3]

The 4400h × 3500v–pixel resolution mentioned above, however, needs to be slightly improved if one wants to retain the full level of resolution in an electronic display. In converting an optical display to progressive scan electronic display, one introduces a visual loss due to the Kell factor. This factor implies that the perceived image has an apparent vertical resolution that is only 70 percent of the nominal resolution. If one aims at compensating for this factor, one actually needs 4400h × 5000v pixels (or line pairs), equating to 22 million pixels.

Interlacing is an important factor to consider. In television it is customary to display successive frames by alternating the lines shown. If in frame $i$ the odd-numbered lines are displayed, then in frame $i + 1$ the even-numbered lines are displayed. This is known as *2:1 interlacing*. The initial reason for interlacing was to reduce the required transmission bandwidth compared to the bandwidth needed for progressive display of full frames. Interlacing obviously introduces image degradation, since useful information is "thrown away." It is estimated that the resolution loss due to interlacing is 35 percent. Some new TV sets utilize frame storage to present full frames progressively scanned at 60 frames per second, or twice the previous rate required for two successive fields.

Table 3.1, based partially on Ref. 3, depicts the nominal resolution of some display systems (note that the table does not include the added dimension of gray scale* and/or color). The effective resolution is from 30 to 60 percent less than the nominal resolution. For example, NTSC TV nominally carries 525 lines; however, some lines have no information (e.g., blanking interval that takes 40 lines); other lines are over-

---

*Some use *grayscale* or *grey-scale*; we use *gray scale* per Ref. 4. A gray scale is a series of achromatic tones having varying proportions of white and black, to give a full range of grays between white and black; a gray scale is usually divided into 10 steps.

TABLE 3.1    Nominal Resolution of Some Display Systems

| System | Nominal resolution | Total pixels, nominal* |
|---|---|---|
| Vision (referenced to a 10 × 12 window) | 4400h × 3500v | 15.5 million |
| MegaScan display† | 2560h × 2048v | 5.2 million |
| HDTV | 1920h × 1125v | 2.1 million |
| High-quality monitor | 1280h × 1024v | 1.3 million |
| Super-VGA | 800h × 600v | 0.48 million |
| VGA | 640h × 480v | 0.31 million |
| Macintosh Classic | 640h × 400v | 0.26 million |
| EGA | 640h × 350v | 0.22 million |
| CGA | 640h × 200v | 0.13 million |
| TV (NTSC) | 525h × 336v | 0.18 million |

*Effective resolution varies from 30 to 60 percent of the nominal resolution; e.g., effective resolution for HDTV is 0.9 million pixels.
†Used for medical imaging applications supporting a 12-bit gray scale.

scanned and are not normally displayed (about 41 lines—overscanning is utilized to maintain the screen fully painted even under voltage reduction situations that lead to picture shrinkage; overscanning is not used in PC monitors). Therefore, only 444 are visible in the vertical axis. In addition, there is the interlacing factor, where only 202 lines are shown in any one frame. This means that instead of a resolution of 525h × 336v (176,400 pixels), one only gets 202h × 336v (67,872 pixels). (In fact, the horizontal resolution is only 309 lines.)

Two points worth noting from the table are that (1) television is two orders of magnitude less "clear" than what the human eye can see (250 times, or 0.06 million pixels versus 15.5 million pixels), and (2) even the much touted high-definition television (HDTV) is relatively poor, although it is 15 times better than existing television (0.06 million pixels of actual resolution versus 0.9 million pixels of actual resolution[3]).

There continues to be controversy in the industry as to the successor technology to NTSC. Some argue that the quality of HDTV is not sufficient for CAD/CAM and medical imaging applications; others argue that it would be adequate for entertainment if a noninterlace 1125-line/60 fps (frames per second) version could be adopted. In the meantime, high-quality cinema formats are emerging. For example, the ShowScan system uses 65-mm film and is projected at 60 (rather than the usual 24) fps, offering an order of magnitude improvement over regular cinematography.

In addition to the pixel density, there is the issue of gray-scale digitization and of color. In terms of gray scale, the commercial norm now is 256 levels (8-bit words); see Ref. 3 for a rationalization. Medical imaging requires a more accurate digitization: 4096 levels (12-bit words are used). For color images, each of three primary color components (or color difference components) also requires a 256-level quantization; this is expressed by saying that 24 bits per pixel are required (for medical applications $3 \times 12 = 36$ bits would be used). However, it should be noted from an optimization point of view that the number of bits for the three colors does not necessarily have to be the same. This is because green contributes about 59 percent to the combined color resolution, red contributes 30 percent, and blue contributes only 11 percent.[5,6] Some of the issues related to color are discussed next.

## 3.2  Basic Color Principles

Many DISs, EISs, and SISs require capture and display of color material. This and the next section discuss basic aspects of color. Methodologies for expressing color measurements are discussed in the material that follows, as background information. Color scanners, covered in Chap. 4, may or may not utilize all these techniques directly; however, as the science of imaging progresses to more sophisticated applications, particularly in SIS environments, these considerations may begin to play a more important role. PC and workstation monitors, discussed at the end of this chapter, as well as other output systems covered in Chap. 5, also utilize many of the principles discussed herewith. Some readers may wish to skip some or all portions of this and the following subsections on first reading. Table 3.2 provides a summary (glossary) of some key concepts on color used in this chapter.

Color is not a direct property of an object or of physical energy, but it is the perceptual experience of the human observer.[7] There are physical, psychophysical, and perceptual factors. Since color itself is a perceptual response, it cannot be directly measured. Although the visual process begins with physics, as radiant energy reaching the eye, it is in the mind of the observer that the stimuli produced from this radiant energy are interpreted and organized to form meaningful perceptions, including the perception of color.[8] Table 3.3 depicts some of the factors involved in color analysis. Physical factors affect the transmitting side of the light system and cover spectral distribution and radiance. Psychophysical attributes include luminance, dominant wavelength, and excitation purity (see Table 3.2 for some quick definitions). Perceptual factors are related to hue, brightness, and saturation. No color description model can take into account all the factors that determine a color response; these models, however, are successful at capturing some key aspects.

Techniques have been developed to arrange colors in systematic order (e.g., the Munsell system), based on color appearance. Such approaches are based strictly on subjective human perception. A summary of these approaches is provided first (Sec. 3.2.2). More "analytical" approaches use the variations in spectral composition of the light reflected or transmitted by a specimen of such color(ed material) (Secs.

**TABLE 3.2   Key Concepts Pertaining to Color**

| | |
|---|---|
| Achromatic versus chromatic color | An image (object) that exhibits a specific hue, such as red or green, is said to have chromatic color; an image (object) that stands out from its background on the basis of lightness, such as black or gray, is said to have an achromatic color; objects in the visual environment that reflect or emit distributions of wavelengths in unequal amounts are chromatic |
| Brightness | That attribute of visual sensation indicating that an area appears to emit more or less light; if the total amount of light illuminating an object is increased, the lightness stays the same while the brightness increases |
| Chromaticity | The quality of light expressing hue and saturation features; typically shown in a 2-D (two-dimensional) plane in some coordinate system (the third coordinate is obtained from subtracting the other two from 1, since their sum is normalized to 1) |
| Color | The characteristics of radiant energy in the visible domain (380–700 nm) by which an observer can distinguish between two fields of view of different spectral compositions |
| Color appearance | What colors look like to a human observer (as contrasted with color matching) under nonstandardized (viz., normally available) lighting conditions |
| Color matching | The process of comparing, under standardized viewing conditions (lighting, viewing angle, surroundings, etc.), a sample to either another sample or a given mix of light from specified primaries, until the observer is unable to distinguish any color difference in the two samples |
| Colorimeter | An instrument that enables one to measure color by determining the intensity of the three primary colors that will give that color |
| Colorimetry | Color matching under standardized conditions of comparison (observation) |
| Discrimination | A human's ability to perceive a difference between two colors; it entails the luminance and chromaticity differences between sources, the ambient environment, the level of adaptation of the eye, and the information field size |
| Distribution of spectral energy | The variation of the spectral concentration of visible energy |
| Dominant wavelength (complementary wavelength) | The dominant wavelength of a color is the wavelength of the spectral color that, when additively mixed in appropriate proportions with the specified reference white, yields a match with the color under investigation |

TABLE 3.2    Key Concepts Pertaining to Color (*Continued*)

| | |
|---|---|
| Excitation purity | $L_1/L_2$ on a chromaticity diagram, where $L_1$ is the distance from a specified achromatic color to the color sample and $L_2$ is the distance along the same direction as $L_1$ and running from the achromatic point through the color sample to the edge of the chromaticity diagram; ranges from 0 (achromatic sample) to 1 for a spectrally pure color |
| Hue | That attribute of visual sensation such that a stimulus appears to be similar to the perceived colors of purple, blue, green, red, orange, yellow, etc. |
| Lightness | That attribute of visual sensation indicating that an area appears to reflect or transmit, to a greater or smaller extent, a fraction of the incident light |
| Luminance | A measurement of the intensity response of a typical human observer of the light (image) source; defined as the instantaneous luminance of the light field—namely, if $V(\lambda)$ represents the spectral response of human vision, and $C(x,y,t,\lambda)$ represents the spatial energy distribution of a light (image) source at spatial coordinates $(x,y)$, time $t$, and wavelength $\lambda$, then it is the (integral) accumulation of the product $C(x,y,t,\lambda) \times V(\lambda)$ over the visible domain |
| Munsell renotation system | A system that specifies the color of a collection of chips by hue, lightness (also known as *value*), and saturation (also known as *chroma*), mapped to a chromaticity coordinate space |
| Radiance | The radiant intensity per unit area (measure made as the source is projected to a perpendicular plane from which the observation is made) |
| Saturation | That attribute of the perceived color that indicates how different that color is from an achromatic color; spectral colors have high saturation, while pastel colors have low saturation |

3.2.3 and beyond). These approaches are based on the electromagnetic spectrum; hence, the discussion starts with an overview of the electromagnetic spectrum.

### 3.2.1    Spectral composition of light

Figure 3.2 depicts portions of the electromagnetic spectrum identifying where visible light fits in. The parameters of the spectrum are either frequency $f$ or wavelength $\lambda$; the two variables are related by the equation $\lambda = c/f$, with $c$ the speed of light, $c = 3 \times 10^8$. At these ranges, wavelength can be quoted as micrometers, nanometers, or angstroms (Å). For example, fiberoptics communication takes place in the infrared region, typically at 8300 Å (0.83 µm or 830 nm; 1 Å = $10^{-10}$ m), 13,500 Å or 15,500 Å. These signals are not visible to the human eye, since the

TABLE 3.3    Key Factors Affecting Color Images

| Factors | Color | Intensity | Temporal | Spatial |
|---|---|---|---|---|
| | | Domain | | |
| Visual | Chromatic aberration Chromaticity Color aftereffects Color contrast Color mixing Color purity Display convergence Number of colors Visual abnormalities of observer | Brightness Contrast Retinal adaptation | Flicker (CRT display of image) Eye movement | Background Image aspect Image convergence Image resolution Image size Viewing angle Viewing distance |
| Perceptual | Color discrimination (relative process) Color identification (absolute process) | Image visibility | Stability of image information | Color integrity Image quality (clarity, sharpness) |

eye's response is between 6900* Å (red) and 4300† Å (violet); these infrared systems operate just below the visible area.

Figure 3.2 also provides a view of the hue variation in the normal sunlight spectrum. Violet is generally positioned to range from 4000 to 4240 Å; blue, 4240 to 4912 Å; green, 4912 to 5750 Å; yellow, 5750 to 5850 Å; orange, 5850 to 6470 Å; and red, 6470 to 7000 Å. Maximum visibility is achieved at 5500 Å. As a side observation, note that when sunlight is examined through a spectroscope it is found that the spectrum is traversed by 31 dark lines parallel to the length of the slit. These dark lines, some of which are shown in Fig. 3.2, are known as *Fraunhofer lines* (these dark lines arise from the absorption of the solar energy by layers of vapors that act as filters). For example, the B line is at 6869.995 Å; the C line at 6562.816 Å; the D line at 5895.944 Å, etc. Measurement of the spectral composition of light in terms of constituent wavelengths requires appropriate instrumentation. Figure 3.3 depicts some examples of light source spectra, other than sunlight.

### 3.2.2 Human perception of color

The Commission Internationale de l'Eclairage (CIE) has established several standards to help establish relatively precise measurements of

---

*Nominally 7000 Å.
†Nominally 4000 Å.

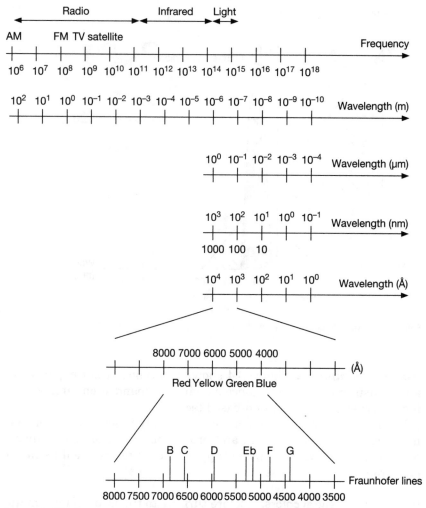

**Figure 3.2**  Electromagnetic spectrum, focusing on the visible range.

color based partially on spectral composition. The CIE color system is a worldwide color mixture system for specifying any color, recommended in 1931 by the International Commission on Illumination (i.e., Commission Internationale de l'Eclairage), (1) by giving the amounts (tristimulus values) $X,Y,Z$ of three primary colors required by a standard observer to match the color in question, which are calculable from the spectral composition of the radiant energy leaving the color specimen or (2) by giving one of the tristimulus values $Y$, expressing the luminance value of the color, combined with two of the fractions: $x = X/(X + Y + Z)$, $y = Y/(X + Y + Z)$, $z = Z/(X + Y + Z)$, known as *chro-*

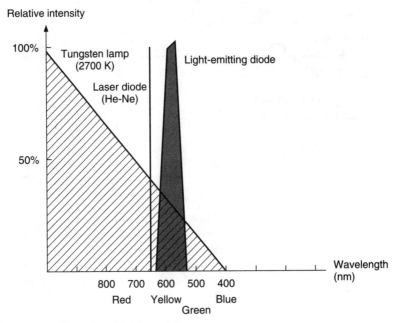

**Figure 3.3**  Examples of light spectra.

*maticity coordinates.* Figure 3.4 shows two typical color experiments and measurements. These concepts will be expanded on later, following a discussion of perception-based techniques.

Before discussing this and other analytically based models for color measurement, classification, and processing, two approaches based only on qualitative perception (appearance) are provided as initial background to the discussion.

**Perception of neutral colors.**  Before turning to the issue of (chromatic) color, a brief discussion of neutral colors is provided. The terms *achromatic color* and *black-and-white* are both used in this text.

When the source illuminating an object contains all of the wavelengths to which the eye is sensitive and when the object reflects all such wavelengths equally, the color of the object is achromatic. The object will appear to be white, black, or some intermediate level of gray. The amount of light reflected determines, to a large extent, the lightness of the object. Objects reflecting ≥80 percent of the light appear white, while those reflecting ≤3 percent appear black; levels of gray are represented by reflectance between 4 and 79 percent.

Two aspects of neutral color perception are *lightness* and *brightness.* Lightness is that attribute of visual sensation (white or black) indicating that an area appears to reflect or transmit, to a greater or lesser

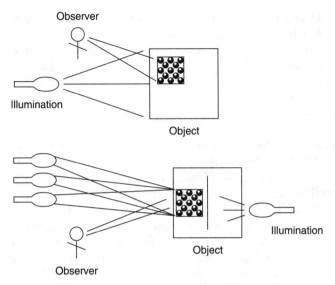

**Figure 3.4**  Typical color experiments and measurements.

extent, a fraction of the incident light. Brightness is that attribute of visual sensation (bright or dark) indicating that an area appears to emit more or less light. Lightness and brightness are generally perceptually distinguishable; however, under certain conditions the separation of the two is difficult, since increases in lightness are often connected with increases in brightness.

For a black-and-white achromatic printing system, in support, for example, of a BIS, where the reflectance of the surface and the lightness can be varied, one must develop a lightness scale where different degrees of lightness appear evenly spaced throughout the gamut of lightness levels. In developing such a lightness scale, the illumination is held constant while the reflectance of the surface is varied. The scale depends on illumination of the surface, the measurement technique employed, and the type of surface. Nonetheless, lightness is found to increase as a logarithm of reflectance. For printed images, an increase or decrease in illumination has been shown to have little perceptual effect on the *relative* lightness of areas of differing lightness. Since the percentage of light reflected from different areas remains unchanged with variations in illumination, the ratios of reflected light also remain the same. An increase in illumination makes the entire image appear brighter, but the contrast between elements of the image remains constant. Therefore, on a hard copy, the ratios of reflected light determine lightness.

The situation for a CRT-based PC monitor is not as clearcut. The luminance of the monitor is a measure of combined lightness and brightness. As the electrical signal to the monitor's electron gun is increased, a change in both lightness and brightness takes place. The images vary from black to white (lightness) and from dark to bright (brightness). When the illumination is increased, an equal amount of light is added to all areas of the image on the CRT. (Unfortunately, the increase in light output or luminance from the display is not a linear function of applied energy.) Conversely, decreasing the illumination increases the contrast as an equal amount of light is removed from all areas.

**Perception of (chromatic) colors.**   Three perceptual descriptors of light are commonly used to describe its sensation: hue, brightness (or lightness, per Table 3.2), and saturation. The perceptual attribute of light that distinguishes light coming, for example, from a yellow traffic light as contrasted to a red traffic light is called the *hue* of the light. *Saturation* describes the "whiteness" of a light source; it distinguishes a dark tone from a pastel tone of light of the same hue. *Brightness* is a perceptual interpretation of light intensity, although physical energy intensity alone is not an adequate quantitative measure of brightness.

The light reflected or emitted by typical objects is generally multi-chromatic; namely, it contains a number of different wavelengths. If an observer looks at a source emitting a narrow band of wavelengths, a dominant hue will be evident. This dominant hue often remains the same even with an increase in the spectral width; however, increasing the spectral width causes the sensation to be modified, so that the hue becomes less distinct or clear. In this case, the hue is said to be less saturated. Saturation is related to the number of wavelengths contributing to the color sensation. The narrower the band of wavelengths in the light reflected or emitted, the more highly saturated the resulting color sensation; the wider the band of wavelengths, the less saturated will be the resulting color. Achromatic colors are completely desaturated; namely, no amount of a hue is present. Mixing an achromatic color with a specific hue produces a desaturated hue with the level of saturation depending on the relative amounts of achromatic color and hue[7] (see Fig. 3.5).

*Lightness* refers to the range of achromatic colors running from white through gray to black; such range also referred to as *gray level*. Increasing the level of illumination of both achromatic and chromatic colors produces a qualitative change in appearance on the aspect of dark to bright, namely, a change in perceived brightness. As in the case with achromatic colors, however, the distinction between lightness and brightness can become difficult as brighter colors appear lighter. As the intensity of the illumination light increases or the luminance of the emitted light is raised, the colors appear brighter and the saturation increases. The saturation reaches a maximum at levels dependent on the color in question. (Yellow obtains maximum saturation at a higher

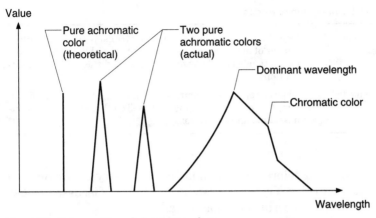

**Figure 3.5**   Achromatic and chromatic colors.

level of illumination than the rest of the visible hues.) Increases in intensity beyond the point of maximal saturation produce higher levels of brightness but a reduction in saturation. Eventually, the brightness level becomes dazzling, but the hues appear washed out and approach a luminescent white.[7]

Although color appearance has been studied in order to establish standardized measures for quantifying color appearance, no standardized measures have yet emerged. This is due partially to the complexity of the phenomenon: the perceived appearance of a color depends on factors such as

- Spectral power distribution of the source of light illuminating the object.

- Spectral reflectance and/or transmittance of all objects in the scene under observation, including the particular object of interest.

- Spatial arrangement of objects in the scene.

Color appearance is classified in the two modes listed in Table 3.4. Wavelength (spectrum, to be more inclusive) is not a completely adequate measure of the human perception of color. (In fact, some colors found in nature are not even included in the sunlight decomposed by a glass prism.)

The intricacies of the relationship between hue, saturation, lightness, and brightness have led to the development of a number of descriptive systems that attempt to model these relations. The purpose of such a system is to provide a mechanism for characterizing color samples in an orderly way in such a manner that relations between colors can be identified. In practical terms, such systems aid in the speci-

TABLE 3.4    Color Appearance Modes

| Object color mode | Objects appear to be reflecting or transmitting light; luminances of environment are similar to the object under study; perception is based on three factors—lightness, hue, and saturation |
|---|---|
| Light source mode | Objects appear to be emitting light (e.g., CRTs, TV monitors, lamps, sun, etc.); perception is based on three factors—brightness, hue, and saturation |

fication of particular colors for uses in art and industry by providing a numeric index for color. Two such systems are briefly discussed below. (One such system is described in more detail.)

At the turn of the century, the artist Alfred Munsell introduced the first version of a color description system, known as the *Munsell system*. Munsell was motivated by the ambiguity between colors afforded by the variety of names assigned to different sensations. The goal of the descriptive system was aimed at providing interrelated scales of hue, lightness, and saturation in which the size of the perceptual change in each dimension was spaced in equal steps. This system has experienced a number of modifications over the years. In the current version published by the Munsell Color Company, the system consists of an ordered array of color chips that vary in hue, lightness (here called "value"), and saturation (here called "chroma"). The lightness scale consists of nine shades of gray, visually equally spaced and bounded by white and black. Hue is represented by a circular locus in which a total of 40 steps divides the circle into equal units (e.g., 2.5B, 5B, 7.5B, 10B, four subdivisions for each of 10 hues). The dimension of saturation relates the scales of hue and lightness with a maximum of 16 gradations. CIE *x,y* coordinates (discussed later) have been derived and published for most of these color chips; these values are known as the *Munsell renotation*.

Another approach to color description is taken in the *natural color system* developed in Sweden.[7] This system emphasizes qualitative variations in color sensation rather than equally spaced visual scales as in the Munsell system. The underlying concept in the natural color system is that all colors can be described in terms of three pairs of polar coordinates: black-white, red-green, and yellow-blue. Just as with the Munsell system, this system includes a consideration of intrinsic lightness and saturation differences but fails to incorporate brightness and contrast effects. CIE *x,y* coordinates have been derived and published for over 15,000 color samples. While both systems provide a means of specifying the appearance of colors, each emphasizes a different element of color. The purpose of both the Munsell system and the natural color system is to provide a means of expressing the relationship between colors in an orderly fashion.

### 3.2.3  The Munsell color system—
### a more-detailed view

The Munsell color system is a system of specifying colors in terms of appearance on scales of hue and chroma, established first in 1915 by a collection of color chips. In 1943 it was standardized and defined to the theoretical limits by tables and diagrams in terms of the internationally adopted CIE color mixture system. (This more analytical approach is discussed later.) The system is also know as *Munsell renotation system.* It uses an approach that specifies the color of a collection of chips by hue, lightness (also known as *value*), and saturation (also known as *chroma*). The three attributes of color discussed above—hue, lightness, and saturation—may be considered as dimensions of color that can be related in the three-dimensional form suggested in Fig. 3.6.

In terms of appearance, colors have a hue that resembles the hue circle shown in Fig. 3.7. (For the sake of cost containment, the figure is in black and white, letting the reader imagine the actual colors.) The purple hues, while not found in the sunlight spectrum itself, show a resemblance to the blue and red ends and complete the hue circuit. (Purple light can be produced by combining equal amounts of red and blue lights.) Such colors are *chromatic* and differ from a pure gray scale,

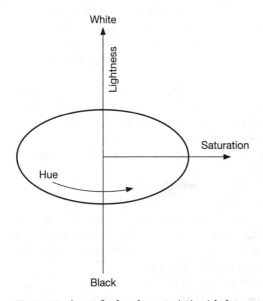

**Figure 3.6**  Axes of color characteristics (skeleton form).

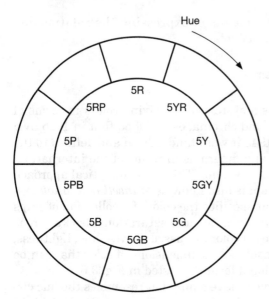

**Figure 3.7** Poor person's version of the hue circle. $R$ = red; $YR$ = yellow red; $Y$ = yellow; $GY$ = green yellow; $G$ = green; $GB$ = blue green; $B$ = blue; $PB$ = purple blue; $P$ = purple; $RP$ = red purple. [*Note:* Each hue can be further divided into four elements (e.g., 2.5$R$, 5$R$, 7.5$R$, 10$R$).]

which has no hue, and hence is called *achromatic* or *neutral,* as discussed earlier. Thus, an object that exhibits a specific hue, such as blue or yellow, has a chromatic color; an object that stands out from its background on the basis of lightness, such as gray or black, has achromatic color.

If a number of chromatic colors are selected to be constant in hue and lightness, for example, with a series of reds, some of these red colors stand out more vividly than others. Such a series may be arranged in an order of difference that increases from the grayest color to the most vivid. This difference is one of *color saturation.* Figure 3.8 provides a poor person's version of this effect.

The Munsell chips form an atlas of charts that shows scales in which two of the three variables are constant, the hue scale containing five principal and five intermediate hues (to provide a color notation in the decimal system), the value scale containing 10 steps from black to white, and the chroma scales showing 10 or more steps from the equivalent gray. The 10 hues are $R, YR, Y, GY, G, BG, B, PB, P,$ and $RP.$ Each of these has 10 subdivisions; the four most common are 2.5 (e.g., 2.5$R$), 5, 7.5, and 10. The value (lightness) has 10 subdivisions, with 0 being dark and 10 being pure white. Chroma has 20 subdivisions (or

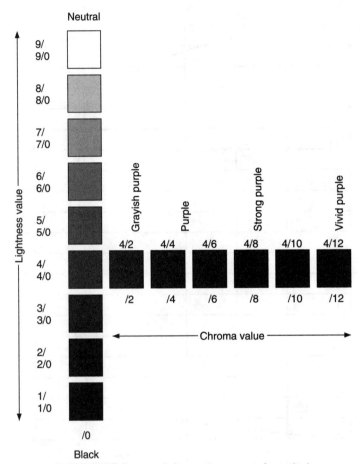

**Figure 3.8**  Scale of lightness and chroma (poor person's version).

more), with 0 representing a neutral color and 20 (or more) representing a color of high saturation. These three scales are intended to present equal visual (not physical) intervals for a normal observer and daylight viewing with gray-to-white surroundings, so that under these conditions hue, lightness value, and chroma of the color chips correlate closely with hue, lightness, and saturation of color perception. (Under other conditions the correlation for these chip is lost, and their hue, value, and chroma designations become terms of psychophysical significance since they refer to their appearance only under these standard conditions.)

Figure 3.9 shows an example of a Munsell chart; note in the figure, as implied by the discussion above, that the color "zones" are limited to a number of discrete values, being tied, in this figure, to a 20 × 14 grid. (As indicated above, the chroma can go higher.) In a study, a respondent may

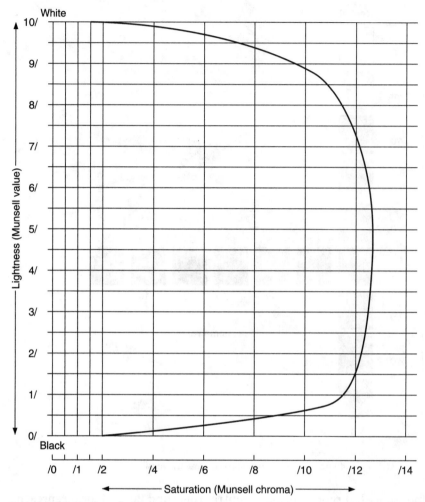

**Figure 3.9** Munsell graduation.

classify a color as being 7.5R 8/10, which means that the Munsell chip corresponding to the hue of 7.5R with a value of 8 and chroma of 10 is perceived to have the same color as the color under study.

Hue, lightness, and saturation can be mapped on a solid like the one shown in Fig. 3.10. In this color solid, hue extends in a circular direction about the neutral axis; lightness extends in the vertical direction from black at the bottom through a series of grays to white at the top of the solid; and saturation extends in a radial direction horizontally from the neutral axis, at which the saturation is zero, out to the strongest saturation, as far as this may extend from the central axis.

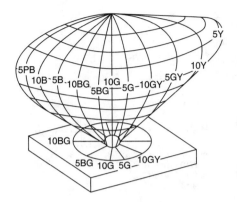

**Figure 3.10**   Color representation solid (poor person's rendition).

One needs a "discourse-friendly" approach to talk about colors in practical settings (e.g., for selecting a dye or paint) even in the context of the Munsell system; this issue is discussed next. Color can be defined in terms of names that depend on this three-dimensional analysis of color. This method has been standardized, developed, and published by the InterSociety Color Council and (what used to be) the National Bureau of Standards (now the National Institute of Standards and Technology). It is known as the *ISCC-NBS Method of Designating Colors and a Dictionary of Color Names* (NBS Publication 553, 1955). The terms "light," "medium," and "dark" designate decreasing degrees of lightness, and the adverb "very" extends the lightness scale to "very light" and "very dark." The adjectives "grayish," "moderate," "strong," and "vivid" designate increasing degrees of saturation. These and a series of hue names, used both as nouns and in adjective form, are combined to form names for describing color in terms of its three perceptual attributes. Certain other adjectives cover combinations of lightness and saturation, as *brilliant* for "light, strong," *pale* for "light, grayish," and *deep* for "dark, strong."

There are 267 ISCC-NBS name blocks in the complete system, and each defines a block in the color solid. This number is sufficient for naming colors in writing and in discourse, but since the human eye can distinguish several million colors, it follows that each name block contains a number of distinguishable colors. The important characteristic of this method that distinguishes it from other methods is that the boundaries of each color term are specified. These boundaries are in terms of the numeric scale of hue, value, and chroma of the Munsell color notation just described. (Under standard daylight conditions these scales correlate closely with the hue, lightness, and saturations scales of color perception.) Each ISCC-NBS color designation defines a block in the color solid bounded by vertical planes of constant hue, horizontal planes of constant values, and cylindrical surfaces of constant

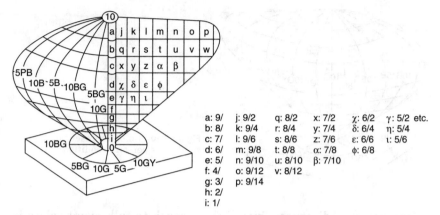

| | | | | |
|---|---|---|---|---|
| a: 9/ | j: 9/2 | q: 8/2 | x: 7/2 | χ: 6/2   γ: 5/2 etc. |
| b: 8/ | k: 9/4 | r: 8/4 | y: 7/4 | δ: 6/4   η: 5/4 |
| c: 7/ | l: 9/6 | s: 8/6 | z: 7/6 | ε: 6/6   ι: 5/6 |
| d: 6/ | m: 9/8 | t: 8/8 | α: 7/8 | φ: 6/8 |
| e: 5/ | n: 9/10 | u: 8/10 | β: 7/10 | |
| f: 4/ | o: 9/12 | v: 8/12 | | |
| g: 3/ | p: 9/14 | | | |
| h: 2/ | | | | |
| i: 1/ | | | | |

**Figure 3.11**  Vertical planes of constant hue, horizontal planes of constant values, and cylindrical surfaces of constant chroma.

chroma. Figure 3.11 shows one quarter of the Munsell solid removed to demonstrate the relation of the interior sampling for color charts of constant hue, in which lightness (value) changes in a vertical direction and saturation (chroma) varies in a horizontal direction from the center to outside limits. (Actually, this color solid has no rigid boundary for saturation—except in terms of theoretical limits, which are approached today only for yellow pigment and dyes.)

Table 3.5 contains the hue names and abbreviations used in the ISCC-NBS system. Figure 3.12 shows graphically the scheme of hue modifiers, the "-ish" grays and the neutrals with their modifiers.

To illustrate the relation of ISCC-NBS color names to the color solid, a diagram of the purple section is depicted in Fig. 3.13. (The outside limits would have to be expanded if colors were found saturated enough to extend beyond the surface indicated.) The same limits in relation to Munsell value-chroma charts which represent vertical slices cut through the neutral center of the solid, as illustrated in Fig. 3.11, are used in this figure; two diagrams included here illustrate how this is accomplished: Fig. 3.14 represents an uncomplicated name diagram in the Munsell 3P-to-9P hue range, while Fig. 3.15 represents a more complicated diagram in the 5YR-to-7YR hue range in which the pale colors are yellowish pinks, the light and strong yellow-reds are oranges, and the dark yellow-reds are browns.[9]

Table 3.12 (in the Appendix at the end of this chapter) provides the list of the 267 color name pockets grouped by hue names. (It should be noted that color samples, within tolerances close enough to be useful in illustrating these names, are not possible with usual conditions of color printing.) The ISCC-NBS naming method does not aim at describing

TABLE 3.5    Key ISCC-NBS Colors

| Color | Symbol |
|-------|--------|
| Red | $R$ |
| Reddish orange | $rO$ |
| Orange | $O$ |
| Orange-yellow | $OY$ |
| Yellow | $Y$ |
| Greenish yellow | $gY$ |
| Yellow-green | $YG$ |
| Yellowish green | $yG$ |
| Green | $G$ |
| Bluish green | $bG$ |
| Greenish blue | $gB$ |
| Blue | $B$ |
| Purplish blue | $pB$ |
| Violet | $V$ |
| Purple | $P$ |
| Reddish purple | $rP$ |
| Purplish red | $pR$ |
| Purplish pink | $pPk$ |
| Pink | $Pk$ |
| Yellowish pink | $yPk$ |
| Brownish pink | $brPk$ |
| Brownish orange | $brO$ |
| Reddish brown | $rBr$ |
| Brown | $Br$ |
| Yellowish brown | $yBr$ |
| Olive-brown | $OlBr$ |
| Olive | $Ol$ |
| Olive-green | $OlG$ |
| Black | $K$ |
| White | $W$ |

colors to a close tolerance, but it does provide a description that is useful for basic color discourse. For colorimetry, when it is important to distinguish to a very close tolerance among the thousands of colors that in the ISCC-NBS system might have an identical designation, a numeric notation must be used, preferably one that is as internationally standardized as the CIE colorimetric coordinate system, or, if nothing else, the Munsell system of notation, both of which are included in the group of standards adopted in 1951 by the American Standards Association to specify a method to measure and specify a color.

### 3.2.4  Color vision model

The previous sections provided a simple color description methodology based wholly on appearance. Models for monochrome and color vision aid the field of computer-based imaging. Appearance-based models (such as the ones described earlier) may be made to become quantita-

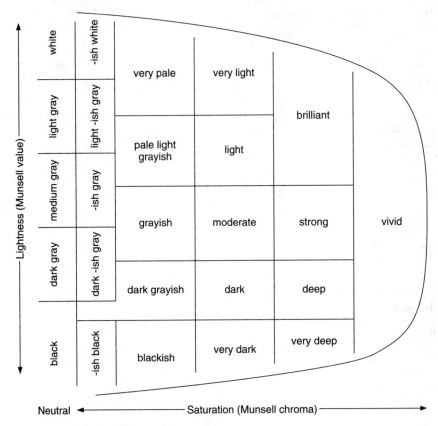

**Figure 3.12**  Scheme of hue modifiers.

tive by measuring aspects of human light perception. Photometry is the science dealing with luminance, while colorimetry is the science of color measurements. This and the following subsections cover issues pertaining to color perception and colorimetry. The "chromaticity" results (i.e., the chromaticity diagrams shown later) are based on objective, yet psychophysical, senses; namely, they are based on color matches, not subjective color appearance discussed earlier.

As already discussed, light of many wavelengths produces the psychophysical visual sensation of color. Different spectral distributions generally, but not always, give rise to a different perceived color, particularly when there is a high degree of peakedness in some region of the electromagnetic spectrum (see Fig. 3.16). In other words, color is that aspect of visible energy that enables an observer to distinguish between radiant energy of different spectral compositions (in the visible range). A color stimulus is defined by a specified radiant energy of a given intensity and spectral distribution (composition). To facilitate discourse, color is described by attaching names to key differing sensa-

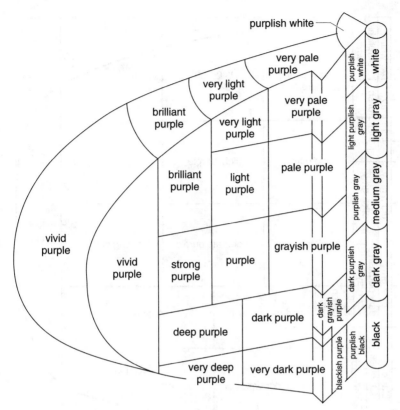

**Figure 3.13**   Slice of color solid for purple.

tions, such as red, black, and blue (as discussed in the previous subsection).

In dealing with colors, three basic elements are involved in the quest of specifying it:

- What are the characteristics of two colors that make them appear identical under specified conditions of observation? This is called *color matching*.

- How and how much are two colors different? This covers *color differences*.

- How does a color look to the observer? These nuances deal with *color appearance*.

These facets are examined in detail as the chapter progresses.

**Mathematical machinery.**   The material that follows briefly presents some needed mathematical machinery. As an aid, recall that the integral function can be thought of as representing the area under the

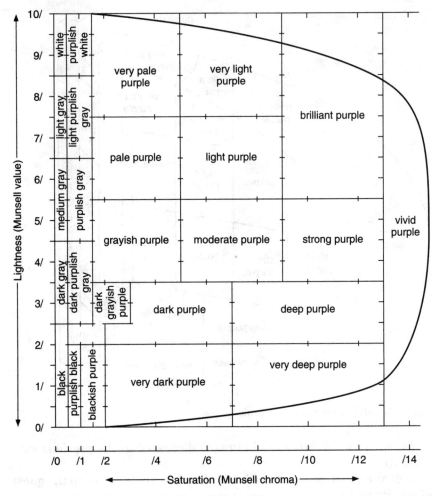

**Figure 3.14** Name diagram in the Munsell 3P-to-9P hue range.

curve of the specified function. (Such function may be shown as the product of two or more other functions.)

Let $C(x,y,t,\lambda)$ represent the spatial energy distribution of a light (image) source at spatial coordinates $(x,y)$, time $t$, and wavelength $\lambda$. This function is a bounded (based on physical considerations) four-dimensional function with bounded (based on physical considerations) independent variables. A key measure of interest is the intensity response $Y(x,y,t)$ of a typical human observer of the light (image) source. It is defined as the instantaneous luminance of the light field; namely, if $V(\lambda)$ represents the spectral response of the human vision, then

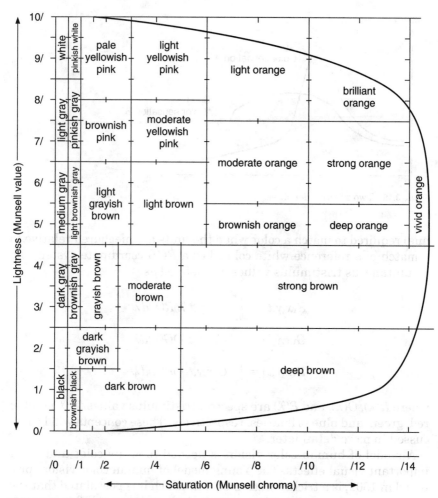

**Figure 3.15**  Name diagram in the Munsell 5YR-to-7YR hue range.

$$Y(x,y,t) = \int_0^\infty C(x,y,t,\lambda)V(\lambda)d\lambda$$

In the imaging systems discussed in this book, the image does not usually change with time; hence, the time variable may be dropped from many of the relevant equations.

The color response of a typical observer is commonly measured in terms of what are called *tristimulus values*. These values are linearly proportional to the amount of (for example) red, green, and blue light needed to "match" a colored light signal. These values represent units of energy. Put differently, the tristimulus values of a color specify the amounts of the three (given) primaries (three light sources of given

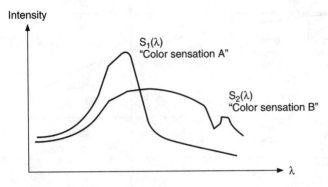

**Figure 3.16**  Two spectral densities.

hue) required to match a color when the units are measured relative to a match of a reference white color. For a $RGB$ coordinate system the instantaneous tristimulus values are defined as

$$R(x,y,t) = \int_0^\infty C(x,y,t,\lambda)R(\lambda)d\lambda$$

$$G(x,y,t) = \int_0^\infty C(x,y,t,\lambda)G(\lambda)d\lambda$$

$$B(x,y,t) = \int_0^\infty C(x,y,t,\lambda)B(\lambda)d\lambda$$

where $R(\lambda)$, $G(\lambda)$, and $B(\lambda)$ are spectral tristimulus values for the set of red, green, and blue primaries, respectively. These concepts will be discussed in more detail later.

A model of human color vision is needed to study color and other important visual effects. The Young model of human color vision, proposed in 1802, is a trichromatic model in which it is postulated that the eye possesses three types of sensors, each sensitive to a different wavelength band. Physiological evidence of this assumption emerged (only) in the 1960s. Figure 3.17 depicts the results of sensitivity studies.

The measured peaks in these retinal color receptors and cones experiment are 445 nm (quasi-blue), 535 nm (quasi-green), and 570 nm (quasi-red). Figure 3.18 depicts a relatively simple color vision model (compared with more sophisticated models proposed more recently based on more refined spatial frequency response measurements). In this model, the signals $d_2$ and $d_3$ are related to the color (chromaticity) and $d_1$ is proportional to the luminance. The model is a reasonably accurate one for both color vision phenomena and colorimetry. Figure 3.19 shows an example of an arbitrary spectral energy distribution $C(\lambda)$ that may be arriving at such a modeled system.

As shown in the model in Fig. 3.18, each type of cone integrates the energy of the incident light consisting of the spectral energy distribu-

Relative response

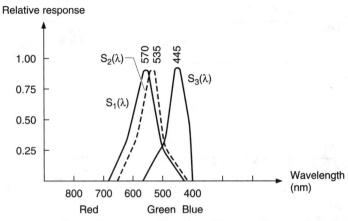

**Figure 3.17** Spectral sensitivity functions of the retinal cones, based on Konig's studies.

tion $C(\lambda)$, in proportion to its own sensitivity to that wavelength; in the model above this is $s_i(\lambda)C(\lambda)$, for $i = 1,2,3$. The integration of a function between two endpoints is a single number (i.e., the area under that function). The three resulting numbers from the integrations shown in the figure are the principal factors in perception of color. In other words, our perception of color is reducible to an amazingly simple mechanism of only *three numbers*.

These models and the subtending research gave rise to the tricometric theory of color, which states that the color of the light entering the brain (the eye, for that matter) may be specified by only three numbers rather than the entire curves of spectral density (see Fig. 3.20). There is a companion, and equally important, principle. This principle, developed by Maxwell in 1855, declares that light of any color can be obtained by an appropriate mixture of three (properly) selected primary colors (also known as *primaries*). The ensuing body of knowledge is known as *colorimetry*.

### 3.2.5  Photometry

Photometry deals with measures of luminance. This topic is of interest in physics and photography. It also has some relevance to imaging and related support systems. Photometric measurements aim at describing quantitatively the perceptual brightness of visible light.

The quantity $C(\lambda)$ representing the spectral energy distribution, already encountered in Fig. 3.19, specifies the time rate of energy the source emits per unit wavelength interval. $C(\lambda)$ is important in photometric calculations because, as indicated, the luminance $Y(C)$ is obtained by integrating $C(\lambda)*V(\lambda)$ over the visible range. For example,

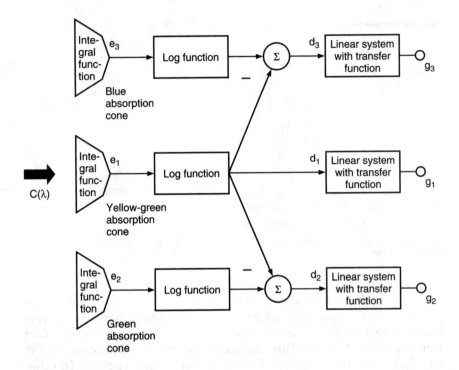

C(λ) = observed light spectral energy distribution
    = t(λ)*E(λ) (for transmittive object)
    = r(λ)*E(λ) (for reflective object)
where E(λ) represents the spectral energy distribution of light
        emitted from a primary light source
    t(λ) represents the wavelength-dependent transmissivity
    r(λ) represents the wavelength-dependent reflectivity
$e_1 = \int C(\lambda)s_1(\lambda)d\lambda$
$e_2 = \int C(\lambda)s_2(\lambda)d\lambda$
$e_3 = \int C(\lambda)s_3(\lambda)d\lambda$
where $s_1(\lambda)$, $s_2(\lambda)$, $s_3(\lambda)$ represent the spectral sensitivities of the three receptors
(absorption pigments of the retina)
$d_1 = \log e_1$
$d_2 = \log e_2 - \log e_1 = \log (e_2/e_1)$
$d_3 = \log e_3 - \log e_1 = \log (e_3/e_1)$
$g_s$ = signals for color perception in brain

**Figure 3.18**  Frei's color vision model.

in the visible segment of the electromagnetic spectrum, the (approximate) spectral energy distribution for a blackbody is

$$C(\lambda) = \frac{C_1}{\lambda^5} \exp \frac{C_2}{\lambda T}$$

where $T$ is the temperature of the body in kelvins and $C_1$ and $C_2$ are constants.

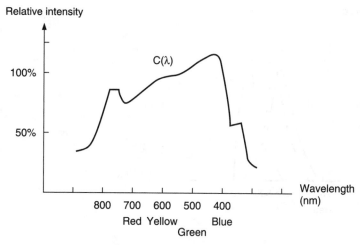

**Figure 3.19**  Example of arriving signal of arbitrary spectral energy.

The CIE defines several standard sources of light with specified luminance characteristics, including a tungsten filament lamp (source $S_A$), a source (source $S_B$) that approximates sunlight, a source (source $S_C$) that approximates an overcast day, and an ideal source $E$ often used in colorimetric calculations (referred to later) that emits constant radiant energy at all wavelengths (see Fig. 3.21). Other sources discussed later are $D_{6500}$ and $D_{9300}$.

Of passing interest is the spectral energy distribution for phosphors for computer monitors (used, for example, in imaging applications) and television sets. Figure 3.22 depicts the distribution for phosphor mixture P22 often included on the inside surface of the cathode-ray tube (CRT) (other phosphor mixtures are also used). Red, green, and blue emitting phosphor elements are arranged in strips or dots (see Sec. 3.3.12).

## 3.3   Colorimetry

The concept of colorimetry also plays a role in DISs, EISs, and SISs. Hence, this issue is covered here in some detail. Colorimetry aims at measuring color quantitatively; color measurements are expressed in terms of the tristimulus values of a color, or some function thereof. Although the trichromatic theory of color vision is based on physiological processes, precise measurements can be made to study color matches.

### 3.3.1   Color matching

It is possible to match an arbitrary color by superimposing appropriate amounts of three (designated) primary colors. This observation forms

Relative response

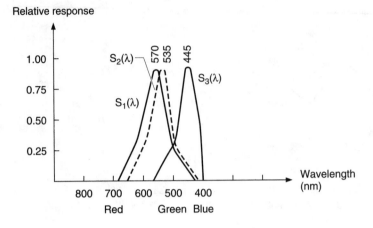

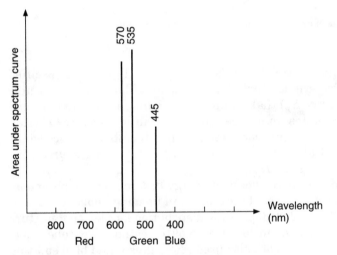

**Figure 3.20**  Equivalency of spectral densities and derived signal factors. Top: spectral densities. Bottom: derived signals.

the basis for the "trichromatic theory of color." There are two basic methods for color matching:

- *Additive color reproduction systems* (TV monitors, *RGB* computer monitors, etc.).    In these systems, the three primary colors are red, green, and blue. Light sources generating these primaries are projected onto a shared region of space (e.g., a monitor screen) to obtain a colored light. The red primary is usually centered at 700 nm with an approximate triangular distribution of 100 nm on each side; the green primary is usually centered at 546 nm with an approximate

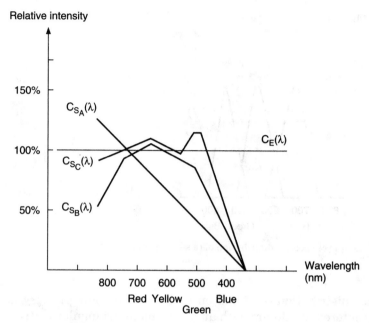

**Figure 3.21**   CIE spectral energy distribution for reference illumination sources.

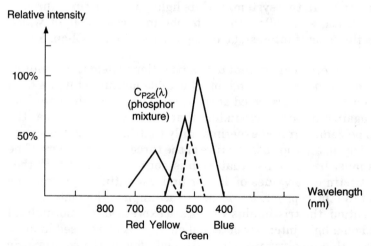

**Figure 3.22**   Spectral properties for phosphors used in monitors and television sets.

Relative intensity

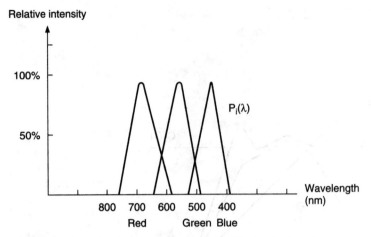

**Figure 3.23**  Example of spectral distribution of (a set of) primaries.

triangular distribution of 75 nm on each side; the blue primary is usually centered at 436 nm with an approximate triangular distribution of 75 nm on each side (see Fig. 3.23).

- *Subtractive color reproduction systems* (color photography, color printing, etc.).   In this system, a white light passes, in turn, through cyan, magenta, and yellow filters to obtain a colored light which matches the color of interest. (This topic is revisited in Chap. 5.)

A typical colorimetric experiment uses a partitioned field that contains the test color on the left side and an adjustable mixture of lights from three primaries that is projected at the right. The entire bipartite field is viewed against a dark surrounding that subtends a 2° angle at the eye. It can be demonstrated experimentally that "most" test colors can be matched by an appropriate mixture of the three primary colors. (The primaries must be chosen so that each is not a mixture of the other two.) The tristimulus values of a color under scrutiny represent the amounts of the three primaries needed to accomplish the match.

By convention, the tristimulus values are expressed in a normalized form based on a light intensity of "equal energy." As discussed in more detail below, this involves two steps. The left side of the colorimetric experiment described earlier is allowed to radiate light of unit intensity having a spectral distribution that is constant with respect to the wavelength. [This is $C_E(\lambda)$, described in Sec. 3.2.5 as an example.] Then, the amount of each primary required to achieve a match is taken to be the reference unit value; the amounts of primaries required to match other test colors are expressed in terms of these normalized units.

**TABLE 3.6    Grassman's Axioms**

| Axiom | Color matching rule |
|---|---|
| 1 | Any color can be matched by a mixture of no more than three colors |
| 2 | A color match at a radiance level holds over a (wide) range of levels |
| 3 | Components of a mixture of colored lights cannot be resolved by the human eye |
| 4 | The luminance of a color mixture is equal to the sum of the luminance of the components |
| 5 | If color $M$ matches color $N$ and color $P$ matches color $Q$, then color $M$ mixed with color $P$ matches color $N$ mixed with color $Q$ (law of addition) |
| 6 | If the mixture of color $M$ and color $P$ matches the mixture of color $N$ and color $Q$, and if color $P$ matches color $Q$, then color $M$ matches color $N$ (law of subtraction) |
| 7 | If color $M$ matches color $N$ and if color $N$ matches color $P$, then color $M$ matches color $P$ (transitive law) |
| 8 | Either of the following is true (color matching): <br> $C$ units of color $C$ match the mixture of $M$ units of color $M$ plus $N$ units of color $N$ plus $P$ units of color $P$ <br> A mixture of $C$ units of color $C$ plus $M$ units of color $M$ matches the mixture of $N$ units of color $N$ plus $P$ units of color $P$ <br> A mixture of $C$ units of color $C$ plus $M$ units of color $M$ plus $N$ units of color $N$ matches $P$ units of color $P$ |

There are eight classical axioms that support trichromatic color matching, known as *Grassman's axioms*.[10] These are listed in Table 3.6.

Brute-force color matching proceeds by the following seven steps for additive color matching (this method cannot be easily automated because it depends on perceptual factors):

1. Consider a light source $C$ with a color of spectral distribution $C(\lambda)$ (e.g., as shown in Fig. 3.19.) Assume that the light is projected onto an ideal reflector at some point $\alpha$. Next, project light $W$ [white reference with spectral distribution $W(\lambda)$] onto an adjacent point ß on the reflector. Next, project and overlap onto another adjacent point $\gamma$ on the reflector the $P_1$ (primary 1) light, with spectral distribution $P_1(\lambda)$, the $P_2$ (primary 2) light, with spectral distribution $P_2(\lambda)$, and the $P_3$ (primary 3) light, with spectral distribution $P_3(\lambda)$ (the spectral distribution of the primaries is similar to those just described above), while adjusting the intensities of the primaries to match perceptually the brightness, hue, and saturation of $W$. The values of the intensities $A_1(W)$, $A_2(W)$, and $A_3(W)$ are noted in some convenient measure, e.g., milliwatts. Next, adjust the intensities of the primaries to match perceptually the brightness, hue, and saturation of $C$. If a match is found, the values of the intensities $A_1(C)$, $A_2(C)$,

and $A_3(C)$ are noted in the same convenient measure, e.g., milliwatts. (If a match is not found, go to the other steps below.) The tristimulus values are then calculated as

$$T_i(C) = \frac{A_i(C)}{A_i(W)} \quad \text{for } i = 1,2,3$$

2. If a match was not found in step 1, proceed as follows. Superimpose primary $P_1$ with light $C$. Next, adjust the intensity of the three primaries until a match is achieved between $(a)$ the overlapping region between $P_2$ and $P_3$ and $(b)$ the overlapping region of $P_1$ and $C$. If a match is found, the values of the intensities $A_1(C)$, $A_2(C)$, and $A_3(C)$ are noted. (If a match is not found, go to the other steps below.) The tristimulus values are then calculated as

$$T_1(C) = \frac{-A_1(C)}{A_1(W)}$$

$$T_2(C) = \frac{A_2(C)}{A_2(W)}$$

$$T_3(C) = \frac{A_3(C)}{A_3(W)}$$

3. If a match was not found in step 2, proceed as follows. Superimpose primary $P_2$ with light $C$. Next, adjust the intensity of the three primaries until a match is achieved between $(a)$ the overlapping region between $P_1$ and $P_3$ and $(b)$ the overlapping region of $P_2$ and $C$. If a match is found, the values of the intensities $A_1(C)$, $A_2(C)$, and $A_3(C)$ are noted. (If a match is not found, go to the other steps below.) The tristimulus values are then calculated as

$$T_1(C) = \frac{A_1(C)}{A_1(W)}$$

$$T_2(C) = \frac{-A_2(C)}{A_2(W)}$$

$$T_3(C) = \frac{A_3(C)}{A_3(W)}$$

4. If a match was not found in step 3, proceed as follows. Superimpose primary $P_3$ with light $C$. Next, adjust the intensity of the three primaries until a match is achieved between $(a)$ the overlapping region between $P_2$ and $P_1$ and $(b)$ the overlapping region of $P_3$ and $C$. If a match is found, the values of the intensities $A_1(C)$, $A_2(C)$, and $A_3(C)$

are noted. (If a match is not found, go to the other steps below.) The tristimulus values are then calculated as

$$T_1(C) = \frac{A_1(C)}{A_1(W)}$$

$$T_2(C) = \frac{A_2(C)}{A_2(W)}$$

$$T_3(C) = \frac{-A_3(C)}{A_3(W)}$$

5. If a match was not found in step 4, proceed as follows. Superimpose primaries $P_1$ and $P_2$ with light $C$. Next, adjust the intensity of the three primaries until a match is achieved between $(a)\,P_3$ and $(b)$ the overlapping region of $P_1$ and $P_2$ and $C$. If a match is found, the values of the intensities $A_1(C)$, $A_2(C)$, and $A_3(C)$ are noted. (If a match is not found, go to the other steps below.) The tristimulus values are then calculated as

$$T_1(C) = \frac{-A_1(C)}{A_1(W)}$$

$$T_2(C) = \frac{-A_2(C)}{A_2(W)}$$

$$T_3(C) = \frac{A_3(C)}{A_3(W)}$$

6. If a match was not found in step 5, proceed as follows. Superimpose primaries $P_1$ and $P_3$ with light $C$. Next, adjust the intensity of the three primaries until a match is achieved between $(a)\,P_2$ and $(b)$ the overlapping region of $P_1$ and $P_3$ and $C$. If a match is found, the values of the intensities $A_1(C)$, $A_2(C)$, and $A_3(C)$ are noted. (If a match is not found, go to the other steps below.) The tristimulus values are then calculated as

$$T_1(C) = \frac{-A_1(C)}{A_1(W)}$$

$$T_2(C) = \frac{A_2(C)}{A_2(W)}$$

$$T_3(C) = \frac{-A_3(C)}{A_3(W)}$$

7. If a match was not found in step 6, proceed as follows. Superimpose primaries $P_2$ and $P_3$ with light $C$. Next, adjust the intensity of the three primaries until a match is achieved between ($a$) $P_1$ and ($b$) the overlapping region of $P_2$ and $P_3$ and $C$. If a match is found, the values of the intensities $A_1(C)$, $A_2(C)$, and $A_3(C)$ are noted. The tristimulus values are then calculated as

$$T_1(C) = \frac{A_1(C)}{A_1(W)}$$

$$T_2(C) = \frac{-A_2(C)}{A_2(W)}$$

$$T_3(C) = \frac{-A_3(C)}{A_3(W)}$$

A brute-force subtractive color matching process is fundamentally similar to the additive method. The process deals with varying dye concentrations, as the spectral absorption of the dye filter depends on the dye concentration. The dye concentrations needed to obtain a filtered light through the three filters that has the same perceptual match with the reference light $W$ are noted as $A_1(W)$, $A_2(W)$, and $A_3(W)$. Then the three dye concentrations are varied until a perceptual match with light $C$ is reached. The concentrations are noted as $A_1(C)$, $A_2(C)$, and $A_3(C)$. The tristimulus values are calculated as in step 1 above.

### 3.3.2 Basic colorimetry equations

From Grassman's axioms one can derive the following two equations that are at the base of colorimetry:

$$C(\lambda) \approx \sum_{i=1}^{3} T_i(C)A_i(W)P_i(\lambda) \qquad (1)$$

where $T_i(C)$ is the $i$th tristimulus value, $A_i(W)$ is the $i$th reference value for the white source, $P_i(\lambda)$ is the spectral energy distribution of the $i$th primary signal, and $\approx$ means color equivalence (i.e., provides the same perceptual response in the eye); and

$$Y(C) = \int C(\lambda)V(\lambda)d\lambda = \sum_{i=1}^{3} \int A_i(C)P_i(\lambda)V(\lambda)d\lambda$$

$$= \sum_{i=1}^{3} \int T_i(C)A_i(W)P_i(\lambda)V(\lambda)d\lambda \qquad (2)$$

where $Y(C)$ is the luminance of the mixture (refer to Sec. 3.2.4) and $V(\lambda)$ is the spectral response of the human vision (i.e., the relative luminous efficiency).

### 3.3.3  Calculation of tristimulus values

One wants to be able to calculate the tristimulus quantities $T_i(C)$, $i = 1,2,3$, without having to go through the matching procedure discussed above. This is possible if the tristimulus values of the spectral colors of the primaries are known. These values must be known as a function of $\lambda$ over the visible range. Let these specific tristimulus functions be denoted as $T_{S_1}(\lambda)$, $T_{S_2}(\lambda)$, and $T_{S_3}(\lambda)$. Then it can be shown that

$$T_i(C) = \int C(x) T_{S_i}(x) dx$$

for $i = 1,2,3$. It turns out that these tristimulus values may be mathematically negative; this may be interpreted in two ways:

1. The color match is obtained by adding the primary color with the negative tristimulus value to the original color and then matching the result with the remaining primaries.

2. Certain colors cannot be matched given a practical color delivery mechanism (e.g., a PC screen) given a fixed set of primaries. This, in turn, can be amplified as follows:

   - A different set of primaries may be needed to match a specific color to obtain positive tristimulus values.
   - Choose an appropriate set of primaries so that the most important and/or commonly recurring colors can be directly matched.

### 3.3.4  Tristimulus space

The three tristimulus values $T_i(C)$ may be considered to form three axes of a color space. In this representation a particular color can be described as a vector in the space. Note, however, that the *vector*, that is, $(T_1, T_2, T_3)$, represents the color, not the length of the vector itself. (Two distinct colors may have the same vector length.) See Fig. 3.24.

A color $C$ is viewed as the vector $\mathbf{C}$ with coordinates $(T_1, T_2, T_3)$ in the space defined by the chosen primaries, e.g., $R,G,B$. Vectorially, if we define

$$\mathbf{R} = (1,0,0)$$

$$\mathbf{G} = (0,1,0)$$

$$\mathbf{B} = (0,0,1)$$

then

$$\mathbf{C} = T_1 \mathbf{R} + T_2 \mathbf{G} + T_3 \mathbf{B}$$

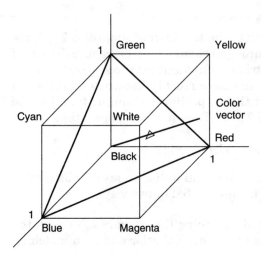

**Figure 3.24** Color space generated by red, green, and blue primaries.

Some of the Grassman's axioms identified earlier are consequences of vector algebra. For example, a mixture **S** of two colors **A** and **B** is given by **S = A + B,** and the respective coordinates are

$$\mathbf{S} = (s_1, s_2, s_3)$$

with

$$s_1 = a_1 + b_1$$
$$s_2 = a_2 + b_2$$
$$s_3 = a_3 + b_3$$

where $\mathbf{A} = (a_1, a_2, a_3)$ and $\mathbf{B} = (b_1, b_2, b_3)$.

Also, when performing a color matching experiment, only positive amounts of primary colors can be used in the physical experiment. In the abstract, negative amounts of primary colors may be needed; since this cannot be realized in practice, the match is done by adding positive amounts of the primary color in question to the test, as described earlier. This is clear in vector notation; consider the problem of matching **S**, which may need a negative tristimulus value. Then one could find a match as follows:

$$\mathbf{S} + 4\mathbf{G} = 3.2\mathbf{R} + 1.9\mathbf{B}$$

that is to say, in representational form

$$\mathbf{S} = -4\mathbf{G} + 3.2\mathbf{R} + 1.9\mathbf{B}$$

with tristimulus values $(-4, 3.2, 1.9)$.

A plane can be defined in this space by the three primary colors; usually one shows only the piece of the plane that resides inside the cube, known as the *Maxwell triangle* (see Fig. 3.24). The intersection point of a specific color vector with this triangle provides an indication of the saturation and hue of the color with respect to the distance of such point from the vertices of the triangle.

### 3.3.5 Chromaticity coordinates

In many situations, the luminance of a color is not of principal interest in the process of color match. In these cases, the saturation and hue of the color under scrutiny can be described in terms of chromaticity coordinates. The chromaticity coordinates are defined in terms of normalized tristimulus values, as follows: $t_i = T_i/(T_1 + T_2 + T_3)$ for $i = 1,2,3$. Since $t_3 = 1 - t_2 - t_1$, one typically employs only two coordinates to describe a color match. This gives rise to the chromaticity diagrams similar to those of Figs. 3.25 and 3.26 (corresponding to different chromaticity coordinates; Fig. 3.26 represents the basic CIE diagram developed in 1931 and still used today). Luminance is factored out of the two-dimensional chromaticity graph; however, luminance can be determined from the tristimulus values, as covered later. (Luminance can also be measured by photometric means.)

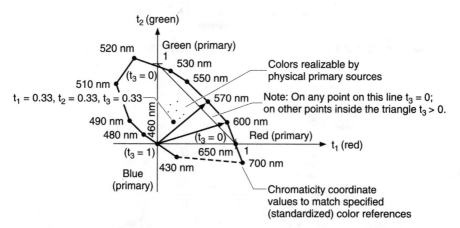

**Figure 3.25** Generic example of chromaticity diagram. [*Notes:* (1) The diagram can show only two of the three dimensions of a mixture. (2) The three primaries (460, 530, and 650 nm) are connected by straight lines to form a triangle. All points within the triangle can be produced by an additive combination of the three primaries. All areas outside the triangle, which may include parts of the visual spectrum, cannot be produced by an additive combination of the three primaries. (3) An earlier system initially studied by Guild in 1925 used primaries at 436, 547, and 700 nm.]

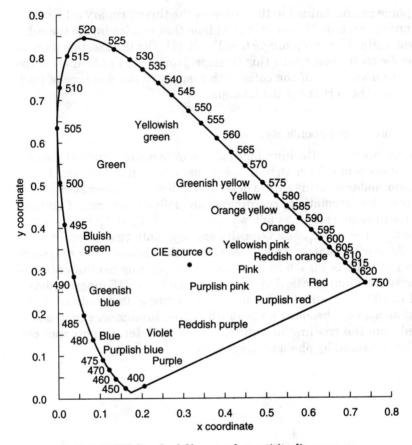

**Figure 3.26**    1931 2° CIE Standard Observer chromaticity diagram.

In particular, one defines

$$r = \frac{R}{R + G + B}$$

$$g = \frac{G}{R + G + B}$$

$$b = \frac{B}{R + G + B}$$

For example, in the NTSC system (indicated by the subscript N), if $R_N$ = 0, $G_N$ = 1, and $B_N$ = 1 (cyan), then $r_n$ = 0/2 = 0, $g_n$ = 1/2 = 0.5, and

$b_n = 1/2 = 0.5$. If $R_N = 1$, $G_N = 1$, and $B_N = 1$ (white), then $r_n = 1/3 = 0.333$, $g_n = 1/3 = 0.333$, and $b_n = 1/3 = 0.333$.

Since the diagram of Fig. 3.25, which is representative of CIE $RGB$ shown as $R_C G_C B_C$, leaves a large number of desirable colors outside the unit triangle, the CIE decided to utilize an approach developed by Maxwell at an earlier time, where a set of imaginary primaries called $X$, $Y$, and $Z$ was used to encompass the entire visual spectrum. The imaginary primaries do not exist as physical colors but are mathematical abstractions. Nonetheless it is possible to indicate the position of any real primaries (such as $R_C B_C G_C$), and other real colors that can be mixed by their additive combination, within this space.

These diagrams are based on averaged observers under specified illumination and field-of-view conditions. It is to be noted that as soon as some of these standard assumptions are changed, the color descriptions provided by the chromaticity diagrams become less accurate. For sources smaller than 4° (e.g., a PC monitor) the 1931 CIE system may be used to assess color characteristics, while the 1964 $U^*V^*W^*$ system should be used for larger fields of view. Two widely used definitions of white are $D_{6500}$ and $D_{9300}$, where the number represents the temperature in degrees Kelvin. The white mixture approaching $D_{6500}$ is usually used as the reference white for color television, while PC monitors frequently use the $D_{9300}$ source. $D_{9300}$ contains a higher proportion of blue and, for most viewers, produces a better white under the fluorescent illumination found in the workplace.

The tristimulus values of spectral colors, that is, light of a single but specified wavelength, having unit intensities, are called *color matching functions*. Stated in other words, the color matching functions $\{r(\lambda), g(\lambda), b(\lambda)\}$ are the tristimulus values with respect to three given primaries of unit monochromatic light of wavelength $\lambda$. The tristimulus values corresponding to specific monochromatic colors (e.g., 770, 650, 620, 600 nm) plot a curve of particular interest in the chromaticity diagram. (This is the horseshoe curve seen in the previous figures.)

These color matching functions can also be used to express the tristimulus values of a generic color $C(\lambda)$, as follows:

$$R_C = \int C(\lambda)r(\lambda)d\lambda$$

$$G_C = \int C(\lambda)g(\lambda)d\lambda$$

$$B_C = \int C(\lambda)b(\lambda)d\lambda$$

(Nominally, the integration limits are from 0 to infinity; more precisely, they correspond to the visible range, say, 380 to 780 nm.)

Two colors $C$ and $D$ are matched if $R_C = R_D$, $G_C = G_D$, and $B_C = B_D$. It is to be noted by the equations just given that the distribution functions $C(\lambda)$ and $D(\lambda)$ could be different and yet the tristimulus values could be the same (as long as the *integrals*—say, the area—are the same). This says that it is not necessary for $C(\lambda) = D(\lambda)$ for all $\lambda$. In a way, this is explained by the trichromatic theory of vision: If colors are converted at the retina into three distinct types of response, the eye-mind is unable to detect the difference between two stimuli that give the same response to the retina, yet have different spectral compositions. Hence, there are many colors having different spectral distributions that have the same tristimulus values. These colors are called *metamers.* (This is in contrast to two colors that have identical spectral distributions and are known as *isomers.*) Figure 3.27 shows a "concocted" example of metamers to make the calculation obvious.

In some coordinate spaces, color perception is not uniform across the space. This is in fact a drawback of the 1931 CIE color space. New coordinate systems were introduced in 1960 and in 1976, in which equal distances within a chromaticity diagram correspond more closely to perceptual differences. (This topic will be reexamined later.) Currently, the CIE $L^*u^*v^*$ system is the recommended chromaticity space for discussion of color-related matters for video, multimedia, and imaging applications. (These coordinates are shown in the sections that follow.)

The chromaticity coordinates $t_i$ can be used in conjunction with the luminance of a matched color to derive the tristimulus values $T_i$. This can be done by defining the luminosity coefficients of the primaries $Y(P_i)$ as follows [based on Eq. (2) in Sec. 3.3.2]:

$$Y(P_i) = \int A_i(W)P_i(\lambda)V(\lambda)d\lambda$$

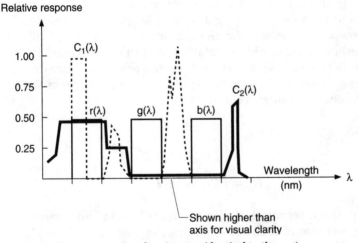

Figure 3.27 Two metameric colors (appear identical to the eye).

Then, letting $Q = t_1(C)Y(P_1) + t_2(C)Y(P_2) + t_3(C)Y(P_3)$, one has

$$T_i(C) = \frac{t_i Y(C)}{Q} \qquad i = 1,2,3$$

where $Y(C)$ is the luminance of the matched color.

Luminance may be obtained by a separate match from the color match. Luminance aims at putting a quantitative measure on the aspect of visible energy that produces the sensation of brightness. It turns out that radiation at different wavelengths makes different contributions to the sensation of brightness; as noted earlier, maximum brightness is perceived by light emitted or radiated at 550 nm. This observation is based on studies plotting the brightness sensation against a monochromatic light at wavelength $\lambda$. The relative response, termed *relative luminous efficiency* $y(\lambda)$, is shown in Fig. 3.28 for the CIE Standard Observer.

In conclusion, a color $C$ can be matched, that is, specified, by its (1) tristimulus values $T_i(C)$, $i = 1,2,3$ or (2) chromaticity values $t_i(C)$, $i = 1,2$ and its luminance $Y(C)$.

Earlier we noted that if $\mathbf{A} = (A_1,A_2,A_3)$ and $\mathbf{B} = (B_1,B_2,B_3)$ are mixed to form a color $\mathbf{M} = (M_1,M_2,M_3)$, then $M_i = A_i + B_i$, $i = 1,2,3$, where $A_i$ and $B_i$ are the tristimulus values. However, the chromaticity coordinates do not simply add. If the chromaticity coordinates of $\mathbf{A}$ are $(x_1,y_1,Y_1)$ and for $\mathbf{B}$ are $(x_2,y_2,Y_2)$, with $Y$ representing the luminance, one has the following chromaticity-luminance coordinates for $\mathbf{M}$:

$$x_m = \frac{x_1(Y_1/y_1) + x_2(Y_2/y_2)}{(Y_1/y_1) + (Y_2/y_2)}$$

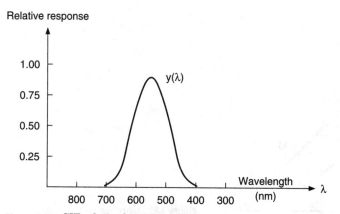

Relative response

**Figure 3.28**  CIE relative luminous efficiency.

$$y_m = \frac{Y_1 + Y_2}{(Y_1/y_1) + (Y_2/y_2)}$$

$$Y_m = Y_1 + Y_2$$

Hence, the chromaticity coordinates of the mixture are the weighted linear sum of the chromaticity coordinates of the components. Stated in another way, the chromaticity coordinates of the mixture lie on the straight line connecting the points $(x_1, y_1)$ and $(x_2, y_2)$; interestingly, the exact location of the coordinates depends on the luminance $Y_1$ and $Y_2$. See Fig. 3.29 for an example.

The concept of dominant wavelength is shown in Fig. 3.30. This figure can also be used to define the concept of excitation purity. *Excitation purity* is defined as the ratio between the distance from the achromatic reference to the color sample and the total distance from the reference to the boundary (the locus of spectral colors).

### 3.3.6 Multiple sets of primaries and tristimulus value transformations

As noted in the discussion above, color matching does not require a unique set of primaries. So, while some approach (system) may use $P_1$, $P_2$, $P_3$, and $W$, another system may use $P_1'$, $P_2'$, $P_3'$, and $W'$. Hence, there is a need to transform one set of tristimulus values obtained in one system to another set appropriate for that system.

It can be shown that if the tristimulus values are known for a given set of primaries, conversion to another set of primaries involves only a linear transformation:

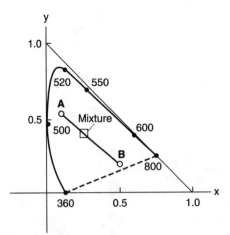

**Figure 3.29** Chromaticity coordinates of mixture.

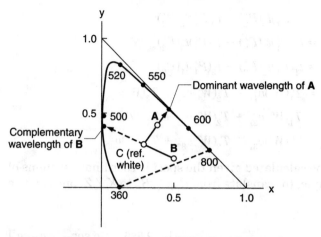

**Figure 3.30** Dominant wavelength. [*Note:* For colors in the lower right-hand portion of the chromaticity diagram, the straight line connecting the color under consideration with the reference white needs to be projected backward (this is now known as *complementary wavelength*).]

$$T'_1 = w_{11}T_1 + w_{12}T_2 + w_{13}T_3$$
$$T'_2 = w_{21}T_1 + w_{22}T_2 + w_{23}T_3$$
$$T'_3 = w_{31}T_1 + w_{32}T_2 + w_{33}T_3$$

Namely, $w_{ij}$ are the entries of the matrix

$$
\begin{bmatrix} T'_1(C) \\ T'_2(C) \\ T'_3(C) \end{bmatrix}
=
\begin{bmatrix}
\dfrac{v_{11}}{v_1} & \dfrac{v_{12}}{v_1} & \dfrac{v_{13}}{v_1} \\[2ex]
\dfrac{v_{21}}{v_2} & \dfrac{v_{22}}{v_2} & \dfrac{v_{23}}{v_2} \\[2ex]
\dfrac{v_{31}}{v_3} & \dfrac{v_{32}}{v_3} & \dfrac{v_{33}}{v_3}
\end{bmatrix}
\begin{bmatrix} T_1(C) \\ T_2(C) \\ T_3(C) \end{bmatrix}
$$

with

$$v_{11} = t_2(P'_2)t_3(P'_3) - t_3(P'_2)t_2(P'_3)$$
$$v_{12} = t_3(P'_2)t_1(P'_3) - t_1(P'_2)t_3(P'_3)$$
$$v_{13} = t_1(P'_2)t_2(P'_3) - t_2(P'_2)t_1(P'_3)$$
$$v_{21} = t_3(P'_1)t_2(P'_3) - t_2(P'_1)t_3(P'_3)$$
$$v_{22} = t_1(P'_1)t_3(P'_3) - t_3(P'_1)t_1(P'_3)$$
$$v_{23} = t_2(P'_1)t_1(P'_3) - t_1(P'_1)t_2(P'_3)$$

$$v_{31} = t_2(P_1')t_3(P_2') - t_3(P_1')t_2(P_2')$$

$$v_{32} = t_3(P_1')t_1(P_2') - t_1(P_1')t_3(P_2')$$

$$v_{33} = t_1(P_1')t_2(P_2') - t_2(P_1')t_1(P_2')$$

$$v_1 = T_1(W')v_{11} + T_2(W')v_{12} + T_3(W')v_{13}$$

$$v_2 = T_1(W')v_{21} + T_2(W')v_{22} + T_3(W')v_{23}$$

$$v_3 = T_1(W')v_{31} + T_2(W')v_{32} + T_3(W')v_{33}$$

These values can be calculated given the specific coordinate systems of interest. For example, to translate from $R_C, G_C, B_C$ to $X, Y, Z$, one can use the conversion

$$[T_X(C), T_Y(C), T_Z(C)] = [R_C(C), G_C(C), B_C(C)] \begin{bmatrix} 2.365 & -0.897 & -0.468 \\ -0.515 & 1.426 & 0.089 \\ 0.005 & -0.014 & 1.009 \end{bmatrix}$$

or

$$T_X(C) = 2.365R_C(C) - 0.515G_C(C) + 0.005B_C(C)$$

$$T_Y(C) = -0.897R_C(C) + 1.426G_C(C) - 0.014B_C(C)$$

$$T_Z(C) = -0.468R_C(C) + 0.089G_C(C) + 1.009B_C(C)$$

To translate from $X, Y, Z$ to $R_C, G_C, B_C$, one can use the relation

$$[R_C(C), G_C(C), B_C(C)] = [T_X(C), T_Y(C), T_Z(C)] \begin{bmatrix} 0.490 & 0.310 & 0.200 \\ 0.177 & 0.812 & 0.011 \\ 0.000 & 0.010 & 0.990 \end{bmatrix}$$

or

$$R_C(C) = 0.490T_X(C) + 0.177T_Y(C) + 0.000T_Z(C)$$

$$G_C(C) = 0.310T_X(C) + 0.812T_Y(C) + 0.010T_Z(C)$$

$$B_C(C) = 0.200T_X(C) + 0.011T_Y(C) + 0.990T_Z(C)$$

For example, if $R_C = 1$, $B_C = 0$, and $G_C = 0$, then, by using the first set of equations, one gets $T_X = 2.365$, $T_Y = -0.897$, and $T_Z = -0.468$. Conversely, if $T_X = 2.365$, $T_Y = -0.897$, and $T_Z = -0.468$, then, by using the second set of equations, one gets $R_C = 1$, $B_C = 0$, and $G_C = 0$.

### 3.3.7  Common color coordinate systems

Several well-known coordinate systems have been used over the years, in addition to other secondary systems (see Table 3.7). These systems are briefly discussed in the sections that follow.

**TABLE 3.7    Key Color Coordinate Systems (Alphabetical List)**

| |
|---|
| $L*a*b*$ |
| $L*u*v*$ |
| $R_C G_C B_C$ (C = CIE) |
| $R_N G_N B_N$ (N = NTSC) |
| $R_S G_S B_S$ (S = SMPTE) |
| $U*V*W*$ |
| $UVW$ |
| $XYZ$ |
| $YIQ$ |
| $YUV$ |

As we undertake this discussion of available color coordinate systems, it should be noted that there is no best method to deal with color in the sense that a system is the optimal one for a number of ultimate applications. The practitioner is left with the task of assessing the characteristics of each candidate system, particularly its limitations, and then determining if these limitations are reasonable given the intended application.

**$R_C G_C B_C$ coordinate system.** The $R_C G_C B_C$ coordinate system was developed in 1931 by the CIE, by specifying a standard reference system of three primaries: red (peak at 700 nm), green (peak at 546.1 nm), and blue (peak at 435.8 nm) (see Fig. 3.31). When different observers match a given color, there are slight differences in the resulting tristimulus values. The 1931 CIE established the Standard Observer by averaging

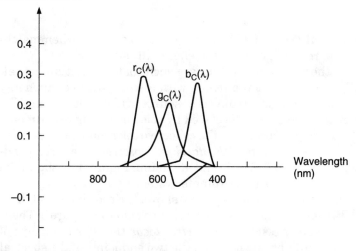

**Figure 3.31**    Tristimulus values for CIE spectral primaries (Standard Observer); units such that equal quantities of the primaries match $E$.

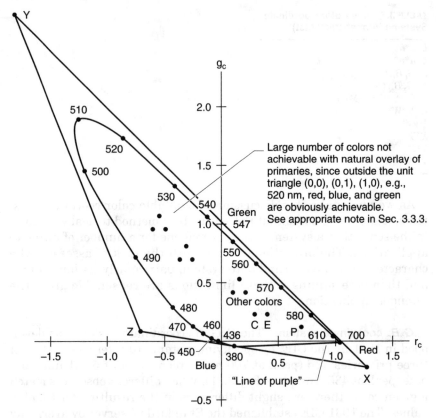

**Figure 3.32** Chromaticity diagram for $R_C, G_C, B_C$ CIE system (based on 1925–1926 studies by Guild). E: Equal-energy white. C: Illuminant $C$ (standard bluish-white source). P: A specific color sample irradiated by illuminant $C$. X,Y,Z: Standard CIE primaries.

the tristimulus values from a large number of observers, when matching colors compared to light from the energy illuminant $E$.

The units of the tristimulus values are such that the tristimulus values $R_C, G_C, B_C$ are equal when a match with a white with equal energy throughout the visible spectrum (i.e., source $E$) is undertaken. The curves of Fig. 3.31 have been developed by color matching experiments performed by a group of observers; the collective color matching response of these observers is called the *CIE Standard Observer*. The corresponding wavelengths are 700.0, 546.1, and 435.8 nm. Figure 3.32 shows the chromaticity diagram for this coordinate system.

A chromaticity diagram also typically shows the coordinates of (key) spectral colors (light of single wavelength, also said to be "pure"). These spectral colors usually reside on a *spectral locus* that has the shape of a horseshoe; the straight line between the two endpoints of the spectral locus is the *line of purples*. The spectral locus of the chromaticity diagram extends outside the triangle formed by the red, green, and blue primaries located at points (0,0), (1,0), and (0,1), respectively. (This is contrasted, for example, with the $xy$ chromaticity diagrams discussed later where the spectral locus is contained completely inside the triangle formed by the $X$, $Y$, and $Z$ primaries.)

The horseshoe diagram of the spectral colors (pure colors of a single wavelength), that is, the spectral locus, can also be shown by another diagram (not to be confused with the spectrum distribution of the primaries). In this diagram one can find, for a given wavelength, the chromaticity coordinates of the color of that wavelength (see Fig. 3.33). Note that for some wavelengths these values are negative.

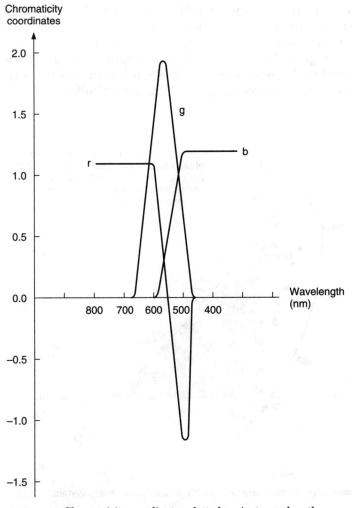

**Figure 3.33** Chromaticity coordinates plotted against wavelength.

**NTSC $R_N G_N B_N$ color coordinate system.** Television receivers in the United States employ cathode-ray tubes coated with three phosphors that glow in the red $(R_N)$, green $(G_N)$, and blue $(B_N)$ regions of the spectrum [N refers to NTSC (National Television System/Standards Committee)]. Modern televisions use improved phosphors; however, the NTSC standard remains the reference. A standard camera produces *RGB* outputs. Figure 3.34 shows the chromaticity diagram for NTSC systems. (The units of the tristimulus values are not normalized, so that the three values are equal when matching illuminant *C* white reference.)

See also Fig. 3.35.

Since the reference phosphors are not sharply monochromatic light sources, they are not able to produce the range of colors possible with the CIE spectral primaries shown in Fig. 3.32. Figure 3.36 superimposes the range of CIE primary derivable colors (from Fig. 3.32) with NTSC colors plotted in the same coordinate space. Clearly, NTSC standard phosphors are not as encompassing. See also Table 3.8.[11]

One disadvantage of this system is that the tristimulus values are highly correlated with one another. In developing efficient sampling, quantization, coding, and processing techniques, particularly for digi-

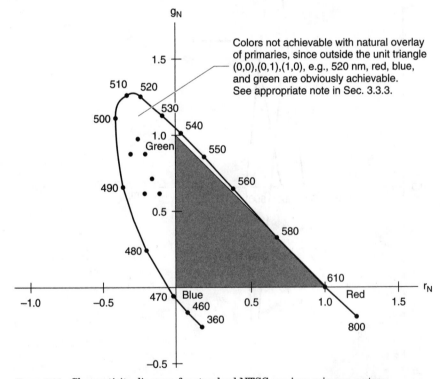

**Figure 3.34**   Chromaticity diagram for standard NTSC receiver primary system.

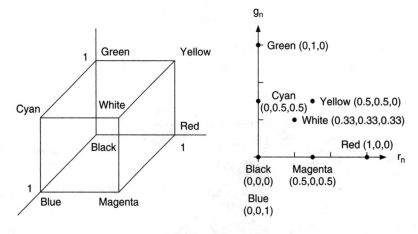

| | NTSC red | NTSC green | NTSC blue | NTSC cyan | NTSC magenta | NTSC yellow | NTSC white | NTSC black |
|---|---|---|---|---|---|---|---|---|
| $R_N$ | 1 | 0 | 0 | 0 | 1 | 1 | 1 | 0 |
| $G_N$ | 0 | 1 | 0 | 1 | 0 | 1 | 1 | 0 |
| $B_N$ | 0 | 0 | 1 | 1 | 1 | 0 | 1 | 0 |
| $r_n$ | 1 | 0 | 0 | 0 | 0.5 | 0.5 | 0.33 | 0 |
| $g_n$ | 0 | 1 | 0 | 0.5 | 0 | 0.5 | 0.33 | 0 |
| $b_n$ | 0 | 0 | 1 | 0.5 | 0.5 | 0 | 0.33 | 0 |

**Figure 3.35**  Tristimulus space and chromaticity coordinates for NTSC colors.

tal imaging, it is desirable to have tristimulus values that are not correlated (i.e., are orthogonal); these aspects will be addressed later.

**SMPTE $R_s G_s B_s$ color coordinate system.**  The SMPTE (Society of Motion Picture and Television Engineers) has promulgated a coordinate system for a standard receiver that uses primaries that match modern phosphors more accurately than the NTSC system.

***YIQ* NTSC transmission color coordinate system.**  NTSC formulated a color coordinate system to be used for transmission. The system uses three tristimulus values: $Y$, $I$, and $Q$. $Y$ represents the luminance of a color; $I$ and $Q$ describe (in a combined manner) the hue and saturation aspects of an image. This enables the development of a modulation scheme supporting color television on the same bandwidth as monochrome television. Table 3.9 maps the NTSC colors to $YIQ$.[11]

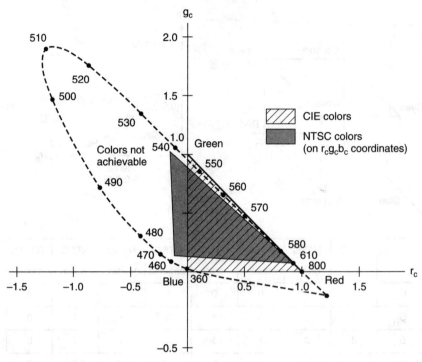

**Figure 3.36** Comparison of colors possible with NTSC versus CIE (red, green, and blue primaries).

**TABLE 3.8  Maps of the Major $R_N G_N B_N$ Colors into the $R_C G_C B_C$ Space**

|  | NTSC red | NTSC green | NTSC blue | NTSC cyan | NTSC magenta | NTSC yellow | NTSC white |
|---|---|---|---|---|---|---|---|
| $R_C$ | 0.207 | −0.026 | −0.026 | −0.052 | 0.180 | 0.181 | 0.154 |
| $G_C$ | 0.020 | 0.133 | 0.028 | 0.161 | 0.048 | 0.153 | 0.181 |
| $B_C$ | 0.000 | 0.010 | 0.200 | 0.210 | 0.199 | 0.010 | 0.210 |
| $r_c$ | 0.912 | −0.222 | −0.129 | −0.163 | 0.422 | 0.526 | 0.283 |
| $g_c$ | 0.088 | 1.137 | 0.139 | 0.505 | 0.112 | 0.445 | 0.332 |
| $b_c$ | 0.000 | 0.085 | 0.990 | 0.658 | 0.466 | 0.029 | 0.385 |

**TABLE 3.9  NTSC Colors in *YIQ* Space**

|  | NTSC red | NTSC green | NTSC blue | NTSC cyan | NTSC magenta | NTSC yellow | NTSC white |
|---|---|---|---|---|---|---|---|
| $Y$ | 0.299 | 0.587 | 0.114 | 0.701 | 0.413 | 0.886 | 1 |
| $I$ | 0.596 | −0.274 | −0.322 | −0.595 | 0.272 | 0.322 | 0 |
| $Q$ | 0.211 | −0.523 | 0.312 | 0.207 | 0.526 | −0.312 | 0 |

The conversion factors are[1]

$$Y = 0.299R_N + 0.587G_N + 0.144B_N$$

$$I = 0.596R_N - 0.274G_N - 0.322B_N$$

$$Q = 0.211R_N - 0.523G_N + 0.312B_N$$

and

$$R_N = 1.000Y + 0.956I + 0.621Q$$

$$G_N = 1.000Y - 0.272I - 0.647Q$$

$$B_N = 1.000Y - 1.106I - 1.703Q$$

**YUV color coordinate system.**   PAL (phase-alternation line) and SECAM utilize color-difference methods with luminance $Y$ and

$$U = 0.493\,(B_N - Y)$$

$$V = 0.877\,(R_N - Y)$$

See Table 3.10 for a mapping of the NTSC colors.

**XYZ color coordinate system.**   CIE's $R_C G_C B_C$ system and the NTSC systems of primaries may require negative tristimulus values to match a color. CIE has promulgated a system of (artificial) primaries so that all tristimulus values required to match standardized reference colors are positive. The $X$, $Y$, and $Z$ primaries are shown in Fig. 3.37. Figure 3.38 depicts the chromaticity space. Figure 3.39 provides some additional details on NTSC colors in the $xy$ space. A large value of $x$ implies a substantial amount of red (matched by colors that appear red, orange, or reddish-purple); a large value of $y$ implies that the color can be matched by a green, bluish-green, or yellowish-green color. When $x$ and $y$ are small, $z$ must be large; this means that the color can be matched by colors appearing violet, blue, or purple.

The primaries are defined so that the $Y$ tristimulus value is equivalent to the luminance of the color to be matched. A color can be speci-

**TABLE 3.10   NTSC Colors in YUV Space**

|   | NTSC red | NTSC green | NTSC blue | NTSC cyan | NTSC magenta | NTSC yellow | NTSC white |
|---|---|---|---|---|---|---|---|
| $Y$ | 0.299 | 0.587 | 0.014 | 0.701 | 0.413 | 0.886 | 1 |
| $U$ | 0.147 | −0.289 | 0.437 | 0.147 | 0.289 | −0.437 | 0 |
| $V$ | 0.615 | −0.515 | −0.100 | −0.615 | 0.515 | 0.100 | 0 |

Tristimulus values

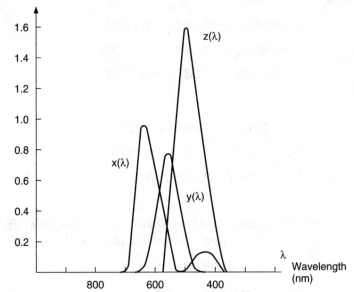

**Figure 3.37**    Color matching functions for the 2° CIE Standard Observer.

fied by the chromaticity coordinates $x,y$ and the luminance $Y$, namely, $(x,y,Y)$. This last representation can be thought of as the color of the stimulus stripped of brightness.[12]

Figure 3.40 shows the chromaticity coordinates of the spectral colors; note that they are all positive. The fact that the $X$, $Y$, and $Z$ primaries are positive results in the fact that they are imaginary (nonreal). This means that they cannot be realized by any actual color stimuli. Additionally, the primaries are represented in the tristimulus vector space by vectors that are outside the domain of real colors (i.e., the unit triangle).

The conversion factors between $XYZ$ and $R_N G_N B_N$ were provided earlier. Figure 3.41 depicts a mapping of the $R_N G_N B_N$ color space into the $XYZ$ color space. As can seen, the gamut of colors realizable with $R_N G_N B_N$ is smaller than that possible with the $XYZ$ primaries.

The table in Fig. 3.41 is obtained as follows. To translate from $R_N, G_N, B_N$ to $X,Y,Z$ one has

$$[T_X(C),\ T_Y(C),\ T_Z(C)] = [R_N(C),\ G_N(C),\ B_N(C)]\begin{bmatrix} 0.607 & 0.299 & 0.000 \\ 0.174 & 0.587 & 0.066 \\ 0.200 & 0.114 & 1.116 \end{bmatrix}$$

or

$$T_X(C) = 0.607R_N(C) + 0.174G_N(C) + 0.200B_N(C)$$

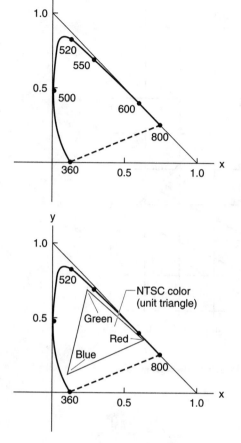

**Figure 3.38** Chromaticity graph for CIE *XYZ* primary color system and comparison with NTSC colors.

$$T_Y(C) = 0.299R_N(C) + 0.587G_N(C) + 0.114B_N(C)$$

$$T_Z(C) = 0.000R_N(C) + 0.066G_N(C) + 1.116B_N(C)$$

To translate from $X,Y,Z$ to $R_N,G_N,B_N$, one can use the relation

$$[R_N(C), G_N(C), B_N(C)] = [T_X(C), T_Y(C), T_Z(C)] \begin{bmatrix} 1.910 & -0.985 & 0.058 \\ -0.532 & 2.000 & -0.118 \\ -0.288 & -0.028 & 0.898 \end{bmatrix}$$

or

$$R_N(C) = 1.910T_X(C) - 0.532T_Y(C) - 0.288T_Z(C)$$

$$G_N(C) = -0.985T_X(C) + 2.000T_Y(C) - 0.028T_Z(C)$$

$$B_N(C) = 0.058T_X(C) - 0.118T_Y(C) + 0.898T_Z(C)$$

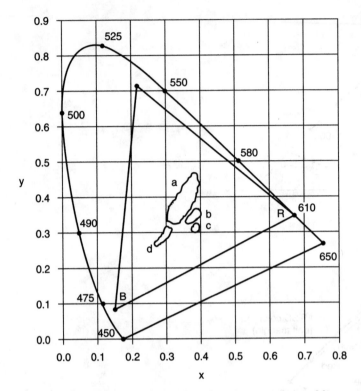

**Figure 3.39** Some details of the NTSC color scheme. a = green foliage; b = soil; c = human skin; d = sky.

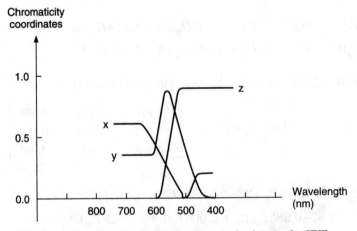

**Figure 3.40** Chromaticity coordinates of spectral colors in the $XYZ$ system plotted against the wavelength.

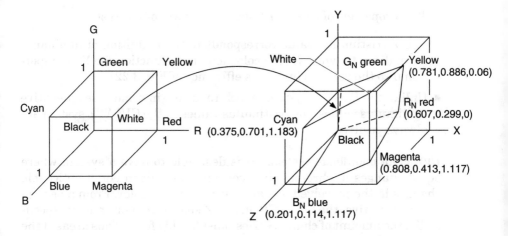

| | NTSC red | NTSC green | NTSC blue | NTSC cyan | NTSC magenta | NTSC yellow | NTSC white |
|---|---|---|---|---|---|---|---|
| X | 0.607 | 0.174 | 0.200 | 0.375 | 0.808 | 0.781 | 0.982 |
| Y | 0.299 | 0.587 | 0.114 | 0.701 | 0.413 | 0.886 | 1.000 |
| Z | 0.000 | 0.066 | 1.117 | 1.183 | 1.117 | 0.066 | 1.183 |
| x | 0.670 | 0.210 | 0.140 | 0.166 | 0.346 | 0.451 | 0.310 |
| y | 0.330 | 0.710 | 0.080 | 0.310 | 0.177 | 0.511 | 0.316 |
| z | 0.000 | 0.080 | 0.780 | 0.524 | 0.478 | 0.038 | 0.374 |

**Figure 3.41** Smaller $R_N G_N B_N$ color space compared to the $XYZ$ space.

Therefore, looking at the previous set of equations, for a red $R_N$ value (1,0,0), one gets $T_X(C) = 0.607$, $T_Y(C) = 0.299$, and $T_Z(C) = 0$. Note that these are all positive. Therefore $x = 0.670$, $y = 0.330$, and $z = 0$.

For a green $G_N$ value (0,1,0), one gets $T_X(C) = 0.174$, $T_Y(C) = 0.587$, and $T_Z(C) = 0.066$. Note that these are all positive. Therefore $x = 0.210$, $y = 0.710$, and $z = 0.080$. For a $B_N$ blue (0,0,1), one gets $T_X(C) = 0.200$, $T_Y(C) = 0.114$, and $T_Z(C) = 1.116$. Note that these are all positive. Therefore $x = 0.140$, $y = 0.080$, and $z = 0.780$.

Note that these values are consistent with Fig. 3.38 (showing the NTSC colors inside the $xy$ diagram with the coordinates just derived), with Fig. 3.41 for the transformation of the $R_N G_N B_N$ space into the $XYZ$ space, and with the table included in that figure. (*Observation:* Different sources quote slightly different matrix values for these and other transformations.)

Two properties of this coordinate system are of interest:

- The $Y$ tristimulus value corresponds to the definition of luminance normalized to white $E$ (the color matching function for $Y$ is proportional to the relative luminous efficiency of Fig. 3.22).

- Unlike the $R_C G_C B_C$ system, which requires (in some cases) negative tristimulus values, the tristimulus values in the CIE $XYZ$ system are always positive.

**UVW color coordinate system.** It is desirable to have a system where equal changes in chromaticity coordinates result in equal noticeable changes in the perceived hue and saturation of a color. From a perceptual perspective, the CIE $RGB$ and $XYZ$ spaces are nonuniform; specifically, the amount of change varies considerably for various areas of the diagram. Large changes are required in the top areas that correspond to green, while very small differences are detectable in the lower portion corresponding to blue. Now a transformation of the CIE 1931 color space has been adopted which produces a more uniform color space. Such system, known as the *uniform chromaticity scale,* was introduced by CIE in 1960. The tristimulus variables are $U$, $V$, and $W$. (Note, however, that these $U$ and $V$ are not the same as the $U$ and $V$ of the $YUV$ coordinate system.) Here $V$ represents luminance. See Fig. 3.42 and also Table 3.11.

The relationships to the $XYZ$ tristimulus values are as follows:

$$U = \tfrac{2}{3}X$$

$$V = Y$$

$$W = -\tfrac{1}{2}X + \tfrac{3}{2}Y + \tfrac{1}{2}Z$$

The inverse transformation is

$$X = \tfrac{3}{2}U$$

$$Y = V$$

$$Z = \tfrac{3}{2}U - 3V + 2W$$

In terms of chromaticity coordinates one has

$$u = \frac{4x}{-2x + 12y + 3}$$

$$v = \frac{6y}{-2x + 12y + 3}$$

with the inverse transformations

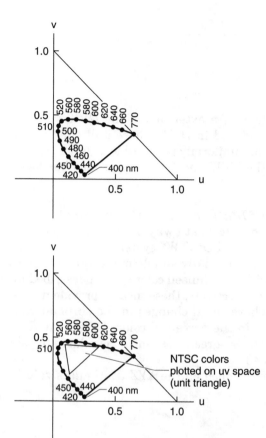

**Figure 3.42** Chromaticity graph for uniformity chromaticity scale primary color system and comparison with NTSC colors.

TABLE 3.11    Basic NTSC Colors in *UVW* Space

|   | NTSC red | NTSC green | NTSC blue | NTSC cyan | NTSC magenta | NTSC yellow | NTSC white |
|---|---|---|---|---|---|---|---|
| $U$ | 0.405 | 0.116 | 0.133 | 0.259 | 0.539 | 0.521 | 0.655 |
| $V$ | 0.299 | 0.587 | 0.114 | 0.701 | 0.413 | 0.880 | 1.000 |
| $W$ | 0.145 | 0.827 | 0.627 | 1.456 | 0.774 | 0.972 | 1.601 |
| $u$ | 0.477 | 0.076 | 0.152 | 0.107 | 0.312 | 0.220 | 0.201 |
| $v$ | 0.352 | 0.384 | 0.130 | 0.290 | 0.239 | 0.371 | 0.307 |
| $w$ | 0.171 | 0.541 | 0.717 | 0.603 | 0.448 | 0.410 | 0.492 |

$$x = \frac{1.5u}{u - 4v + 2}$$

$$y = \frac{v}{u - 4v + 2}$$

**U\*V\*W\* color coordinate system.**  An extension of the $UVW$ system, known as $U*V*W*$, was introduced in 1964, where unit changes in luminance and chrominance are uniformly perceptible. A large body of color information based on the $UVW$ and $U*V*W*$ systems has been collected.

**L\*a\*b\* color coordinate system.**  $L*a*b*$ and $L*u*v*$ were introduced by CIE in 1976 to provide a more accurate way of measuring colors, thereby superseding the $UVW$ and $U*V*W*$ systems. In particular, these systems provide a computationally simple measurement technique that is in agreement with the Munsell color system described in the beginning of this chapter; effectively, these models provide a perceptually uniform system where equal changes in the chromaticity space produce equal changes in the perceived color. $L*$ is related to brightness, $a*$ is related to redness-greenness, and $b*$ is related to yellowness-blueness. See Fig. 3.43.

The "forward" equations positioned on the $XYZ$ tristimulus values are[11,12]

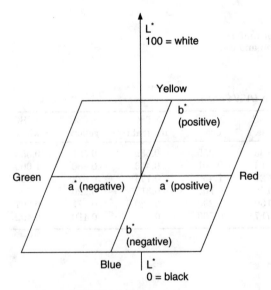

**Figure 3.43**  $L*a*b*$ coordinate system.

$$L^* = 25 \left( \frac{100Y}{Y_0} \right)^{1/3} - 16$$

$$a^* = 500 \left[ \left( \frac{X}{X_0} \right)^{1/3} - \left( \frac{Y}{Y_0} \right)^{1/3} \right]$$

$$b^* = 200 \left[ \left( \frac{X}{X_0} \right)^{1/3} - \left( \frac{Z}{Z_0} \right)^{1/3} \right]$$

where $X_0$, $Y_0$, and $Z_0$ are the tristimulus values for the reference white. The "reverse" equations are

$$X = X_0 \left[ \frac{a^*}{500} + \left( \frac{1}{100} \right)^{1/3} \frac{L^* + 16}{25} \right]^3$$

$$Y = Y_0 \left( \frac{L^* + 16}{25} \right)^3$$

$$Z = Z_0 \left[ \left( \frac{1}{100} \right)^{1/3} \frac{L^* + 16}{25} - \frac{b^*}{200} \right]^3$$

**L\*u\*v\* color coordinate system.** $L^*u^*v^*$ has evolved from $L^*a^*b^*$ and $U^*V^*W^*$, and became a CIE standard in 1976. $L^*u^*v^*$ is commonly referred to by the abbreviation *CIELUV*. The color coordinates are for self-luminous sources referenced to the $D_{6500}$ white. The equations are

$$L^* = \begin{cases} 25 \left( \dfrac{100Y}{Y_0} \right)^{1/3} - 16 & \dfrac{Y}{Y_0} \geq 0.008856 \\[4mm] \dfrac{903.3Y}{Y_0} & \dfrac{Y}{Y_0} < 0.008856 \end{cases}$$

$$u^* = 13L^* \left( \frac{4X}{X + 15Y + 3Z} - u_0' \right)$$

$$v^* = 13L^* \left( \frac{9Y}{X + 15Y + 3Z} - v_0' \right)$$

where $u_0'$ and $v_0'$ are obtained by substitution of the tristimulus values $X_0$, $Y_0$, and $Z_0$ for the reference white (it turns out that if $Y$—luminance—is represented by a precision of $\leq 8$ bits, the second branch of the equation can be ignored); that is

$$u'_0 = \frac{4X_0}{X_0 + 15Y_0 + 3Z_0}$$

$$v'_0 = \frac{9Y_0}{X_0 + 15Y_0 + 3Z_0}$$

The "reverse" equations are

$$X = \frac{9}{4} \left( \frac{u^*/13L^* + u'_0}{v^*/13L^* + v'_0} \right) Y$$

$$Y = Y_0 \left( \frac{L^* + 16}{25} \right)^3$$

$$Z = Y \left[ \frac{12 - 3(u^*/13L^* + u'_0) - 20(v^*/13L^* + v'_0)}{4(v^*/13L^* + v'_0)} \right]$$

As noted, two uniform color spaces from a perceptual point of view are the Munsell renotation system (also called *Munsell book of color*) and the Optical Society of America Uniform Color Scale. The $L^*a^*b^*$ and $L^*u^*v^*$ systems are an attempt to find an analytical machinery supporting such perceptually uniform color organization. This topic is revisited in Sec. 3.3.10.

**Other color coordinate systems.**    A coordinate system that has been used by the image processing community is the intensity, hue, and saturation (*IHS*) system. In this system blue is the reference point for hue ($H = 0$ for blue). The system uses three coordinates, $I$, $V_1$, and $V_2$, defined on the basis of $R_N$, $G_N$, and $B_N$, as follows:

$$I = \frac{1}{3} R_N + \frac{1}{3} G_N + \frac{1}{3} B_N$$

$$H = \tan^{-1} \frac{V_2}{V_1}$$

$$S = [(V_1)^2 + (V_2)^2]^{1/2}$$

with

$$V_1 = -\frac{1}{\sqrt{6}} R_N + \frac{-1}{\sqrt{6}} G_N + \frac{2}{\sqrt{6}} B_N$$

$$V_2 = \frac{1}{\sqrt{6}} R_N + \frac{-2}{\sqrt{6}} G_N$$

The inverse transformations are

$$R_N = \frac{4}{3} I + \frac{-2\sqrt{6}}{9} V_1 + \frac{\sqrt{6}}{3} V_2$$

$$G_N = \frac{2}{3} I + \frac{\sqrt{6}}{9} V_1 + \frac{-\sqrt{6}}{3} V_1$$

$$B_N = I + \frac{\sqrt{6}}{3} V_1$$

where

$$V_1 = S \cos(H)$$
$$V_2 = S \sin(H)$$

As noted earlier, it is desirable to have a set of tristimulus values that are orthogonal. This can be done by the Karhunen-Loeve (K-L) color coordinate system. As the mathematics gets more involved, the interested reader is referred to any number of advanced imaging textbooks, including Ref. 11.

### 3.3.8  Limitations of some of the key color systems

There are two physical limitations in the representation of natural colors in imaging systems:

1. Physical primaries can emit only positive amounts of light; this implies that a color match requiring a negative tristimulus value cannot be achieved with additive color mixtures. In other words, colors with tristimulus values cannot be generated.

2. Colors in natural objects may result from diffuse illumination reflected from an opaque object or through a transparent material. Non-self-luminous objects suffer from restrictions in brightness that is dependent on the object's color.

There are certain limitations in the experiments described thus far. One issue is that color matching depends to some (mild) degree on the condition of observation. Also, it depends on the (just) previous exposure of the eye. For example, the desensitization of the eye based on previous exposure to white can be measured experimentally; there is also desensitization based on the color of the surroundings. This is called *persistence of color match*. Yet another issue is the fact that color matching must be averaged over a number of observers.

### 3.3.9  Color temperatures

The CIE has specified certain sources of light that are important in colorimetry. This issue was already discussed in an earlier section; however, color temperature aspects were not discussed. The reason for having to deal with temperature is that as the temperature of a blackbody increases, the blackbody begins to emit visible radiation. Figure 3.44 shows the change in chromaticity coordinates as the temperature of the blackbody is increased.

Several radiant sources on or close to the locus of Fig. 3.44 are taken as standard CIE sources. Illuminant *A*, already introduced, represents light from a tungsten lamp; it has a temperature of 2856 K and resides at (0.447,0.407). Illuminant *B* represents direct sunlight; it has a temperature of 4870 K and resides at (0.384,0.352). Illuminant *C* represents average sunlight; it has a temperature of 6770 K and resides at (0.310,0.316). A new source, illuminant $D_{6500}$, is being positioned as a new reference for average daylight; it has a temperature of 6500 K and resides at (0.312,0.330). Source *E* has a temperature of 5500 K and resides at (0.333,0.333).

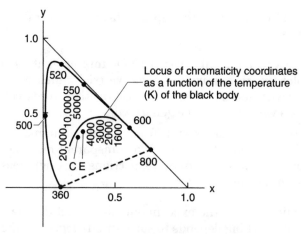

**Figure 3.44**  Chromaticity coordinates as function of temperature.

### 3.3.10    Some relationships to Munsell's renotation

As noted earlier in this chapter, the chips in the Munsell system (based on color appearance) have been calibrated on the basis of the *xyz* chromaticity coordinates under the source *C* illuminant. Figure 3.45 depicts an example: the loci of constant hue and constant chroma for value (lightness) of /1 are shown. Figure 3.46 depicts an actual "spider" diagram for /5.

The problem with the *xyz* coordinates is that the loci of constant hue and constant chroma do not show uniformity in the sense that a change $\Delta x \, \Delta y$ in some radial direction for *xy* close to the point representing illuminant *C* does not equate to a change in chroma when the same change $\Delta x \, \Delta y$ occurs at the fringes of the diagram. As discussed earlier, the CIE *UVW* coordinates transform the *xy* space into the *uv* space where the Munsell lines are nearly uniform. (The change $\Delta u \, \Delta v$ results in the same change of the Munsell values, regardless of the value of *u* and *v*.) See Fig. 3.47; Fig. 3.48 depicts the actual color mapping in the *uv* space.

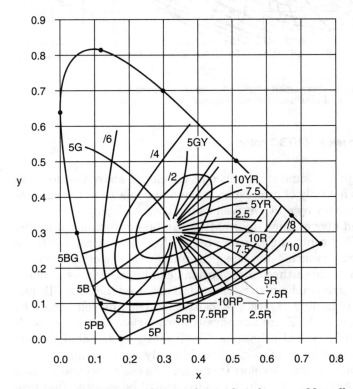

**Figure 3.45**  *xy* chromaticity diagram showing loci of constant Munsell hue (radial "lines") and constant Munsell chroma ("ovals") for lightness value /1.

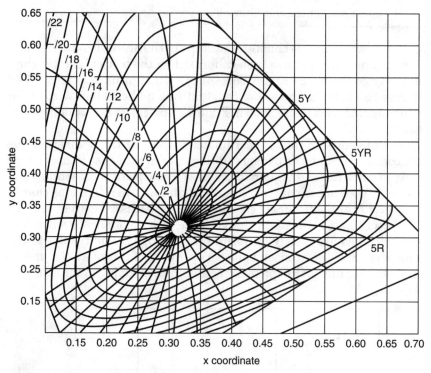

**Figure 3.46**  Actual $xy$ chromaticity "spider" diagram showing loci of constant Munsell hue (radial "lines") and constant Munsell chroma ("ovals") for lightness value /5.

### 3.3.11  Some basics of NTSC color television

This section applies some of the concepts developed above to color television. This is not only of interest on its own but relates to the capture of images off the air by a PC, as well as the for the display of images.

As discussed above, color information can be approximated by the summation of light intensities generated by three primaries. Any three nonoverlapping primaries (not being the mixture of the other two) can be used. Each of these three distributions can be treated as a monochrome image that can be raster-scanned. If one used the $XYZ$ CIE primaries, the tristimulus values are positive, and so any color could be realized. However, $XYZ$ are nonphysical primaries. One is left with $RGB$ as a set of physical primaries. The limitation, as noted, is that since the physical primaries can provide only positive amounts of energy, there always will be colors that cannot be shown on real TV and PC monitors. Additionally, primary sources must be selected that produce enough luminance; the actual sources that produce such adequate luminance may generate only a reduced spectral output compared to

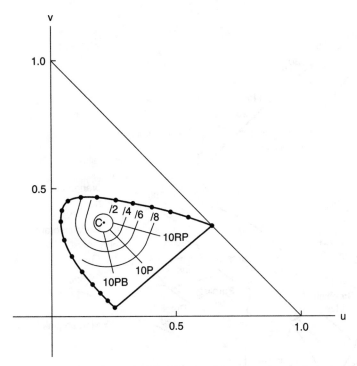

**Figure 3.47**   Munsell system in $uv$ chromaticity space (approximate).

even the definition of an idealized $R_N G_N B_N$ primary, thereby further restricting the scope of the color space.

For a TV camera to measure three tristimulus values at every pixel in the image, three calculations (as per Sec. 3.3.5) must be undertaken, as implied in Fig. 3.49. In this figure, the purpose of the camera filters $r_C(\lambda), g_C(\lambda)$, and $b_C(\lambda)$ is to perform the wavelength averaging according the spectral distribution of a set of potential chosen primaries; the monochromatic raster device produces the tristimulus value by integration.

As seen in Fig. 3.31, the spectral distribution for the $R_C G_C B_C$ primaries, namely, the matching function, can be negative; this precludes utilizing them as filtering mechanisms since real filters do not have negative characteristics. One way around this is to employ the $XYZ$ system, which has all positive matching functions $x(\lambda), y(\lambda), z(\lambda)$, to obtain the tristimulus values $X(t), Y(t), Z(t)$, and then perform the appropriate matrix multiplication to obtain the $R(t), G(t), B(t)$ values for the $RGB$ system of primaries. This approach has a number of problems. Negative $RGB$ tristimulus values may arise. Even more importantly, the original scene illumination and the viewing conditions do

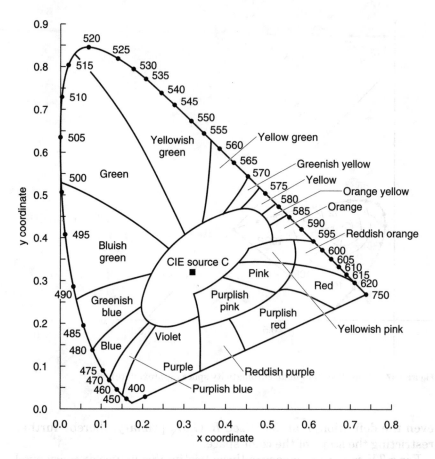

**Figure 3.48** Color mapping in the $xy$ space and $u^*v^*$ space.

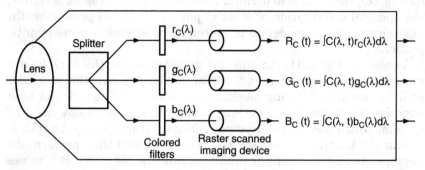

**Figure 3.49** TV camera producing tristimulus values. (*Note:* In this figure the subscript C stands for camera, not CIE as in $R_C G_C B_C$.)

not match the conditions at the display end. It follows that the correct recreation of the signal to achieve the desired perceived color is not achieved simply by correct delivery of the tristimulus values.

The practical approach is to design cameras with nonnegative filtering functions $r_C(\lambda)$, $g_C(\lambda)$, $b_C(\lambda)$ that do not correspond to any particular set of primaries. The values $R_C(t)$, $G_C(t)$, $B_C(t)$ are then transformed using an optimization matrix $T$ with

$$
\begin{bmatrix} R(t) \\ G(t) \\ B(t) \end{bmatrix} = T \begin{bmatrix} R_C(t) \\ G_C(t) \\ B_C(t) \end{bmatrix}
$$

where $T$ is selected to minimize the average error in the perceived color at the display equipment or to optimize the reproduction of (say) human skin. The camera outputs are then $R(t)$, $G(t)$, and $B(t)$.

From the earlier discussion of the equivalence of (matrix) transformed tristimulus values, various transformations (really, linear combinations) of the $R(t)$, $G(t)$, and $B(t)$ values are utilized in television, as needed. The transformed values are called $Y(t)$, $C_1(t)$, and $C_2(t)$; these are the values that are transmitted to the user. In most cases $Y(t)$ is selected to approximate the luminance; the other two values contain the color information (chrominance). (There may yet be additional compromises on the signals transmitted due to bandwidth and other engineering considerations.)

**NTSC.**    The 1952 NTSC system defines standard display phosphors and color primaries in terms of the CIE $xyz$ chromaticity coordinates:[12]

$$
\begin{array}{c c c c}
 & x & y & z \\
R & 0.67 & 0.33 & 0.00 \\
G & 0.21 & 0.71 & 0.08 \\
B & 0.14 & 0.08 & 0.78
\end{array}
$$

Several earlier figures (in particular under the CIE $XYZ$ discussion) showed the NTSC realizable colors as mapped over the $xyz$ chromaticity space. As those figures revealed, there is an extensive range of colors that cannot be reproduced by this system. One attenuating factor, however, is that many colors in nature have low saturation, so that saturated hues are less of a troubling problem. Also, newer monitors use nonstandard phosphors that support higher color saturation and luminance. Note that the reference white for NTSC is chosen to be approximate daylight as standard illuminant $C$.

**PAL.**  The phase-alternation line color television system used in western Europe was developed after NTSC. Consequently, the display primaries used in PAL support high-luminance phosphors used in PC displays. They are defined in terms of the CIE *xyz* chromaticity coordinates:

$$
\begin{array}{c}
 & x & y & z \\
R & \left[\begin{array}{ccc} 0.64 & 0.33 & 0.03 \\ G & 0.29 & 0.60 & 0.11 \\ B & 0.15 & 0.06 & 0.79 \end{array}\right]
\end{array}
$$

Figure 3.50 shows the chromaticity diagram.

### 3.3.12    Color issues as related to display monitors

Some aspects of color reproduction on a PC or workstation monitor are also important for imaging applications, for example, in displaying or

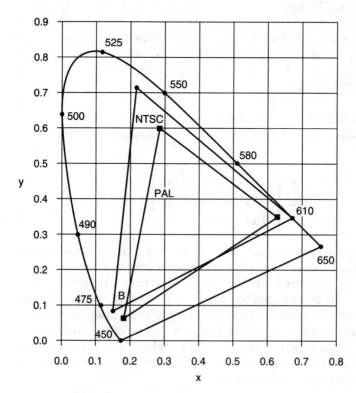

**Figure 3.50**  PAL colors.

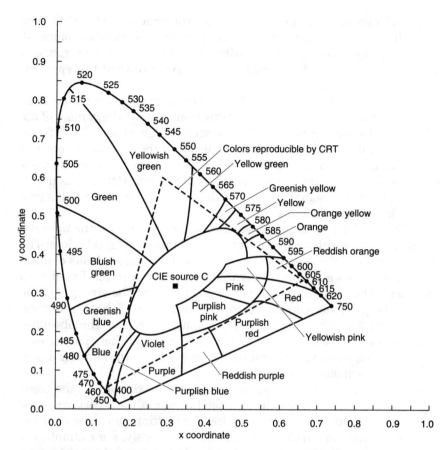

**Figure 3.51**   Color space of a typical monitor. (*Note:* Since the chromaticity diagram does not show the luminance, transformations are needed to determine the proportional luminous value of each primary to achieve the desired color.)

visualizing a high-resolution image for editing or analysis purposes. The amount of light emitted by a PC or workstation monitor is usually expressed as luminance and is measured in foot-lamberts (fl). It ranges from about 25 to 35 fl for computer monitors to 160 fl for a TV monitor.

The range of colors available on a CRT depends on the phosphors used as well as the method of beam superposition. Phosphors are usually specified in terms of the 1931 CIE chromaticity coordinates. (The 1976 Uniform Chromaticity Scale is also used because of the uniformity of the chromaticity space.) Figure 3.51 depicts the color space of a typical monitor that uses phosphor P43 for green and P22 for red and blue on the 1931 CIE *xy* space. As in the cases above, the corners of the triangle correspond to the chromaticity coordinates of the primaries realized by specific phosphors used in the construction of the CRT. The colors inside the triangle correspond to physically achievable colors. As noted, the human eye is most sensitive to light in the 550-nm range (a yellowish green) with decreasing sensitivity toward the spectral extremes (see Fig. 3.28).

Voltage and luminance of a CRT are normally plotted on a logarithmic scale. The *slope* of the resulting function is called the *gamma of the display*. For a monochrome CRT, a relatively high gamma level (2.8 to 3.0) is desirable; this allows the dark levels of the display to appear a deep black. For a color monitor a high gamma produces strong color distortions as luminance is increased or decreased. Hence, it is necessary to modify the signals to each of the display's three guns; this procedure is known as *gamma correction*.

Additive color mixture methods discussed earlier form the underlying principle by which PC and workstation monitors "mix" colors. The inside surface of the color monitor consists of hundreds of dots of phosphor. Phosphors are compounds that emit light when radiated with electrons. The amount of light emitted depends on the strength of the beam. The phosphors on the screen are in groups of three: red phosphors, blue phosphors, and green phosphors. Because the phosphor dots are small, the output of the three elements of the triad appears amalgamated when viewed from a distance, so that the result is a field of color that appears homogeneous.

To display a green object on the screen, as an example, all the green phosphors forming the outline and the interior of the object are made to emit light. Other hues are produced by making two or more of the three phosphors in a triad emit light simultaneously. For example, the simultaneous activation of a green and red phosphor field in the immediate proximity results in the perception of a yellow or orange color, depending on the luminance of the individual phosphors. As implied by the discussion in the early part of the chapter, when the energy distribution of a blue phosphor and the energy distribution of a green phosphor are additively superimposed, the mixture consists of a broader set of wavelengths; this implies that the mixture will be less saturated than the blue or green alone. When the energy distribution of a red phosphor is additively superimposed with the energy distribution of a green phosphor, the resulting hue is yellow. All three phosphors' signals superimposed together produce a distribution containing all the visible wavelengths which are perceived as white. Varying the intensity of the three phosphors produces differing levels of lightness.

The total number of colors that can be produced by the monitor depends on the number of steps of gray level obtainable for each phosphor. If the electron gun can be stepped over four levels, the resulting palette has 64 colors. Many PC and workstation monitors are capable of

256 steps of gray from each gun, resulting in a palette of over 16 million unique combinations. However, the eye is not capable of discriminating many of the small changes in color. The viewable palette has fewer colors: under optimal conditions, a total about 3 million discriminable colors (colors that are recognizably different when placed adjacent to one another) can be produced in a PC monitor. The scope of the palette decreases to about 7000 when colors located at different PC and workstation monitor areas must be recognized as different from one another.

A common CRT technology is shadow mask. In this case color is achieved by a spatial additive process: color mixture occurs by juxtaposition of small primary color dots that cannot be individually perceived (i.e., resolved) by the observer (see Fig. 3.52). The shadow-mask CRT consists of (1) three electron guns in close proximity, (2) a shadow mask, and (3) a screen painted with regular zones of three types of phosphors. The guns can be arranged in a straight line (called *in-line*) or in a delta arrangement (called *delta gun*); the gun can also be a single three-beam gun (see Fig. 3.53). The interested reader is referred to Refs. 7 and 13, which provide an extensive treatment of this topic.

**Descriptive color systems used for PC monitors.**  A commonly used *descriptive* system in the context of PC and workstation monitors is to describe colors in terms of the additive proportions of red, green, and blue. This approach is the *RGB* system. This system is a straightforward and direct approach that incorporates the additive principles discussed in the body of this chapter. It specifies the triplets of values ranging from 0 to 100 percent for each of the three primaries.

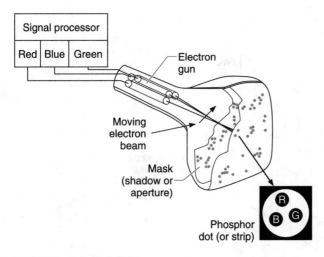

**Figure 3.52**  A typical CRT.

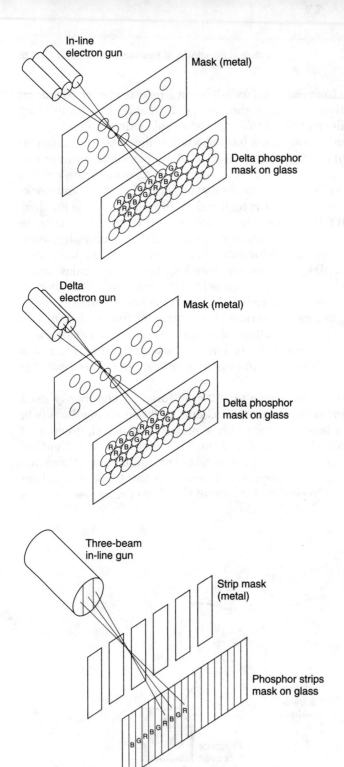

**Figure 3.53** Various CRT gun configurations.

Another commonly used color descriptive system for PC and workstation monitors is Tektronix's *HLS* (hue, lightness, and saturation) system. In this system the hues are conceptualized as a circle surrounding the midpoint of the lightness scale. The hues are arranged so that complementary colors are located across from each other on a circle. Hue specification is given in degrees starting with blue at 0°, magenta = 60°, red = 120°, yellow = 180°, green = 240°, and cyan = 300°. Lightness and saturation are expressed as percentages along a continuum ranging from 0 to 100 percent. Thus, a yellow of medium lightness and high saturation would be specified as 180, 50, 100 percent.

Another color descriptive system for PC and workstation monitors is the color naming system. This system uses common English names for colors, similar to the system described in Table 3.5 and related text. A set of seven generic color names (red, orange, brown, yellow, green, blue, and purple) along with white, black, and gray is used. A total of 31 hue names are derived by using adjacent hue names together to indicate a hue half way between two generic hues (i.e., brown-yellow ) and the suffix *-ish* to denote quarter-way hues (i.e., brownish yellow). Five lightness levels (very dark, dark, medium, light, and very light) and four saturation levels (grayish, moderate, strong, and vivid) can be specified. A color specification could read "light, grayish, brownish yellow." The number of specifiable colors is 627. (Note, however, that many PC and workstation monitors have palettes of 4096 and more.)

### 3.3.13  Colorimetric calibration

Colorimetric calibration for electronic imaging devices is becoming important given the advances in color photocopying and desktop publishing, particularly for printing. The repertoire of desktop imaging systems now appearing includes color monitors, devices that expose photographic paper, offset printing devices, ink-jet printers, dye diffusion thermal transfer printers, and wax thermal transfer printers. Accurate colorimetric calibration enables the generation of image material that enjoys high fidelity when compared to the original.

Models have been developed to calibrate devices colorimetrically. Two classic examples of color prediction methods using analytical techniques are Beer's law and the Neugebauer equations. These models enable prediction with a few measurements; however, they may not be accurate enough for practical systems.[14] Empirical models have been developed to take over where the theory leaves off. A well-known method is the polynomial regression model. Here the system is assumed to be a black box and the parameters are obtained from input-output relationships. This method can be used in scanner and printer systems; the method, however, cannot guarantee high accuracy across the entire color spectrum. (In general, colors close to the measurement point used for regression are predicted reasonably well, but points far away are predicted less well.)

There is a second empirical approach that has been widely applied. This technique uses a matrix of color patches, along with measurements, and a method for interpolation. Multidimensional [three-dimensional (3-D) in particular] interpolation techniques have been developed for color scanners and printers. The first patent for the cubic interpolation techniques (also known as *trilinear interpolation*), which uses eight corners of a cube to interpolate, was awarded in Great Britain in 1972. A second interpolation method is known as *tetrahedral interpolation* and was patented in Japan in 1978. With this method, interpolation could be performed in fewer and simpler multiplications.

The basic concept in interpolation-based calibration is that any smooth function can be approximated by many successive linear elements. Generally there are two steps: (1) division of the space and (2) acquisition of the values in a transformed space. To obtain a point in the color space corresponding to a point in the signal space, the algorithm performs the following actions:

- Search a set of points surrounding the given point.

- Calculate the corresponding values in the counterpart space for the set of points.

To obtain a set of color values from a set of signal values, step 1 undertakes a check of the position of the signal value in a lattice. The division of the multidimensional space can be done using cubic subspace division and tetrahedral subspace division (see Fig. 3.54 for a 2-D example). Step 2 continues by obtaining weighted averages based on eight (or four) subdivided volume values. For the cubic interpolation, the calculation is performed using the following transformation:

$$P' = \frac{1}{V} \sum_{i=0}^{7} P'_i V_i$$

where $V$ is the total volume of the cubic subspace, $V_i$ is the volume of the subdivided subspace, and $P$ and $P_i$ are the coordinates of the points.

For the inverse transformation, to obtain a set of signal values from a set of color values, the cube division is utilized a priori. Since no firm criterion exists for showing the inclusion of a given point $P$ in a solid formed with eight points, the procedure requires an iterative calculation by dividing the nominated solids and renominating. (Note that the six surfaces of the solid need not be a plane.) Hence, the process requires an iterative calculation to reach an acceptable level of error; this, in turn, implies more calculation time.

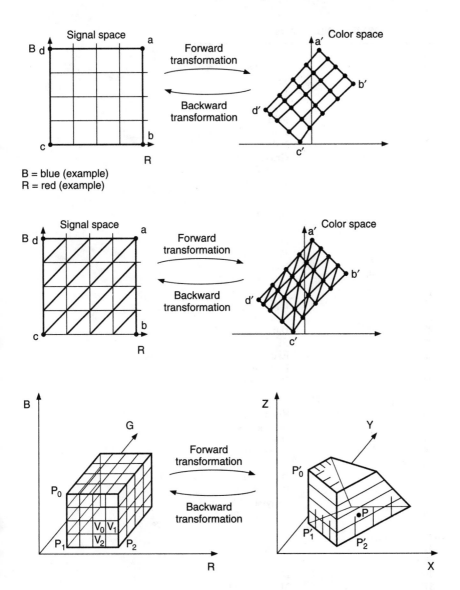

**Figure 3.54** Colorimetric calibration. Top: cubic subspaces. Middle: tetrahedral subspaces. Bottom: 3-D transformation.

## Appendix    ISCC-NBS Colors

Table 3.12 depicts the ISCC-NBS colors described in Sec. 3.1. These colors should not be confused with, for example, a 24-bit *RBG* color system, where filters are allocated to each of the sampled colors (three), and intensity values are determined. The 24-bit codepoint space is not

**TABLE 3.12   267 ISCC-NBS Colors**

Pinks
| | |
|---|---|
| 1 | Vivid *Pk* |
| 2 | Strong *Pk* |
| 3 | Deep *Pk* |
| 4 | Light *Pk* |
| 5 | Moderate *Pk* |
| 6 | Dark *Pk* |
| 7 | Pale *Pk* |
| 8 | Grayish *Pk* |
| 9 | Pinkish white |
| 10 | Pinkish gray |

Reds
| | |
|---|---|
| 11 | Vivid *R* |
| 12 | Strong *R* |
| 13 | Deep *R* |
| 14 | Very deep *R* |
| 15 | Moderate *R* |
| 16 | Dark *R* |
| 17 | Very dark *R* |
| 18 | Light grayish *R* |
| 19 | Grayish *R* |
| 20 | Dark grayish *R* |
| 21 | Blackish *R* |
| 22 | Reddish gray |
| 23 | Dark reddish gray |
| 24 | Reddish black |

Yellowish pinks
| | |
|---|---|
| 25 | Vivid *yPk* |
| 26 | Strong *yPk* |
| 27 | Deep *yPk* |
| 28 | Light *yPk* |
| 29 | Moderate *yPk* |
| 30 | Dark *yPk* |
| 31 | Pale *yPk* |
| 32 | Grayish *yPk* |
| 33 | Brownish *Pk* |

Reddish oranges
| | |
|---|---|
| 34 | Vivid *rO* |
| 35 | Strong *rO* |
| 36 | Deep *rO* |
| 37 | Moderate *rO* |
| 38 | Darkish *rO* |
| 39 | Grayish *rO* |

Reddish browns
| | |
|---|---|
| 40 | Strong *rBr* |
| 41 | Deep *rBr* |
| 42 | Light *rBr* |
| 43 | Moderate *rBr* |
| 44 | Dark *rBr* |
| 45 | Light grayish *rBr* |

**TABLE 3.12    267 ISCC-NBS Colors**
**(Continued)**

Reddish browns
| | |
|---|---|
| 46 | Grayish *rBr* |
| 47 | Dark grayish *rBr* |

Oranges
| | |
|---|---|
| 48 | Vivid *O* |
| 49 | Brilliant *O* |
| 50 | Strong *O* |
| 51 | Deep *O* |
| 52 | Light *O* |
| 53 | Moderate *O* |
| 54 | Brownish *O* |

Browns
| | |
|---|---|
| 55 | Strong *Br* |
| 56 | Deep *Br* |
| 57 | Light *Br* |
| 58 | Moderate *Br* |
| 59 | Dark *Br* |
| 60 | Light grayish *Br* |
| 61 | Grayish *Br* |
| 62 | Dark grayish *Br* |
| 63 | Light brownish gray |
| 64 | Brownish gray |
| 65 | Brownish black |

Orange-yellows
| | |
|---|---|
| 66 | Vivid *OY* |
| 67 | Brilliant *OY* |
| 68 | Strong *OY* |
| 69 | Deep *OY* |
| 70 | Light *OY* |
| 71 | Moderate *OY* |
| 72 | Dark *OY* |
| 73 | Pale *OY* |

Yellowish browns
| | |
|---|---|
| 74 | Strong *yBr* |
| 75 | Deep *yBr* |
| 76 | Light *yBr* |
| 77 | Moderate *yBr* |
| 78 | Dark *yBr* |
| 79 | Light grayish *yBr* |
| 80 | Grayish *yBr* |
| 81 | Dark grayish *yBr* |

Yellows
| | |
|---|---|
| 82 | Vivid *Y* |
| 83 | Brilliant *Y* |
| 84 | Strong *Y* |
| 85 | Deep *Y* |
| 86 | Light *Y* |
| 87 | Moderate *Y* |
| 88 | Dark *Y* |

**TABLE 3.12    267 ISCC-NBS Colors**
**(Continued)**

Yellows
| | |
|---|---|
| 89 | Pale $Y$ |
| 90 | Grayish $Y$ |
| 91 | Dark grayish $Y$ |
| 92 | Yellowish white |
| 93 | Yellowish gray |

Olive-browns
| | |
|---|---|
| 94 | Light $OlBr$ |
| 95 | Moderate $OlBr$ |
| 96 | Dark $OlBr$ |

Greenish yellows
| | |
|---|---|
| 97 | Vivid $gY$ |
| 98 | Brilliant $gY$ |
| 99 | Strong $gY$ |
| 100 | Deep $gY$ |
| 101 | Light $gY$ |
| 102 | Moderate $gY$ |
| 103 | Dark $gY$ |
| 104 | Pale $gY$ |
| 105 | Grayish $gY$ |

Olives
| | |
|---|---|
| 106 | Light $Ol$ |
| 107 | Moderate $Ol$ |
| 108 | Dark $Ol$ |
| 109 | Light grayish $Ol$ |
| 110 | Grayish $Ol$ |
| 111 | Dark grayish $Ol$ |
| 112 | Light $Ol$ gray |
| 113 | $Ol$ gray |
| 114 | $Ol$ black |

Yellow-greens
| | |
|---|---|
| 115 | Vivid $yG$ |
| 116 | Brilliant $yG$ |
| 117 | Strong $yG$ |
| 118 | Deep $yG$ |
| 119 | Light $yG$ |
| 120 | Moderate $yG$ |
| 121 | Pale $yG$ |
| 122 | Grayish $yG$ |

Olive-greens
| | |
|---|---|
| 123 | Strong $OlG$ |
| 124 | Deep $OlG$ |
| 125 | Moderate $OlG$ |
| 126 | Dark $OlG$ |
| 127 | Grayish $OlG$ |
| 128 | Dark grayish $OlG$ |

Yellowish greens
| | |
|---|---|
| 129 | Vivid $yG$ |
| 130 | Brilliant $yG$ |
| 131 | Strong $yG$ |

**TABLE 3.12    267 ISCC-NBS Colors**
*(Continued)*

Yellowish greens

| | |
|---|---|
| 132 | Deep $yG$ |
| 133 | Very deep $yG$ |
| 134 | Very light $yG$ |
| 135 | Light $yG$ |
| 136 | Moderate $yG$ |
| 137 | Dark $yG$ |
| 138 | Very dark $yG$ |

Greens

| | |
|---|---|
| 139 | Vivid $G$ |
| 140 | Brilliant $G$ |
| 141 | Strong $G$ |
| 142 | Deep $G$ |
| 143 | Very light $G$ |
| 144 | Light $G$ |
| 145 | Moderate $G$ |
| 146 | Dark $G$ |
| 147 | Very dark $G$ |
| 148 | Very pale $G$ |
| 149 | Pale $G$ |
| 150 | Grayish $G$ |
| 151 | Dark grayish $G$ |
| 152 | Blackish $G$ |
| 153 | Greenish white |
| 154 | Light greenish gray |
| 155 | Greenish gray |
| 156 | Dark greenish gray |
| 157 | Greenish black |

Bluish greens

| | |
|---|---|
| 158 | Vivid $bG$ |
| 159 | Brilliant $bG$ |
| 160 | Strong $bG$ |
| 161 | Deep $bG$ |
| 162 | Very light $bG$ |
| 163 | Light $bG$ |
| 164 | Moderate $bG$ |
| 165 | Dark $bG$ |
| 166 | Very dark $bG$ |

Greenish blues

| | |
|---|---|
| 167 | Vivid $gB$ |
| 168 | Brilliant $gB$ |
| 169 | Strong $gB$ |
| 170 | Deep $gB$ |
| 171 | Very light $gB$ |
| 172 | Light $gB$ |
| 173 | Moderate $gB$ |
| 174 | Dark $gB$ |
| 175 | Very dark $gB$ |

Blues

| | |
|---|---|
| 176 | Vivid $B$ |
| 177 | Brilliant $B$ |

**TABLE 3.12    267 ISCC-NBS Colors
(*Continued*)**

Blues
| 178 | Strong $B$ |
| 179 | Deep $B$ |
| 180 | Very light $B$ |
| 181 | Light $B$ |
| 182 | Moderate $B$ |
| 183 | Dark $B$ |
| 184 | Very dark $B$ |
| 185 | Pale $B$ |
| 186 | Grayish $B$ |
| 187 | Dark grayish $B$ |
| 188 | Blackish $B$ |
| 189 | Bluish white |
| 190 | Light bluish gray |
| 191 | Bluish gray |
| 192 | Dark bluish gray |
| 193 | Bluish black |

Purplish blues
| 194 | Vivid $pB$ |
| 195 | Brilliant $pB$ |
| 196 | Strong $pB$ |
| 197 | Deep $pB$ |
| 198 | Very light $pB$ |
| 199 | Light $pB$ |
| 200 | Moderate $pB$ |
| 201 | Dark $pB$ |
| 202 | Very pale $pB$ |
| 203 | Pale $pB$ |
| 204 | Grayish $pB$ |

Violets
| 205 | Vivid $V$ |
| 206 | Brilliant $V$ |
| 207 | Strong $V$ |
| 208 | Deep $V$ |
| 209 | Very light $V$ |
| 210 | Light $V$ |
| 211 | Moderate $V$ |
| 212 | Dark $V$ |
| 213 | Very pale $V$ |
| 214 | Pale $V$ |
| 215 | Grayish $V$ |

Purples
| 216 | Vivid $P$ |
| 217 | Brilliant $P$ |
| 218 | Strong $P$ |
| 219 | Deep $P$ |
| 220 | Very deep $P$ |
| 221 | Very light $P$ |
| 222 | Light $P$ |
| 223 | Moderate $P$ |

**TABLE 3.12    267 ISCC-NBS Colors**
*(Continued)*

Purples
| | |
|---|---|
| 224 | Dark $P$ |
| 225 | Very dark $P$ |
| 226 | Very pale $P$ |
| 227 | Pale $P$ |
| 228 | Grayish $P$ |
| 229 | Dark grayish $P$ |
| 230 | Blackish $P$ |
| 231 | Purplish white |
| 232 | Light purplish gray |
| 233 | Purplish gray |
| 234 | Dark purplish gray |
| 235 | Purplish black |

Reddish purples
| | |
|---|---|
| 236 | Vivid $rP$ |
| 237 | Strong $rP$ |
| 238 | Deep $rP$ |
| 239 | Very deep $rP$ |
| 240 | Light $rP$ |
| 241 | Moderate $rP$ |
| 242 | Dark $rP$ |
| 243 | Very dark $rP$ |
| 244 | Pale $rP$ |
| 245 | Grayish $rP$ |

Purplish pinks
| | |
|---|---|
| 246 | Brilliant $pPk$ |
| 247 | Strong $pPk$ |
| 248 | Deep $pPk$ |
| 249 | Light $pPk$ |
| 250 | Moderate $pPk$ |
| 251 | Dark $pPk$ |
| 252 | Pale $pPk$ |
| 253 | Grayish $pPk$ |

Purplish reds
| | |
|---|---|
| 254 | Vivid $pR$ |
| 255 | Strong $pR$ |
| 256 | Deep $pR$ |
| 257 | Very deep $pR$ |
| 258 | Moderate $pR$ |
| 259 | Dark $pR$ |
| 260 | Very dark $pR$ |
| 261 | Light grayish $pR$ |
| 262 | Grayish $pR$ |

Neutrals
| | |
|---|---|
| 263 | White |
| 264 | Light gray |
| 265 | Medium gray |
| 266 | Dark gray |
| 267 | Black |

related to this more fundamental (analog) description of colors. This information is included to complete the discussion of basic color description in Sec. 3.1.

## References

1. J. C. Russ, *The Image Processing Handbook,* CRC Press, Boca Raton, FL, 1992.
2. R. Ford, "Digital Photography: Developing Fast, but Not Yet Fully in Focus," *MACWEEK,* February 15, 1993, p. 38.
3. W. R. Nugent, "Electronic Imaging in High-resolution Gray-Scale for Fine Art and Salon Photography," *Document Image Automation,* September–October 1991, pp. 284 ff.
4. S. P. Parker (ed.), *McGraw-Hill Dictionary of Scientific and Technical Terms,* 3d ed., McGraw-Hill, New York, 1984.
5. G. S. Kimbal, "Color Fundamentals—Part 2: Color Scanning and Data Compression," *Document Image Automation,* May–June 1991, pp. 156 ff.
6. G. S. Kimbal, "Color Fundamentals—Part 3: Color Imaging and Display," *Document Image Automation,* July–August 1991, pp. 224 ff.
7. J. Durrett, *Color and the Computer,* Academic Press, San Diego, 1987.
8. D. B. Dove, *Printing Technologies for Images, Gray Scale, and Color,* SPIE Proceedings, February 26–28, 1991, San Jose, CA, Vol. 1458, SPIE Press, Bellingham, WA, 1991.
9. "Color," *Webster's Third New International Dictionary,* Merriam, Springfield, MA, 1976, pp. 447–449.
10. A. N. Netravali and B. G. Haskell, *Digital Pictures—Representation and Compression,* Plenum, New York, 1988.
11. W. K. Pratt, *Digital Image Processing,* 2d ed., Wiley-Interscience, New York, 1991.
12. A. N. Netravali and B. G. Haskell, *Digital Pictures—Representation and Compression,* Plenum, New York, 1988.
13. G. Wyszecki and W. S. Stiles, *Color Science—Concepts and Methods, Quantitative Data Formulas,* Wiley, New York, 1967.
14. P. Hung, "Colorimetric Calibration in Electronic Imaging Devices Using a Look-up Table Model and Interpolations," *Journal of Electronic Imaging,* January 1993, pp. 53 ff.

# 4

# Imaging
# Entry/Capture
# Systems

*Capture* in this context refers to the process of acquiring information from either a static medium such as paper, microfilm, photograph, or X-ray plate, or a dynamic source such as a frame of a TV signal, a live X-ray scan, a CAT scan, or an MRI scan. The capture phase is very critical, since what can be done with an image in downstream steps depends on the quality and type of image information initially obtained. For business imaging, the sources usually are paper, microfilm, or facsimile documents (hard-copy and/or electronic).

Typically, raw pixel data is gathered by some analog device such as a sensor or camera. The pixels are digitized and then processed for compression and/or for some kind of (sophisticated) analysis. For many applications, processing the digitized image requires no more than filtering out noise or other unwanted features. Simple processing of this kind entails image averaging, convolution, and thresholding. The "cleaned out" image may then be stored and/or manipulated.[1] Image analysis goes beyond this and attempts to obtain an understanding of what the picture is or means. Image analysis requires greater numeric computation power, including greater precision. Functions such as feature extraction classification and pattern recognition need processors operating in the hundreds of MFLOPS (million floating-point operations per second); integer-based processing is not adequate for this type of analysis. (Integer-based processing is adequate for image processing.) Now, RISC (reduced instruction set computer)–based floating-point engines can be included on boards, making more imaging analysis accessible beyond scientific computing.

This chapter examines issues associated with the capture of image information. BIS-level scanners as well as DIS-level capture are discussed. Issues pertaining to the display aspects of DIS and BIS images are also covered, along with a brief discussion of the intersection of imaging and video. This chapter builds on the fundamental concepts discussed in the previous chapter, although the reading of that chapter is not mandatory.

## 4.1   Scanning Systems

Figure 4.1 depicts a basic document scanning system. A light source illuminates the document. Black areas on the page absorb (almost all) light, while white areas reflect it. The gray areas reflect light in proportion to their shade of gray. As the document is scanned line by line, the light reflected from the document is detected by photosensitive cells called charge-coupled devices (CCDs) arranged in a single linear row. (CCDs can be in a single line of sensors as shown in the figure, or in a two-dimensional array, for example, to facilitate TV raster scanning.)

The light collected by each cell is converted into an electrical charge whose magnitude corresponds to the intensity of the light received. The analog values of these charges are then translated into digital signals for further processing. Hence, the image corresponding to the document page is captured as a two-dimensional array (grid) of individual picture elements (pixels) or raster image.

Three key methods are available for scanning of a color image document:[2]

1. In this system the light beam is split into its red, green, and blue components. The scanner generates color separations into three primaries: $R$, $G$, and $B$. Each of these components is captured along with its associated gray scale by individual CCD arrays. In some systems the $RGB$ elements may be converted onto cyan, magenta, yellow, and black ($CMYK$), which is a common format for color reproduction. (Printing is covered in more detail in Chap. 5.)

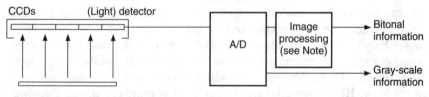

**Figure 4.1**   Business document scanning. CCD = charge-coupled device; A/D = analog to digital conversion. [*Note:* Gray scale to binary conversion (dithering/thresholding).]

2. This system employs sequential color filtering and a single CCD. Although this scanning method is cheaper, it is slower and alignment problems may occur that affect the image.

3. This system uses sequential color illumination and a single CCD. The sequential color illumination is achieved by using a (relatively) large rotating filter as the light source. Deficiencies in filter design degrade the quality of the image that is captured.

There are three key systems for achieving relative movement between the scanning light and the document, each optimized for the application envisioned:

1. *Flatbed scanners.*   Documents are handled as in a standard photocopying machine.

2. *Roll-fed scanners.*   Documents are transported through the unit and over the scanning head. These systems are typically employed for large-format engineering drawings.

3. *Handheld scanners.*   The scanner is moved manually (by hand) over the area to be scanned.

The number of pixels in a line and the number of lines used to create the bitmap determine the resolution of the scanner. Scanner resolution is quoted in terms of linear dots (pixels) per inch. Table 4.1 depicts the data rate associated with business imaging systems, based on compression, resolution, and document type. BISs can use 200- to 300-dpi bitonal scanning, which is the range of typical office printers, and result in about 50 kB per document with 10:1 compression (refer to Table 4.1). OCR-based BISs should use 400 dpi. DISs, EISs, and SISs will require different resolution, as discussed below and shown in Table 4.2.

For bitonal images, each pixel needs to be represented by a single bit (black pixel—1; white pixel—0). Photographic materials, including X-ray plates, contain a continuous range of tones. The capturing process must ascertain that adequate resolution is retained. For some applications assigning a pixel to one of 256 tone levels (i.e., assigning an 8-bit number) is sufficient; for other applications 65,536 tone levels (i.e., assigning a 16-bit number) or even 4,294,967,296 tone levels (i.e., assigning a 32-bit number) may be required. Also note that a color photograph may require that many levels for each component. Graphics art 24-bit color images have a typical uncompressed size of 40 to 50 MB ($4196 \times 4196$ pixels).[3] PACSs require 8 or 12 bits (256 to 4096) levels of gray and $1280 \times 1024$ pixels; a chest X ray is $14 \times 17$ in, so that display monitors of the 21- and 24-in landscape-portrait type are required.[4] As an example, note that a high-resolution scanner such as Microteck

TABLE 4.1    Data Rate Associated with Business Imaging Systems

| Document type and compression | Resolution, ppi | |
| --- | --- | --- |
| | 200 dpi | 400 dpi |
| Uncompressed A0 drawing, bitonal[a] | 7.7 MB | 31 MB |
| 25:1 compressed A0 drawing, bitonal | 0.3 MB | 1.2 MB |
| Uncompressed A4 bitonal | 0.5 MB[b] | 2.0 MB[c] |
| 10:1 compressed A4 bitonal | 0.05 MB | 0.2 MB |
| Uncompressed A4 256 tones (gray scale; 8 bits per pixel) | 3.9 MB[d] | 15.5 MB |
| Uncompressed A4 65,536 tones (gray scale; 16 bits per pixel) | 7.8 MB[e] | 31 MB |
| Uncompressed A4 4,294,967,296 color tones (12 bits per color, i.e., 32 bits per pixel) | 15.5 MB[f] | 61.9 MB |
| Computer monitor | $1000 \times 1000$ pixels, 24-bit color, uncompressed: 24 Mb ($\approx$ 3 MB) | |
| Computer monitor (PACS) | $1280 \times 1024$ pixels, 24-bit color, uncompressed: 31 Mb ($\approx$ 3.9 MB) | |
| DIS for graphic arts | $2048 \times 2048$ pixels, 36-bit color, uncompressed: 150 Mb ($\approx$ 19 MB) | |
| Camcorder-quality digital camera image | 400,000 pixels, 24-bit color, uncompressed: 9.6 Mb ($\approx$ 1.2 MB); compressed: 0.4 MB | |
| HDTV-quality digital camera image | 1,500,000 pixels, 24-bit color, uncompressed: 37.5 Mb ($\approx$ 4.6 MB) | |
| High-quality digital camera image | 4,000,000 pixels, 24-bit color, uncompressed: 96 Mb ($\approx$ 12 MB) | |

[a]Common document sizes: A—$8.5 \times 11$ in; A3—$297 \times 420$ mm; A4—$210 \times 297$ mm; A0—$1189 \times 841$ mm; B—$11 \times 17$ in.
[b]$8.5 \times 11 \times 200 \times 200 \times 1/8 = 0.5$ MB.
[c]$8.5 \times 11 \times 400 \times 400 \times 1/8 = 2.0$ MB.
[d]$8.5 \times 11 \times 200 \times 200 \times 8/8 = 3.9$ MB.
[e]$8.5 \times 11 \times 200 \times 200 \times 16/8 = 7.8$ MB.
[f]$8.5 \times 11 \times 200 \times 200 \times 32/8 = 15.5$ MB.
*Unit abbreviations:* dpi—dots per inch; ppi—pixels per inch; MB—megabytes; Mb—megabits.

MSF-400G providing 400-dpi black-and-white continuous-tone scanning with 256 levels of gray scale generates 15 million pixels for an $8.5 \times 11$-in original, that is, 15 MB of data.[5]

For comparison, note that if a drawing on an A0 original were created and stored using vector methods (e.g., IGES), it would require only about 400 kB rather than 7.7 MB or 31 MB, as shown in Table 4.1.

An important consideration for scanners, implicit in the discussion up to this point, is the scanning pitch representing the pixel size. This is a critical parameter. As the pitch becomes finer, the image is reproduced with greater fidelity; however, the scanning time, the file size, the processing time, and the RAM and storage requirements increase quadratically. For example, if a $4 \times 4$-mm figure were scanned using

**TABLE 4.2 Scanning and Print Resolutions Required for Various Applications**

| Color resolution level | Spatial resolution, (dpi) | | | | | |
|---|---|---|---|---|---|---|
| | 200 × 200 | 300 × 300 | 400 × 400 | 800 × 800 | 1200 × 1200 | 2400 × 2400 |
| 1 (bitonal) | Line art BIS | Line art BIS | Line art BIS | Line art DIS | Commercial* line art | Commercial line art |
| 8 (continuous tone) | DIS (screen) | DIS (screen) | DIS (print) | DIS (print) | | |
| 12 (continuous tone, monochrome) | | DIS, commercial* | DIS, commercial | DIS, commercial | DIS, commercial, EIS, SIS | DIS, commercial, EIS, SIS |
| 24 (continuous tone, color) | | DIS, commercial | DIS, commercial | DIS, commercial | DIS, commercial, EIS, SIS | DIS, commercial, EIS, SIS |
| 36 (continuous tone, color) | | DIS, commercial | DIS, commercial | DIS, commercial | DIS, commercial, EIS, SIS | DIS, commercial, EIS, SIS |

*Commercial here refers to commercial graphics art and/or high-quality printing processes.

pixels of size 1 × 1 mm, then one would generate 16 pixels; if the figure were scanned using pixels of size 0.5 × 0.5 mm, then one would generate 64 pixels; if the figure was scanned using pixels of size 0.25 × 0.25 mm, then one would generate 256 pixels; etc. Most drawings have line widths of 0.2 to 0.5 mm; therefore, 0.1 mm is usually adopted at the standard scanning pitch.[6] Other standards may also be used depending on the application, as seen in Table 4.3. Using 0.1-mm resolution (about 200 dpi) on an A0 document (1189 × 841 mm) yields 11,890 × 8410 = 100 million pixels. Using an 8-bit gray scale, one gets 100 MB; if one uses 24-bit color, one gets 300 MB; and if one had scanned such a document at 400 dpi, one would get 1.2 GB!

The scanner relies on the modulation of light by either reflective paper copy or a film transparency. The input is classified as

1. *Line art.* An input form such as a schematic or drawing that has only one of two states: black or white. The output of the scanning process is a sequence of binary values. This is also called *bitonal.*

2. *Continuous tone.* The image has an infinite number of light states, from pure white, all the way to pure black (see Fig. 4.2). The scanner must map this infinite gray scale into discrete gray levels, and map them to a digital code (assuming that the scanner is digital; see below).

TABLE 4.3    Scanning Pitches

| 200 dpi | 200 dots per inch: 8 lines per millimeter, or 0.127-mm pitch |
|---------|--------------------------------------------------------------|
| 300 dpi | 300 dots per inch: 12 lines per millimeter, or 0.085-mm pitch |
| 400 dpi | 400 dots per inch: 16 lines per millimeter, or 0.064-mm pitch |

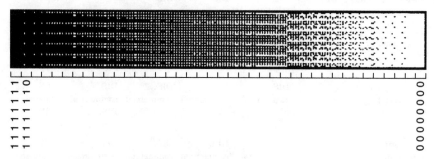

**Figure 4.2**    Gray-tone scale and digital mapping.

Both of these input forms can in turn be monochrome or color. An accepted rule of thumb is that the ratio between pixels and halftone dots should be 2 to 1 (or at least 1.5 to 1).[7] For example, a 2000 × 3000-pixel image printed on 8.5 × 11-in paper results in about 235 dpi (= 2000/8.5); this implies that the ratio of pixels (235) to halftones (256) is slightly less than 1. To improve that ratio (to about 2) one could focus on less pixels (1000 × 1500), or increase the halftone levels to 512.

A light source of constant intensity provides illumination of the material to be scanned. The material modulates the transmitted or reflected light. The modulation is inversely proportional to the density or darkness of the input material. Continuous-tone output is a series of computer "words" corresponding to each spatial position or "pixel." (The word length is a function of the number of gray levels.) Color scanning is an extension of the gray-scale method. In lieu of one density value for each pixel, color scanning produces three values, one for each of the three primary colors contained in the image.

Some scanners are analog. For example, TV cameras do not scan pixel by pixel. Both scanning methods have something in common: both analog and digital methods cover the field of view sequentially in a "raster" fashion, line by line from top to bottom. The TV camera produces a continuously varying (analog) electrical signal, rather that a digital stream. TV pictures (monochrome and/or color) can be captured by "frame grabbers" and converted to digital pictures.

TABLE 4.4    Image Scanning Methods

Direct illumination
  Laser
  CRT

Flying-spot-directed photosensor
  Single sensor
  Multiple sensor

Moving graphic
  Drum
  Flatbed
  Pinch roller

Stationary graphic
  Direct illumination
  Directed sensor

There are a number of ways to physically scan an image, whether a transparency, a paper copy, or a real-life scene, as seen in Table 4.4. Table 4.5 provides some information on these scanning processes.

## 4.2 Color Scanners

Until the early 1990s, color processing in general, and capture in particular, were found only in the high-end prepress world. For example, standalone drum-based color separation scanners cost over $100,000, and were produced by a relatively few vendors (e.g., Crosfield, Hell, Itek Color Graphics, Scitex). Such standalone scanners are not intended to be connected to a mainframe or other computer systems including LANs. These scanners produce *CMYK* four-color separation on film for downstream use in the color printing process. Their output is exposed monochrome photographic film in four segments, one for each of the three primary subtractive colors (*C,Y,M*) and the fourth for black (*K*). Color processing is done in real time.

Now (monochrome) gray-scale as well as color scanners can be found at the desktop, making a number of new applications possible that had previously been too expensive for all but professional environments. These desktop systems not only offer less expensive prepress scanners but can be networked and host-connected. This enables a more synergistic computing environment, where, for example, there is a color scanner in some centrally located room and a mechanism to load the scanned material to a LAN-based server or directly into a user's PC. This desktop publishing system allows a user to scan color pictures in and output fully composed pages with text and color images properly

TABLE 4.5   Key Mechanical Aspects of Scanners

| | |
|---|---|
| Direct illumination | Input document or graphic is illuminated pixel by pixel with a sharply focused beam of light, while photodetector looks at entire scan area—laser can focus on small spot; not widely used, except for aperture card scanning and monochrome applications (laser is inherently single-color and single-wavelength); page may be swept in its horizontal axis by a deflected laser spot while a flatbed transport moves the page in the vertical direction; reflected light is collected by a fiber optic array that delivers the light to a photomultiplier tube |
| | CRT flying spot operates in similar manner; CRT tube uses an unmodulated raster on its face which provides a moving point of light of constant intensity; raster is focused onto image by a lens and the transmitted or reflected light is collected by a (single) sensor |
| Flying-spot-directed photosensor | Illumination is stationary and constant; sensor physically moves and image is deflected mechanically or electrically; alternatively, multiple sensors are sensed electronically in a sequential manner; the multiple-sensor principle is used in TV camera tubes (where a focused electronic beam is swept in two axes across an internal target) and CCDs (where electrical charges are sequentially switched to an output electrode) |
| Moving graphic | Graphic moves in one axis, while the directed illumination (or photosensor) covers the other axis; in a drum scanner, the reflective copy of the image to be scanned moves in one axis past an illumination source and sensor that are stationary with reference to each other; the illumination and sensor are moved together parallel to the drum's axis of rotation; small scanning spots and positional precision are achieved—this is not as easy with a flatbed scanner (e.g., found on older copier machines) |
| | An inexpensive as well as compact moving-graphic system uses pinch rollers: graphic is transported past a line scan system; however, difficult to obtain accurate positional registration; occasionally used in PC desktop systems |
| Stationary graphic | Most common system employed in desktop imaging; it is relatively compact and has few moving parts; similar to copier principle (often manufactured by same companies); usually employs a line scan CCD array and a single lens with fixed focus; object field is moved mechanically in the vertical dimension along a line of illumination |

positioned and registered.[8,9] While the quality of the desktop color processing is not the same as that achieved with traditional color-separation scanners, it is adequate for many, if not most, business applications. Figure 4.3 depicts the color processing aspects of the scanner, based on the principles described in the previous chapter.

A color scanner employs the same mechanical principles described above pertaining to a monochrome gray-scale scanner. It will also have

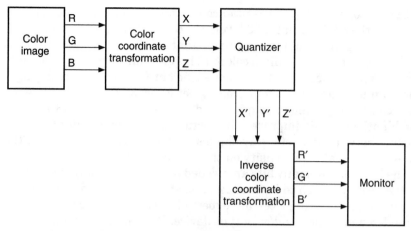

**Figure 4.3**   Tristimulus values generated by a color scanner.

two additional sensor channels or the capability to multiplex to a single sensor. Color scanning requires that the scanning system split the visible light spectrum into three primary parts—usually red, green, and blue—and output three separate signals either simultaneously or sequentially.[8,9] The light source contains the entire visible spectrum, but the sensors are sensitive to a specific color through the use of appropriate filters. The sensing process can consist of (1) a single sensor with sequential filter applications applied during multiple scans or (2) three sensor-filters acting during a single scan.

Table 4.6 depicts key methods utilized by commercially available color desktop scanners.

**TABLE 4.6   Approaches for Color Scanners**

| | |
|---|---|
| Separate CCDs | Three CCDs utilized with a beamsplitter and three stationary filters to separate the color components; issues are cost (three times, based on triple components), coincidence of images |
| Single CCD with movable filters | Motor used to sequentially position three filters over a single CCD; issues are improved registration of colors, expense and potential mechanical failure of moving components |
| Different light sources | Use three distinct illumination sources; each source is pulsed sequentially to illuminate each scan line three times; the reflected light is detected by the CCD array and the time-divided signals are processed to produce *RGB* output |
| Multiple CCD arrays | Four linear arrays are fabricated side by side onto a single substrate, with color filters provided directly onto three linear arrays |

Usually one employs an 8-bit encoding for each of the three primary colors in the *RGB* format (256 levels per color). This allows about 16.77 million codepoint combinations. (Note that this is not the same thing as actually having 16.77 million colors.) This encoding is usually adequate for desktop applications, but is not sufficient for color prepress. High-end scanners support 12-bit encoding per color (36 bits total), allowing each color's gray scale to be quantized into 4096 levels (for 68.7 billion combinations). This improves the picture quality by eliminating contouring between discrete gray shades. *Spatial resolution* refers to the two-dimensional pixel density on the graphic surface.

The issue of how many bits are needed to encode a color image as well as the best approach to be used is somewhat complicated: the optimal selection (i.e., meeting a certain expected quality level) depends on the intended application and/or output device. Basically, images that need to be output only to a video monitor (and/or PC or workstation) require less resolution than do images that need to be printed. *XYZ* and *CMYK* methods are suitable for professional publishing (prepress process); *RGB* is suitable for video display; *L*a*b** (*LAB*) is a color convention suited to textile industry requirements; *YUV* is found in systems with 4:2:2 and 4:4:4 bit configurations (256 and 4096 colors, respectively).

The speed of scanning is also important, as are document feeders. A full-color 300-dpi image can now be scanned in about 20 s or less. It is worth noting that some scientific scanners, such as those used for remote-sensing applications, have a resolution of 20,000 × 20,000 pixels. These scanners require up to 6 h to scan a full frame at maximum resolution (12.5-μm pixels).[10]

**Color calibration problems.**   Color scanners, particularly the less expensive ones, may suffer from calibration-related problems. Although a color scanner generates color separations into three primaries (*R*, *G*, and *B*), these primaries do not typically correspond to what humans see. If the scanner sensitivities were similar to those of the human eye, there would be no problems; however, such sensitivities are difficult to produce in a (low-end) scanner. One way to quantify this discrepancy is to compare the scanner's responses to that of an established primary. Figure 4.4 shows the red sensitivity curve for a typical scanner and the colorimetric curve (based on the CIE $R_C G_C B_C$ from Chap. 3). Note that the wavelength of peak sensitivity for the scanner is too long in the red and there is no sensitivity over much of the rest of the spectrum. This is typical of scanners which do a good job of separating colorants, but which do not emulate the smoothly changing response of the eye to different wavelengths.[11] By looking at this figure one can infer that if the scanner's response (for all three primaries) is similar to a set of colorimetric-based primaries (one of those described in Chap. 3), then the

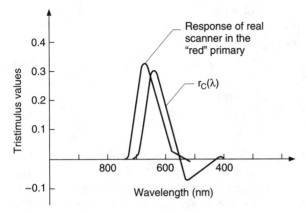

**Figure 4.4**  Colorimetric response of a real scanner.

scanner's specific dependence on the input material is eliminated. In real scanners, the transformation between what the scanner "sees" and what humans see depends on the shape of the spectral reflectance curve of the input; hence, when one calibrates a scanner, the calibration depends on, for example, whether the input is printed material or photographic film. It follows that color aberrations cannot be fixed by calibration, unless the scanning operator is trained to select a different calibration depending on the material in the chosen input. Alternatively, one needs to employ a more sophisticated scanner which has a sensitivity response close to being colorimetric, so that calibration is independent of the input material.[11]

**Higher-color resolution.**    Most desktop scanners are based on CCDs and use a flatbed design. Scanners are the limiting factor for desktop color publishing applications, in terms of producing consistent high-quality work. CCD scanners have insufficent tonal range, introduce significant noise in the shadow areas, and have relatively low resolution for high-end needs (currently, 600 dpi highest). As a result, CCD scanners are typically used in the publishing business (desktop or professional) to scan images at low resolution to provide positioning and cropping information, but not to directly print from.[12] Technology based on drum scanning and photomultiplier tubes provides better resolution; such systems are beginning to appear for desktop applications.

At this time there are two alternative approaches to deal with color prepress:

1. The traditional approach used by the graphics-prepress industry is to utilize a drum scanner to scan images using the *CMYK* format,

obtain 8 bits per color (32 bits total), and pass such a data stream through the entire production system (some of these issues are further discussed in Chap. 5).

2. The newer approach is to utilize transparency scanners, flatbed scanners, or the Kodak Photo CD process, using *RGB* formats, obtain 8 bits per color (24 bits total), and convert to *CMYK* at some intermediate point (using a color management system) for additional processing and printing.

A proposal called *high dynamic range* for a 48-bit *RGB* format was recently advanced by Leaf Systems, Inc.[7] Such a format would allow the movement of color information without corruption or degradation, which is not possible with 24-bit color. The proponents argue that the 24-bit standards arose out of engineering limitations of the past; critics are concerned about the increased storage and transmission requirements.

Earlier discussion indicates that 256 gray levels do not exhaust the limit of human vision; 14 bits of gray levels (16,384 levels, also measurable as 11 f-stops of aperture settings on a camera) are closer to the the limit of human vision. Some use a measure borrowed from continuous-tone film, known as $D_{max}$, to discuss dynamic range in digital devices (scanners and cameras); however, such a measure does not intrinsically include the number of quantization levels.

Fourteen bits of gray levels cannot be reproduced on the printed page, so that the number of bits are reduced. The issue is who does such reduction. The photographer has some initial control by selecting a shutter speed and f-stop. The scanning process further reduces the information content. (In capturing 256 levels out of 16,384, one could say that $^{63}/_{64}$th of the information is lost.) If one aims at being closer to lossless data capture and movement, more than 8 bits are needed. However, even the high-end proponents suggest $12 \times 4 = 48$ bits rather than $14 \times 4 = 56$ bits of color representation. RAM, machine cycles, storage, and communication bandwidth still impose restrictions on the amount of information that can be economically captured. For example, 48 bits of color per pixel is double the amount of storage shown in Table 4.1 for 24 bits (note that images stored as *RGB* with 8 bits per color need only 75 percent of what would be needed for *CMYK* with 8 bits per color). Proponents of higher color resolution claim that $2000 \times 3000$ pixels (175 dpi printed on tabloid-size paper) is adequate for almost all applications.[7] Such an image would need 36 MB for 48 colors per pixel.

With the current approach, a scanner captures 12 or 16 bits per *RGB* channel. The scanner operator adjusts the color thresholds of the scan, reducing it to 8 bits per channel, before saving the image for downstream processing. Such a downstream art director, receiving the image sent from workstation to workstation, manipulates the image, perhaps changing the color space. This may necessitate a downstream rescan. Using a process such as the high dynamic range, the scanner captures 12 or 16 bits per *RGB* channel. The document holds up to 48 bits of color per pixel, tagged with the scanner's color space, as it is moved along the production process from workstation to workstation. The art director can manipulate the image within its original color space, adjusting color thresholds as appropriate for the target output device or medium.

Every time an image undergoes a color-space transformation (e.g., *RGB* to *CMYK, RGB* to CIE *XYZ, CMKY* to CIE *XYZ*), one loses information. One would want to capture all the pertinent data up front and carry it along as needed; a header defining the origin of the color space is stored with the data. This way, one can do a single transformation for output rather than multiple conversions (e.g., printed-quality magazine page). The CIE *XYZ* color space is utilized for definition of the origin space, obviating the need to convert *RGB* to CIE at some downstream point in the process.

Leaf Systems Inc. was in the process of developing ColorShop/High Dynamic Range Macintosh/NeXTstep-based software at press time, to operate with the Leafscan 35 and 45 scanners and LeafDigita Camera. This type of software allows users to perform global tone and color correction, unsharp masking, anamorphic distortion, and color separation with control over undercolor removal, ink limits, and selective-color correction on each plate.[7]

**Scanner equipment samples.**   There are now about two dozen high-resolution color scanners for less than $5000 (offering true optical resolution of more than 300 dpi in at least one direction). Table 4.7 depicts a small set of lower-end scanner equipment to illustrate the type of systems on the market at press time.[13,14] They are employed principally for DIS and BIS applications.

Scanners aimed at transparencies are also available. Typical equipment handling 4 × 5-in transparencies, with 1000-dpi resolution (increasable to 2000-dpi via software interpolation), 24-bit color, are available for $10,000 or thereabout.

Image processing requires loading the image into RAM. A typical PC now can have 8 MB of RAM; this still implies heavy memory pagination to accomplish any desired image edit for high-resolution images. (High-end workstations have higher RAM capacities.) Some image-editing programs allow the user to select a small area for processing, rather that the entire picture; this enables the much smaller file to be directly loaded in RAM, making the editing much faster. Storing the image for transport to a print shop or for other remote delivery requires

TABLE 4.7    Low-end Scanner Equipment*

| Scanner model | Cost, in $1000 | Resolution and other features |
|---|---|---|
| AGFA Arcus | 3.9 | 600 × 600 dpi |
| EPSON ES-600C | 0.8 | 300-dpi (1200-dpi via interpolation), single- or multiple-pass system supporting 24-bit color and/or 8-bit gray scale |
| EPSON ES-800C | 1.1 | 400-dpi (1600-dpi via interpolation), single- or multiple-pass system supporting 24-bit color and/or 8-bit gray scale; optional feeder |
| HP SCANJET IIc | 1.3 | 400-dpi (800-dpi via interpolation), single-pass system supporting 24-bit color and/or 8-bit gray scale; optional feeder |
| HP SCANJET IIp | 0.7 | 300-dpi, 8-bit gray scale for photographs and illustrations |
| La Cie Lmd. SilverScanner | 1.8 | 300 × 450 dpi (interpolated 1200-dpi); on-the-fly sharpening |
| MICROTEK SCANMAKER II | 0.9 | 300-dpi (1200-dpi via interpolation) system supporting 24-bit color and/or 8-bit gray scale |
| Ricoh | 3.5 | 1200-dpi, 30-bit color system (10 bits for each *RGB* color captured and later optimized to 24 bits); 600 × 1200-dpi resolution captured in single pass; SCSI-2 interface; optional feeder |
| Seiko Instruments Spectrapoint | 2.3 | 400 × 400 dpi; single-scan system. |

*Partial list, illustrative of equipment on market at press time.

a 44-MB (SyQuest) cartridge (it would take twenty 2-MB diskettes). Also, local archiving quickly uses up a large amounts of storage. Some utilize StuffIt (lossless) or JPEG (lossy) compression for this task.

**Dithering and thresholding.**    Most scanners capture information using a gray-scale format. This enables the black-and-white or color photograph to be captured and stored in support of the ultimate user application. When such a scanner needs to reproduce line art, *thresholding* is utilized. When there is a need to simulate a gray-scale scanned image on a bitonal laser printer, the gray-scale information must be processed to produce a bit-per-pixel image. This process is called *dithering.*

The lines or text on the original line art document may not be uniform in intensity. In scanning line art a gray-scale scanner needs to set a threshold to discriminate between white and black. The threshold is often established automatically by the scanner. This is done by considering the average density of the background being scanned, as well as the average for the region surrounding the pixel in question. Some scanners also support a dynamic threshold mechanism.

Dithering uses accumulations of solid (printed) dots to create the overall illusion of shades of gray (this is similar to halftone photographic reproduction in newspapers).[2] The printed dots (corresponding to pixels) are arranged in groups called *halftone dots*. The dots of each halftone are composed of a specific mix of white and black pixels. These halftone blocks simulate the shade for each point of the original; 256 gray-scale levels are simulated with blocks of pixels consisting of 16 × 16 solid pixels.

## 4.3   Monitors

Table 4.8 shows some spatial resolutions for PC and workstation monitors utilized in the recent past for imaging and/or multimedia applications. Note for comparison that a Macintosh Classic supported 640 × 400 pixels; with a monochrome bitonal display, this equates to less than 32 kB per screen. Many business applications utilize a 640h × 480v (horizontal × vertical) display; monitors supporting higher resolutions (as high as 1600h × 1200v) are also being introduced in newer imaging systems, not only for DISs, EISs, and SISs but also for BISs.

A 19-in monitor used for high-quality image processing needs a resolution of at least 1152 × 870 pixels, with 24-bit color; this corresponds to about 3 MB per screen, or a 100 increase compared to the Macintosh Classic. Such data I/Os tend to slow down even the faster workstations, often requiring an on-board accelerator. Some workstations (e.g., the Macintosh IIvx and the Performa 600) support 16-bit color as a low-cost option, as a migration upward from a 256 8-bit color arrangement. SVGA monitors cost as little as $350, and VGA monitors cost as little as $250; higher-resolution monitors cost in the $10,000 range.

Individuals in the publishing, advertisement, or artistic fields require 24-bit or 36-bit color. Most of the 24-bit color boards needed to support this requirement are accelerated through special on-board

TABLE 4.8   PC Spatial Resolutions

| | | |
|---|---|---|
| CGA (color graphics adapter) | 320h × 200v | 4 colors |
| EGA (enhanced graphics adapter) | 640h × 360v | 16 colors |
| VGA (video graphics adapter) | 640h × 480v | 16 colors* |
| | | 256 colors* |
| Super-VGA | 800h × 600v | 16 colors* |
| | 1024h × 768v | 256 colors* |

*Depends on controller memory

chips that expedite common video-display tasks. These boards range from $6000 at the high end to $600 at the low end. Typical resolutions supported at 24 color levels include one or more of the following: 640 × 480 pixels, 832 × 624 pixels, 1024 × 68 pixels, and 1152 × 870 pixels. A partial list of companies offering 24-bit color boards includes[15] Apple Computer, E-Machines, Generation Systems, Lapis Technologies, Radius, RasterOps Corporation, SuperMac Technology, and Xceed Technology.

## 4.4  File Formats

There is a plethora of file formats in support of imaging, including but not limited to, the following:[8,9,16,17]

- BMP (bitmap format, e.g., Microsoft Windows, IBM OS/2, or vendor-dependent).

- ITU-T Group 3 and Group 4 (facsimile) standard.

- CLP (Microsoft Windows Clipboard).

- CT2T.

- DCS (desktop color separation).

- DDES.

- DXF is a format that originated with the AUTOCAD software for vector representation of 2-D images.

- EPS (Encapsulated PostScript) (Adobe Systems).

- GIF (Graphic Interchange Format). GIF (sponsored by CompuServe Inc.) defines a protocol for on-line transmission and interchange of raster graphic data independent of the hardware used in the creation or display of such data.

- HFF (Halo File Format) is an extension to TIFF advanced by Media Cybernetics, optimized for image reading and writing.

- HPGL (Hewlett Packard Graphics Language) is an established format for CAD information.

- IGES is a standard for vector representation of 3-D images.

- IMG (GEM) (paint raster graphics—Ventura format).

- ISO's ODA (Office Document Architecture); some vendors consider this standard for electronic publishing of compound documents to be too complex for commercial imaging applications.

- JPEG (Joint Photographic Expert Group—ITU-T/ISO compression standard—see Chap. 6); more specifically, JFIF (JPEG File Interchange Format).

- MO:DCA (IBM's Mixed Object Document Content Architecture) and IOCA (IBM's Image Object Content Architecture).

- MSP (Microsoft Paint raster file format).

- PCX.

- Photo CD format; Kodak's system for scanned photos (discussed below).

- PICT II; used in Macintosh systems.

- RIFF (Resource Interface File Format); developed by IBM as a standard tagged-file format for Windows' multimedia files—now also used by other systems.

- Scitex Handshake; used to permit data exchange between desktop systems and Scitex's high-end prepress equipment.

- TGA (Targa True Color 24-bit format, raster graphics file format, .TGA extension); developed by Truevision, Indianapolis—also handles other color bit values.

- TIFF (tagged image file format); it is a de facto standard adopted by Microsoft and Hewlett-Packard, among others.

- VST.

Scanners typically support one or more of these file formats. As can be inferred from this list, interoperability can be complex and frustrating. For example, sometimes an EPS file generated on one system (e.g., Macintosh/Microsoft Word) does not work on another system (e.g., Sun SPARC/Frame Maker) when ported, when in theory it should very easily.

TIFF has been standardized by Aldus Pagemaker and Microsoft, and is used by many imaging vendors. However, some vendors have developed extensions or other formats to improve the performance and/or store multipage images.

GIF is a common format. CompuServe has granted a limited royalty-free license for the use of GIF in computer software; many products now support GIF. GIF is defined in terms of blocks and subblocks that contain relevant parameters and information used in the reproduction of a graphic. A GIF data stream is a sequence of protocol blocks and subblocks representing a collection of graphics.[18] A data stream may originate locally (e.g., when read from a file), or it may originate remotely (e.g., when received over a network). In the latter case GIF has no provision for error detection and correction; hence, a transport-level protocol ensuring error-free transmission is needed. GIF utilizes color tables to render raster-based graphics. The maximum number of colors supported is 256. Both global and local color tables are supported to enable the optimization of data streams. The decoder may use a color table with as many colors as its hardware can support; if an image contains more colors than the hardware can support, algorithms (not specified in the standard) must be employed to render the image. The documents describing GIF, and software implementing it, are widely available on the Internet via anonymous FTP.

Engineering drawings (line art) coming directly from a CAD/CAM system may be available in vector format. In this format, positional information and geometric shapes are described mathematically. CAD/CAM is now prevalent in many engineering environments. This implies that it may be possible to capture the information directly in vector form for downstream image processing (e.g., storage in CD-ROMs). Software is available to convert CAD information (e.g., IGES) into a raster format, without having to physically scan the image. Proponents support conversion and raster image processing because of their ability to better integrate with other information and facilitate browsing and distribution. In other situations it may be necessary to undertake the opposite conversion, that is, a raster-to-vector conversion, or "vectorization," in order to feed this information into a CAD/CAM system. Software is available to accomplish such a task, at least to some degree. (Another approach is to use digitizing tablets.) Higher-resolution raster scans—say, 400 dpi—are preferred to facilitate such conversion and avoid or minimize distortion problems such as "aliasing." As noted earlier, storage in vector form generally entails less space, compared with an uncompressed image at reasonable resolution (say, 300 dpi), unless the line art is very complex.

## 4.5  Image Processing

Image processing involves the alteration of the pictorial information, based on three techniques: (1) optical, (2) analog, and (3) digital. (This is in contrast to image analysis, e.g., pattern recognition, where more labor-intensive computations are required.)

Optical processing includes actions such as the use of a colored filter, manipulation of the film in a darkroom, and editing. An example of analog processing is provided by a TV image; here the change of a voltage level changes the brightness of the image; changing the amplitude of the signal can change the contrast. In digital processing individual pixels (or blocks of pixels) are manipulated as separate entities. Each pixel has a spatial location value and a brightness value; as noted, in color processing, each of the three primary colors associated with a pixel is assigned a brightness value.

At the application level, image processing can mean a variety of things. In document image processing, it includes geometric operations like scrolling, scaling, rotating, panning, cropping, and enhancement. In machine vision and robotics it includes counting objects and finding outlines.

Now many scanners support some type of image processing; alternatively or additionally, PC-based software can be employed. High-end image editing software systems now on the market (e.g., Adobe Systems' Photoshop DOS 2.5 or higher) offer users higher editing speed, better image control, and advanced features.[3] Software is now also available that enables the display of images from several sources at once. A Microsoft Windows-based or Macintosh PC with this software can acquire CAT, MRI, and PET images from medical scanners and process them into a standard file format for display and/or analysis. The user can access image databases stored on CD-ROMs as well as on PACS used by some medical facilities.[19]

Systems for color correction and retouching range from high-end workstations (e.g., Scitex Prismax, $250,000 range) to midrange (e.g., Kodak Prophecy, $120,000 range) to low-end (e.g., Mac Quadra 950, $30,000 range, 128-MB RAM). Table 4.9 depicts some of the features of color imaging systems.[20]

A different type of image processing, this time as an output media, involves film recorders. These devices attach to a PC in order to translate PC-developed presentations directly into 35-mm slides. Film recorders now can produce slides quickly and inexpensively. There are low-end products in the $5000–$10,000 range, midrange products in the $10,000–$20,000 range, and higher-end products in the $20,000–$50,000 range. They typically support 2000 to 4000 lines of resolution (some go as high as 8000 lines); color depth varies from 24 to 36 bits. Systems are available from a dozen or so vendors, including Agfa/Miles, Polaroid, and Lasergraphics.[21]

TABLE 4.9   Features of Color Imaging Systems

| High-end | Midrange | Low-end |
|---|---|---|
| Dedicated retouching and stripping | Dedicated color correction and retouching | General-purpose |
| Fine controls on complex images | Built-in calibration | Basic image controls |
| Image subsampling | Cost $50,000–$150,000 | Difficult to work with large and/or multiple images |
| Networking | | Wide range of applications available |
| Built-in calibration | | |
| Cost $150,000–$250,000 | | |

## 4.6   Image Acquisition in PC and Workstation Desktop Publishing Environments

The reader is reminded at this point of the slightly different emphasis in processes, goals, and tools between BIS document imaging in workflow contexts versus imaging in desktop publishing and multimedia development (i.e., DIS). Document imaging is characterized by the following factors: it is usually relatively low-resolution, images are bitonal, it may involve workflows, archiving is a key aspect, and flatbed scanners are the principal capture mechanism. Desktop publishing is characterized by the following factors: medium to high resolution, full-color images, archiving less of an issue, and use of a variety of sophisticated capture devices. Table 4.10 depicts some of the capture device options supporting desktop publishing.

Until recently, video-capture boards and still videocameras were the only alternatives, besides scanners, for inputting video to a PC. The introduction of digital videocameras is now drawing many photographers away from these analog methods.[22] The proportion of users employing video-capture boards for still video has dropped. (These boards, however, continue to be used for capture of video.) Nonetheless, the analog-based methods can be cheaper (systems can be assembled for $1000) compared to the use of a digital camera (whose midrange cost is around $10,000).

Budget-conscious users can utilize a camcorder in conjunction with a video-capture board to input images and (live) scenes into their PCs. The use of a low capture board requires either that the subject be still for 3 to 5 s or that a VCR still frame be used instead. The latter degrades the quality to some extent. To capture fast-moving images (e.g., a TV feed), one must employ what are called *frame grabbers* (e.g., Mass Microsystems' QuickImage 24, Super-Mac Technologies' VideoSpigot, Scion's LG-3). The high-end frame grabbers provide full-color full-frame capture (i.e., the two interlaced fields that compose a NTSC TV picture). Very-high-end systems can be used in scientific applications, for example, a board to capture images from a video-recorder attached to a microscope for time-lapse video of cells.[22]

TABLE 4.10   Capture Device Options Supporting Desktop Publishing

| Analog input to PC | Video capture boards for PC |
| | Still video cameras |
| Digital input to PC | Flatbed scanners |
| | Digital cameras |

The next few subsections describe some of the principal image capture hardware for desktop publishing and multimedia development applications.

### 4.6.1  Image acquisition in Photo CD environments

Still photography is in the midst of a transition to digital technologies. Observers claim that this transition lags behind the computer revolution that reshaped word processing; the transition is foreshadowing the changes that are expected to occur in television in the next decade or so.[23] At the moment there is a confusing variety of processes for the capture of digital images. Key components of this process are Eastman Kodak's Photo CD and regular cameras, as well as digital cameras.

The Photo CD process works as follows. A 35-mm picture taken on a conventional camera and conventional film is sent to a properly equipped lab for processing. After the lab develops the film, postprocessing of the image takes place by writing a digitized (scanned) version of the picture onto a CD-ROM. At press time the system supported only 35-mm negatives and slides. (Professional systems for formats of up to $4 \times 5$ in were under development; ProPhoto CD Master is slated to support $4096 \times 6144$ pixels.) Thousands of retail stores and labs in the United States provide Photo CD processing. The typical price per scan is \$1. The Photo CD disk stores copies of each image in one of five sizes, with resolution of up to $2048 \times 3072$ pixels with 24 colors. The images can be displayed on a TV monitor using Kodak's CD player; the images can also be printed on a dye-sublimation printer (see Fig. 4.5).

A typical Photo CD lab consists of a Sun Microsystems workstation, a CD-ROM writer, a dye-sublimation printer, and a color scanner similar to the ones described in earlier sections. A human operator inserts mounted slides or strips of film into the scanner and uses the workstation to enter some parametric information about the image and make any needed color or density adjustments. The scanning process requires 10 s and produces a *RGB* file of 18 MB. This is followed by a workstation-driven compression that encodes the image into the PhotoYCC format (8 bits of brightness and two color channels each requiring 8 bits). The compression reduces the image to about 4.5 MB for storage onto the Photo CD medium. About 100 high-resolution images or several thousand (up to 6000) low-resolution images can be stored on the CD, depending on the Photo CD format utilized. (As noted in the next chapter, a CD-ROM can store 650 MB on the average, thereby supporting in theory up to 144 images, each consisting of 4.5 MB.) The lower-resolution images are aimed at catalog producers.[24]

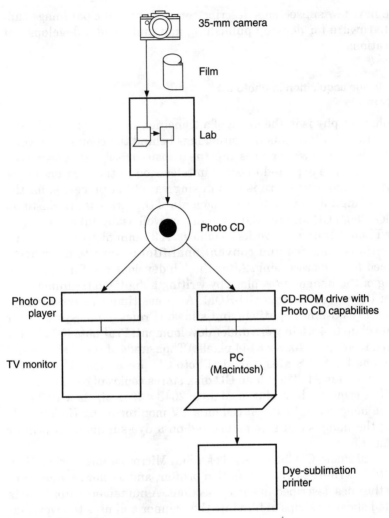

**Figure 4.5**  Photo CD environment.

Relatively good image quality is achievable with the system. Prints can be produced that are almost as good as traditional photographs. This is typically good enough even for magazine publication in a number of instances (except for top-of-the-line magazines such as *National Geographic* or *Vogue*).

Photo CD relies on a particular medium [i.e., CD-ROM; it is not available on the magnetooptical (MO) medium discussed in Chap. 7]. Additionally, it does not use a de facto standard such as TIFF or PICT. Photo CD images can be loaded into a computer (e.g., a Macintosh) with suitable software and a compatible CD-ROM drive. The file format is proprietary to Kodak. A tool kit is licensed to developers to enable their applications to read the images from the Photo CD. Also, Kodak sells an application called *Photo CD Access* that browses images on the Photo CD and converts them, if desired, to a Macintosh-supported format such as TIFF, PICT, and EPS. Adobe Systems has a plug-in for its Photoshop image-editing application that can access images on a Photo CD. Some CD-ROM drives now also include software that shows Photo CD files on a Macintosh desktop and that can be open as if they were PICT files. Even though with appropriate conversion software one can load a Photo CD image onto a PC by converting the image to a standard format, one cannot save a modified image in the Photo CD format.

There always are some disadvantages in proprietary systems. In this case one cannot access the images without a CD-ROM drive and a PC software system that support Photo CD (although, as noted, some CD-ROM drives now automatically include support).[23] Additionally, there is the delay incurred in having to send the negatives to a lab for processing; some applications require an all-in-one all-electronic desktop system (although the quality obtainable with Photo CD may be higher).

At the hardware-volume-directory level, Photo CD uses a fairly standard platform: CD-ROM XA drive, with support for Sony and Philips *Orange Book* standards. A single-session Photo CD disk follows the ISO 9660-1988 standard.

There is considerable interest in archival applications of Photo CD for advertising agencies, book and magazine publishers, catalog producers, real estate agencies, and the government.[24] Some view Photo CD as an intermediary step toward digital photography; photographers can continue to use their favorite film-based cameras and still obtain digital material without expensive high-resolution scanners.

### 4.6.2  Image acquisition with digital cameras

Digital cameras have a digital interface that allows a picture to be uploaded to a PC. A digital camera may be permanently tethered to a PC or workstation, or it may be portable, using a hard disk or memory card to hold images; in the latter case the image can be transferred to the PC at a future time. The advantage of a digital camera compared to a traditional camera is the fact that it provides immediate imaging without the delay of off-line (digital or analog) processing. Once the information is uploaded to the PC, it can be printed at a (color) printer or further processed for inclusion in a newspaper, newsletter, catalog, or (desktop-produced) report (see Fig. 4.6).

Two key subsystems of a digital camera are

- Imaging subsystem (which determines its picture quality).
- Storage subsystem (which determines portability and imaging speed).

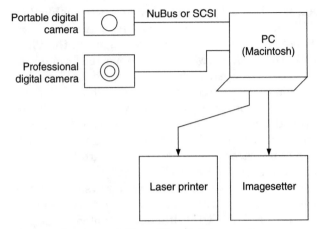

**Figure 4.6**  Image acquisition with a digital camera.

**Imaging subsystem.**  Almost all digital cameras now use CCDs for the imaging subsystem, arranged in a linear array. The linear array handles only a single row at a time, as discussed earlier for other scanners. The advantage of the linear array is its low cost for reasonably high resolution. The price of a digital camera varies, as does the quality of the image. Digital cameras have technological limitations that prevent them from matching the resolution or low cost of film-based cameras.[25] Digital cameras fall in three categories by resolution. The best-area CCDs found in high-end (high-priced) cameras provide resolutions of 2048 × 2048 pixels (about 4 million pixels); this is only one-fifth the pixel density of a 35-mm slide. Midrange cameras provide 1.5 million pixels (equivalent to the resolution of high-definition television). Camcorder-type CCDs used in many (low-end) digital cameras provide low resolutions, in the 400,000-pixel range.

Because CCDs are much smaller than 35-mm images, lenses for digital cameras require shorter focal lengths. Designing a system that provides good color, high resolution, and reasonable cost entails engineering ingenuity and compromise.[25]

The same principles discussed above for stationary color scanners are applicable to digital cameras. Low-end systems use a single CCD row on which (tiny) color filters are stripped. Midrange systems use dual chips that separate brightness and color processing. High-end systems use three chips for separate capture of red, green, and blue. Capturing the image with three passes with a different filter applied for each pass tends to be less desirable because it requires a stationary subject and a steady hand.

**Storage subsystem.** As seen in an earlier table, a camcorder-quality picture requires about 1 MB (400,000 pixels times 24 bits for 24-bit color depth, or 9.6 Mbits); higher-quality images require more (e.g., 4,000,000 × 24, or 10 MB per image). Two engineering challenges must be faced: (1) creating a portable storage system capable of storing a reasonable number of images and (2) reading the data off the CCDs and into the memory (it takes a nontrivial amount of time, exceeding the exposure time) to transfer the data. This limits rapid-fire photography.

Some cameras (particularly those supporting resolution on the 400,000-pixel range) utilize compression and are therefore able to store a few images on RAM cards. Portable systems with higher resolutions rely on battery-powered hard drives, but the low data transfer rate remains a problem; other problems include bulkiness and reliability concerns.[25] Digital studio cameras transfer data directly to a workstation; however, the 10-MB transfer still limits rapid-fire photography. The combination of three-color passes and the data transfer to storage may lead to a 10-s exposure to shoot a high-resolution picture.[26]

Some examples of digital cameras include Dycam's Model 3 (low-end monochrome, $1100), Kodak's DSC 200 (midrange, $9000), Leaf Systems' Leaf Digital Camera (high-end, $29,000), Nikon Electronic Imaging HQ-1500 CF (high-end, $61,500), and Sony's SEPS 1000 (high-end, $41,000—resolution of 133 lines per inch). In a typical configuration, the picture goes from the digital camera to a Macintosh Quadra 700, where it is stored on a 1-GB drive; other networked Quadras and storage devices may be present for additional processing in support of desktop publishing, or for archiving. Pictures can also be stored on tape, such as Digital Audio Tape. One drawback of this kind of high-end arrangement is that the photographic team has to carry around PCs and other peripherals for location shots (i.e., shots outside the studio). As the preceding figures indicate, a high-quality digital videocamera and supporting equipment result in an investment in the neighborhood of $100,000.

Digital cameras are typically used for acquiring pictures for multimedia applications (as these require medium resolution for PC monitor display). They can also be used for print applications, particularly when using a high-resolution system, or for a small-size picture, or for medium-resolution print matter, e.g., a catalog or newsletter. Digital cameras provide a direct link between the subject or object under study and the digitized image, eliminating the processing time and expense that would otherwise be needed to chemically develop the picture and then scan it into a PC-based system. The "shots" can be reviewed immediately, and whatever adjustments are needed can be made on the spot. A photojournalist may take pictures at some remote location and then transfer them to the newspaper assembly location over a telecommunications link. (Cell relay service would be a good choice when this becomes available because of the rates involved.)

Proponents cite ease of use, instantaneous transmission capabilities (particularly when the image is compressed), cost savings (already alluded to above), and environmental conservatism (by bypassing the chemicals-based developing process).[26] With digital technology it is easier to do immediate retouching, edits, collage, special effects, etc.

### 4.6.3 Image acquisition with still videocameras

Still videocameras work approximately the same way as a camcorder (and are in the same price range). They combine CCD imaging techniques discussed in this chapter, with analog electrical standards of camcorders. The standard video connection allows the user to display the images on a TV set (the video can also be sent to a video digitizer for capture on a PC) (see Fig. 4.7). Physically such a camera has the "feel" of a traditional camera. A 2-in magnetic floppy disk stores analog (not digital) information, replacing the camcorder videotape. Up to 50 images can be put on a disk. (This is for a low-resolution single field; full-frame recording reduces the capacity to 25 images.)

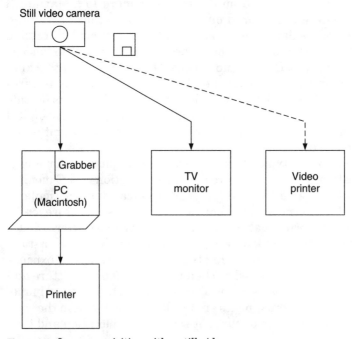

**Figure 4.7**   Image acquisition with a still videocamera.

Still videocameras capture data in analog rather than digital format; therefore, they are better suited to applications intended for TV monitor output. The quality is similar to that obtained on a camcorder, namely, 640 × 480 pixels (or less). Low-end products capture only a single field of video rather that the two interlaced fields that constitute a NTSC TV picture. This reduces the vertical lines to 262, affecting quality (however, 50 images can be saved on the disk). More expensive systems offer full-frame recording. Specially designed equipment (e.g., Canon's RP-733 Color Video Printer) can accept the output of the camera (in either electrical or disk form) and print or digitize the image. The better cameras provide enough quality for TV images and for multimedia applications. Desktop publishers can use still video for pictures printed at small sizes, particularly when time is of the essence.[27] Still videocameras are optimized for the capture of a single frame; capture from video sources may be better handled with a video grabber board.

### 4.6.4  Image acquisition from analog video

VGA-to-NTSC boards allow the user to overlay PC graphics on an input video source and output the combination on videotape. A function called *genlocking* needs to be supported. This is a signal synchronization technique that creates a stable signal to overlay PC graphics with video. These boards range from $500 to $2000. A partial list of products (at press time) includes[28] ADDA VGA-Aver, Aitech ProVGA/TV Plus, Cardinal SNAPplus, Everex Vision VGA with Overlay, Genoa VGA2TV, Magni VGA Producer Pro, Truevision VideoVGA, and Willow VGA-TV GE/O.

Two other types of boards are also available: scan converters and video-in-a-window. *Scan converters* convert a VGA signal into a NTSC signal (but do not provide an overlay capability). They are typically used to display a computerized presentation at a TV monitor or to store it on videotape. They are priced in the $300–$1800 range. *Video-in-a-window* boards (NTSC-to-VGA boards) enable the user to diplay a video on a VGA monitor. In other words, they can capture video input for PC-based handling and storage. They are priced in the $500–2200 range. The boards provide control over the image's hue, saturation, contrast, and brightness. They also allow the user to crop, pan, and zoom in on the image.

### 4.6.5  Directions

In conclusion, proponents see new products for image capture, management, and networking as enabling digital photography to penetrate many newspaper production environments; vendors also expect these technologies to be introduced to a broad base of users over the next 3 to 5 years.[29]

## 4.7  Image-editing Software

Image editing would naturally follow the task of image capture. Although the major theme of this chapter is image capture, a short discussion of some issues, trends, and the commercial status of editing is included for completeness.

Observers note that editing images on the PC is easier than ever; however, heavy-duty hardware and "a lot of patience" is needed.[17] As discussed in the earlier part of this chapter, low-cost scanners and high-resolution PC graphics adapters enable a variety of users, including professional designers, photographers, and business people, to acquire, display, and store high-quality full-color images at a reasonable cost using such DISs. Often, however, the raw output of these processes leaves something to be desired from a high-quality printed-magazine point of view. Here is where image-editing software has a role. These systems aim at taking "less than perfect" scans and transforming them into a more refined image. Table 4.11 shows a short list of what some of the PC image-editing software can do.

To set the discussion in context, note that a DIS image is typically generated from a scanner at 400 dpi, so that a 24-bit color $5 \times 8$-in original results in a $5 \times 8 \times 400 \times 400 \times {}^{24}/_8$ or 19.2-MB file; a PC display version (see Table 4.1) at $2048 \times 2048$ pixels, 24 colors, is a 12.6-MB file. While for transmission and storage one deals with compressed images (e.g., 1:10, 1:25, or even 1:100), for editing and printing one deals with uncompressed images. This implies that fairly powerful PCs and work-

**TABLE 4.11   Some Tasks That Can Be Undertaken with Image-editing Software (Partial List)**

Correct a poor scan

Retouch a photo

Tint a(n antique) picture

Alter the background of a(n antique) picture

Annotate image with text

Integrate two or more (10–15 MB) images into one

Scan a black-and-white halftone and clean up moiré artifacts and other dot patterns

Other "electronic darkroom" effects (e.g., change the color in a picture without changing the saturation or brightness levels)

Four-color separation for print production (e.g., undercolor removal, gray-component replacement, ink absorption, dot grain)

stations are required. A 486, 33-MHz system with 16-MB RAM, 300-MB hard disk, and a 1024 × 768 monitor is a reasonable baseline for this type of work. A rule of thumb employed by practitioners is to use twice as much RAM as the largest image that needs to be edited; 32 MB of RAM is not unusual for some of the high-end editing packages. In addition to the issue of the hardware platform, one must consider the program's own overhead. To accomplish some of the editing functions, a PC may have to run for up to 1 h. For example, a motion blur of only 20 pixels on a 300-dpi image can take 40 min; rotation of a 6 × 9-in 300-dpi image (12.5 MB) can take from 200 to 400 s; a screen redraw (say, shrinking a 400 percent view to 100 percent) can take from 15 to 25 s; to resample a 9 × 7-in 300-dpi image to 4 × 5 in, 150 dpi can take from 50 to 70 s.[17]

Editing packages support a variety of functions, including selection capabilities that let the user limit changes to specific areas of the image. Other functions include area and color masking, rotating, rescaling, resampling, airbrushes, cloning, and special effect filters (e.g., add noise, averaging, blur, despeckle, detect edges, enhance edges, emboss, mosaic, motion blur, sharpen, smooth). Editing enables the user to retouch or artistically enhance pictures. Tonal range or color balance filters are also available. Also, they can perform four-color separation (for commercial printing tasks). Editing packages cost in the $500–1000 range, although high-end professional products can cost somewhat more. Some of the software products support most of the features just identified; others support a subset. A partial list of available systems (at press time) includes[17] (1) for systems running Microsoft's Window: Aldus PhotoStyler, Image-in-Color, Image-in-Color Professional, ImagePals, PhotoFinish, Picture Publisher, PixoFoto, and Publisher's Paintbrush; and (2) for Macintosh systems: Adobe Photoshop and Fractal Design's ColorStudio.

Image-editing programs share some of the functionality of high-end paint products. One of the differences is that the image-editing products support scanner inputs; another difference is the ability to perform substantial alterations to the original image through the use of filters. Image-editing programs also share some of the functionality of image-processing utilities. These utilities usually deal with improvements on an entire image (global enhancements), while the editing programs can perform localized functions, cut-and-paste, etc.

## References

1. P. Dozier, "Scalable Plug-in Multiprocessors Power New Imaging Applications," *Computer Technology Review,* Summer 1992, pp. 97 ff.
2. B. Wiggins, "Document Image Processing—An Overview," *Document Image Automation,* Fall 1992, Vol. 12, No. 3.

3. C. Rubin, "Plug-ins Supercharge Photoshop Functions," *MACWEEK*, March 8, 1993.

4. D. Scheff, "Medical Displays: Challenge and Opportunity," *Information Display*, September 1992, pp. 14 ff.

5 W. R. Nugent, " Electronic Imaging in High-resolution Gray-Scale for Fine Art and Salon Photography," *Document Image Automation*, September–October 1991, pp. 284 ff.

6. R. Kasturi and M. M. Trivedi, *Image Analysis Applications*, Marcel Dekker, New York, 1990.

7. B. Fraser, "Should Mac Users Switch to the 48-Bit-Color Standard?," *MACWEEK*, May 3, 1993, pp. 45 ff.

8. G. S. Kimbal, "Color Fundamentals—Part 2: Color Scanning and Data Compression," *Document Image Automation*, May–June 1991, pp. 156 ff.

9. G. S. Kimbal, "Color Fundamentals—Part 3: Color Imaging and Display," *Document Image Automation*, July–August 1991, pp. 224 ff.

10. J. R. Jensen, *Introductory Digital Image Processing—A Remote Sensing Perspective*, Prentice-Hall, Englewood Cliffs, NJ, 1986.

11. P. G. Roetling, "System Considerations in Color Printing," in *Printing Technologies for Images, Gray Scale, and Color*, SPIE Proceedings, February 26–28, 1991, San Jose, CA, Vol. 1458, SPIE Press, Bellingham, WA, 1991.

12. N. R. Sarker, "Images: From a Printer's Perspective," in *Printing Technologies for Images, Gray Scale, and Color*, SPIE Proceedings, February 26–28, 1991, San Jose, CA, Vol. 1458, SPIE Press, Bellingham, WA, 1991.

13. B. Fraser, "High-res Flatbeds, Part II: Scanning for More Color," *MACWEEK*, November 2, 1992.

14. B. Fraser, "High-res Flatbeds, Part I: Scanning for More Color," *MACWEEK*, June 8, 1992.

15. C. Siter, "24-Bit Color Graphics," *MacWorld*, February 23, 1993, pp. 153 ff.

16. Dataware Technologies Inc., "CD-R: The Next Stage in CD-ROM Evolution," *CD-ROM Professional*, March 1993, pp. 79 ff.

17. L. Simone, "True-Color Image-Editing Software," *PC Magazine*, September 29, 1992, pp. 185 ff.

18. C. Adie, *A Survey of Distributed Multimedia Research, Standards, and Products*, 1st ed., Edinburg University Computing Service, Great Britain, RARE (Reseaux Associes pour la Recherche Europeenne), January 1993.

19. R. Cohen, "MedVision Viewer Can Access CAT, MRI, PET Images for Display," *MACWEEK*, March 8, 1993, p. 10.

20. B. Fraser, "What Does the Future Hold for Color-Imaging Systems," *MACWEEK*, November 16, 1992, pp. 44 ff.

21. C. Goldberg, "Film Recorders: Improving but Not Yet Ready for Big Time," *MACWEEK*, October 5, 1992, pp. 26 ff.

22. L. Stevens, "Don't Abandon That Board Yet—Video Capturing Is Alive and Well," *MACWEEK*, February 15, 1993, p. 42.

23. R. Ford, "Image Acquisition," *MACWEEK*, February 15, 1993, pp. 36 ff.

24. M. Waltz, "Photo CD Technology Widens Archiving and Retrieval Possibilities," *MACWEEK*, February 15, 1993, p. 36.

25. R. Ford, "Digital Photography: Developing Fast, but Not Yet Fully in Focus," *MACWEEK*, February 15, 1993, p. 38.

26. M. Waltz, "Studios Swear by Their Digitals," *MACWEEK*, February 15, 1993, pp. 38 ff.

27. R. Ford, "Imaging Hybrid Blurring the Line Between Video and Photography," *MACWEEK*, February 15, 1993, p. 42.

28. L. Grunin, "VGA-to-NTSC Boards," *PC Magazine*, September 29, 1992, pp. 239 ff.

29. J. Ubois, "Photo Editors Get New Tools at NPPA Digital Conference," *MACWEEK*, March 8, 1993.

# 5

# Output Systems

This chapter explores issues related to output systems supporting BISs, DISs, EISs, and SISs. In particular, aspects of color printing are addressed. Chapter 3 provided an extensive coverage of additive color principles, in the context of methodologies required to support color-based systems in general, and PC and workstation monitors in particular. Because of the intermediate level of mathematical machinery required to understand such principles, the reader was alerted to the possibility of initially skipping that chapter. The present chapter is relatively self-contained and can be read to a large extent without having read Chap. 3; naturally, Chap. 3 affords an enhanced understanding of the topic covered here. As a synopsis of Chap. 3, human color perception is related to three basic factors: hue, saturation, and lightness. Hue is a function of the wavelength at which the subject absorbs light; it is the property that gives rise to a name description of the color, e.g., red, orange, or yellow. Saturation is the colorfulness of an area as a proportion of the brightness of a similarly illuminated area that is uniformly white. Lightness is correlated to the total amount of energy reflected by the object; it represents the brightness of the color in an area relative to a similarly illuminated area that has a uniformly white background.

Color-based creation and printing are beginning to enter the end-user environment, even unrelated to imaging applications (as understood in this text). Color monitors for PCs have led users to raise their expectations for color and, in turn, for color hard copy. At press time, color printers ranged in cost from $700 (ink-jet technology) to about $7000 (dye-sublimation technology); of course, more expensive systems are also available. At the functional level, a color imaging system consists of three stages: color separation, signal processing, and color reconstruction. In the color separation stage, the spectral distributions of the input light are captured and separated into three or more types of color signals. In the signal processing stage, the color signals are processed to generate signals that are suitable for the next stage of the process. This may entail a transformation of the "color space" (also known in this context as "color correction"). In the color reconstruction stage, the signals from the previous stage are used to adjust the amounts of the additive or subtractive color-forming elements of the display medium; the color image is actually produced at this stage.

## 5.1   Principles of Color Basics Related to Printing

### 5.1.1   Background

The printing of color images is now emerging as a result of advances in printer technologies, as well as improved understanding of the image handling required to match the colors actually printed on hard copy to the colors of the original scene, object, or image.[1] Color printers are not only used in BISs, DISs, EISs, and SISs for scanned images, but also for printing of computer-generated graphics. The trend in business, science, and engineering is toward increased use of graphics and increased inclusion of images derived from scanned input. Color printing is already used in specialized areas where color is either beneficial, as in DIS, EIS, and SIS applications, or necessary to replace an already existing technology, as in film-based photography replaced with electronic photography[2] (as discussed in Chap. 4). Proponents of electronic color printing foresee significant growth opportunities for the mid-1990s and beyond. The U.S. market for color hard copy was about $2 billion in 1989 and was expected to reach about $5 billion in 1993. About 10 percent of the market (by revenue) is in the graphic arts area; 30 percent, in the engineering and scientific area; and the balance, in the office.[3] There were an estimated 850,000 color printers deployed in the United States in 1989; the forecast for 1993 was 1.7 million color printers. The introduction of color in desktop systems has been called *desktop color.*

Observers point to rapid and significant changes in the graphic arts industry in general, and output systems in particular, that occurred in the recent past. Some of the key factors affecting this change are[4] (1) the emergence of PostScript (Adobe Systems) as a de facto standard as a page description language (PDL) for both text and art, the continued pace of hardware improvements enabling a variety of sophisticated graphic arts software to perform at acceptable speeds on PCs and workstations, and the now-pervasive presence of laser optics and CCDs in reasonably priced scanners and output devices (including low-resolution printers as well as high-resolution film plotters).

Color is very common in the commercial world of magazine publishing; use of offset lithography is pervasive. The information processing industry has been slower in introducing color. However, observers now expect rapid emergence of color imaging in the next few years; this implies increased penetration of technologies that support generation of quality hard copy.

Color printing is a challenging task, since the eye is sensitive to small shifts in color balance; additionally, there is no assurance that the colors displayed at the PC or workstation monitor match those required for hard copy. Required quality often implies that color printers must operate at 600 dpi or more. There is growing need for color standards for electronic image systems to provide a common approach for the printing of color images from a specified file description, on a variety of systems having different color capabilities, in order to facilitate the introduction of distributed imaging systems in the corporation.

As covered in more detail later, color printing is based on subtractive principles: the desired color is formed via reflection properties by using dyes to absorb differing amounts of the primary *RGB* colors from the incident white light. The primary colors can be printed by placing the correct combination of two of the subtractive colorants superimposed on each other, i.e., overprinting. However, obtaining an exact match of primary colors using commonly available dyes is often a challenging task.

The design of a color imaging system requires knowledge of a number of factors in order to produce and control color. Some aspects of such required knowledge can be derived from measurements of the physical properties of the imaging system at each functional stage of the system discussed earlier (color separation, signal processing, and color reconstruction). However, a thorough understanding of color reproduction requires an understanding of the color perception mechanisms of the user, which include aspects of physics, psychophysics, and psychology, as discussed in Chap. 3.

Physical measurements and mathematical models based on such measurements are often insufficient for the design of a color imaging system when the goal of that system is to produce images that match the appearance of an original scene which an observer has experienced (e.g., a photograph the individual has taken), as contrasted to printing an image for distribution, say, in a magazine, when the observer has not actually witnessed the scene. To create an image to match this mental perception, it is necessary to reproduce both the *tonal aspects* and the *colors* of the original scene; achieving this goal requires control of the physical parameters of the imaging system and proper consideration of the factors that affect the relationships between the physical properties of reproduced images and their resulting visual appearance in specific viewing conditions.[5]

**Tonal considerations.**   At face value one would want to design an imaging system that is able to reproduce in print the absolute luminances of the elements of an original scene; however, often this cannot be done since the illumination level of the original scene may be hundreds of times greater than that of the reproduction (e.g., for a photo at the beach on a bright, sunny day). Fortunately, there is a psychophysical factor of the human visual system, known as *general brightness adaptation,* that can be utilized to work around this problem. It turns out that humans perceive luminances mostly on a relative basis rather than on an absolute basis, implying that tone reproduction can be achieved by the appropriate reproduction of the relative luminance ratios of the elements of the scene in question. However, there are psychophysical factors of the human visual system that can introduce other effects that must be compensated for, or taken into account. These are related to viewing conditions, since such conditions can alter an observer's perception of a reproduction of an image. For example, one may view a color print outdoors, in plain daylight; or one may view it under fluorescent lights; or, one may view it sitting in a chair under an incandescent lamp light; or, as another example, one might view it as a projection from a slide projector. Changes in the sensitivities of adjoining areas of the retina produce a condition called *lateral brightness adaptation,* which impacts an observer's perception of luminance contrast when viewing a projected image in a dark room. The tone reproduction process must take into account such a condition. Another effect that needs to be compensated for is local brightness adaptation. When a person views one object in a real scene and then views another object in the scene, there exists an ability to adjust for brightness differences; this mechanism is greatly reduced when viewing objects within the reproduced scene on hard copy.

**Color reproduction.**   Color reproduction is fairly complex since there are many variables that must be controlled and, at the same time, there are many physical measurements that must be made to get a handle on these variables. Variables include (as discussed in Chap. 3) spectral power distributions of the original scene, viewing illuminants, spectral reflectances of the original object and reproductions, spectral sensitivities of the camera films or camera sensors, signal processing, and spectral characteristics of image-producing elements.[5] However, while the information derived from physical measurements of these variables is needed, that information alone is not sufficient for obtaining effective color reproduction: one must account for the psychophysical factors affecting visual perception. Factors include chromatic adaptation state of the observer, color memory, color preference, and color tolerance.

### 5.1.2 Desktop color

Color printers have already been introduced in niche applications (e.g., CAD/CAM/CAE), but there are expectations that they will soon have a significant penetration into the office automation market as well.[2] As just discussed, color technology is fairly hard to implement at the end-user computing level; this has kept the technology out of many business environments until the recent past. Also, there is the need to deploy a new office infrastructure (color printers, color scanners, color photocopiers, color facsimile machines, color monitors, etc.) if an organization is to foster the growth of color applications in the office environment. Now, one is starting to see the infrastructure being put in place in corporations: color monitors are common, color scanners are getting better and more affordable, and color copiers are finally in the market place at a reasonable cost.

Areas where color may play a significant role include the home market, education market, graphic arts market (supported, e.g., by DISs), engineering and scientific market (supported by EISs and SISs), and office automation market (supported by BISs). The largest of these markets is expected to be the office automation market, in support of word processing, presentations, and electronic publishing. These applications seek to include image graphics in documents with both synthetic and natural color (e.g., digitized photographs). Users need high-quality printers that support both monochrome and color printing on plain paper; indications are that users are willing to pay a modest surcharge for color.

Monochrome desktop publishing entered the market in an aggressive manner in the mid-1980s. Proponents now see desktop color publishing as "poised" to make a similarly strong entry in the corporate or business desktop. There are several factors that enter the discussion of desktop color:

- Which business applications really necessitate color?
- Will desktop color be cost-effective?
- Can high-quality work be produced? How quickly? How easily?
- Will desktop color negatively impact the professional printer industry?
- What hardware and software resources are available to support desktop color?
- Are such systems open? Is there color portability (interchange of files to achieve the same quality in different systems)?

Some horizontal applications (used by generic companies) are generation of color presentations and color-based BISs. Some vertical applications (used by companies with a specific product line) are generation of newsletters or catalogs and digital photography (as discussed in Chap. 4). The answer to the next three questions in the above list is a qualified "yes"; the answer to the last two questions is "to some extent, more so in the future." In terms of hardware, new products have recently entered the market for desktop color, enabling the user to obtain a quality of color that is comparable, to a reasonable extent, to high-end systems. (Some magazines already use desktop color.) As noted in Chap. 4, scanners are the limiting factor for desktop color publishing in producing consistent high-quality work. Some progress can be expected in the next couple of years in this area. At the printing end of things, quality image setters are able to produce halftones of adequate quality (for many applications).

In terms of software, the first generation of desktop color separation software entered the market in the early 1990s. Such systems provide the capability of converting *RGB* scans to *CMYK* needed for printing colors. (The need for this conversion was already discussed in Chap. 4, and will be amplified below.) They also provide other required printing tools such as color corrections, gray-component replacement, undercolor removal, and unsharp masking. These systems enable generation of reasonably good quality in spite of issues related to color standards and calibration techniques.

### 5.1.3  Subtractive color principles

The basic perceptual attributes of color discussed in Chap. 3—hue, saturation, lightness, and brightness—apply to color in any medium. Hence, such principles are the same for printed copy where the physical characteristics of the color are determined by dyes and/or inks, as they would be for a PC monitor, where the colors result from visible light emissions of phosphors. However, CRT displays are based on additive principles of colors; printing is based on subtractive principles.

The color of a surface is related to the capacity of the surface to reflect some wavelengths of the incident light and absorb others. As a surface is dyed or painted with a pigment, a new reflectance characteristic is established according to the pigment's or dye's capacity to absorb some wavelengths and reflect others. A surface painted cyan, for example, absorbs most energy with wavelengths from 400 to 440 nm and the energy with wavelengths above 540 nm, while being able to reflect relatively well energy with wavelengths between these two values. Figure 5.1 depicts the reflectance characteristics of a yellow dye, where the wavelengths between 570 and 700 nm are reflected, and the reflectance characteristics of a cyan dye. Mixing both pigments and painting a sur-

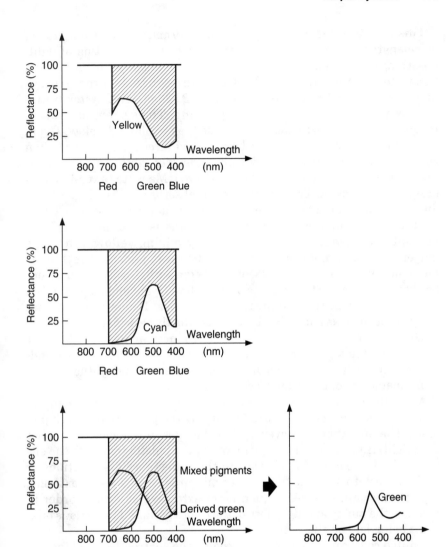

**Figure 5.1** Basic principles of subtractive color methods.

face with the resulting mixture gives rise to a green color. This follows from the fact that the yellow pigment absorbs all the short wavelengths (500 nm and below) and some of the middle band of wavelengths (500 to 550 nm), while the cyan pigment absorbs all the long wavelengths (560 and above) and some of the middle lengths (500 to 550 nm), as seen in the bottom portion of Fig. 5.1. Additional colors can be added to the mixture to create other hues.

This type of color mixture is called *subtractive* because bands of wavelengths are subtracted ("canceled") by the combination of light-absorbing dyes and inks. The minimal number of pigments required in theory to generate the desired colors is three, based on the "trichromatic theory of color" discussed in Chap. 3. The *CMYK* system introduced in Chap. 4 is often used in printing. The system uses cyan, magenta, and yellow; black is also used, as explained below. Cyan, magenta, and yellow colors can be obtained directly. These are often referred to as the *primary colors ("primaries") of subtractive color mixing*. Cyan (a blue-green colorant) absorbs red. Magenta (a red-blue colorant) absorbs green. The yellow colorant absorbs blue (see Fig. 5.1, top diagram). Hence, red is obtained by mixing yellow and magenta; green is obtained by mixing cyan and yellow; blue is obtained by mixing magenta and cyan; black is obtained by mixing yellow, cyan, and magenta. White is not generated, since the assumption is that the surface (such as paper) is already white to begin with. Black can in theory be obtained from the the mixture of the yellow, cyan, and magenta, i.e., overprinting of all three subtractive primaries. However, often pure black is included as a fourth color because the three primaries that produce the best chromatic color seldom produce the best black. Most printing systems use the black dye in order to get a high black-and-white contrast without exercising an excessive demand on the absorption capabilities of the primary color dyes.

A palette of only two pigments, for example, a red and a green, can create all the intermediate hues by varying the proportion of each pigment. The limitation, however, is that the hues thus generated are not very light. Adding additional pigments to the palette improves the situation by increasing the overlap in the reflectance distributions of each; in turn, this means that lighter mixtures emerge (as an extreme, note that a painter uses a much more extensive palette in order to increase the purity and lightness of the colors produced by various mixtures being laid on the canvas).[6]

Printed color copy, then, is produced by the subtractive combination of inks or dyes. *CMYK* provides a minimum palette of eight colors. To augment the hard-copy palette beyond these basic eight colors requires that different levels of color be utilized in each mixture. For example, if one could select from two reflective levels for *each* primary color, then the palette gamut would increase (see Fig. 5.2).

The eight-color system supported by *CMYK* is generally adequate for office applications. Theoretically, a complete palette of colors for continuous tones can be formed by controlling the amount of *CMY* colorant in every small increment to obtain variable shading. (This is analogous to varying the *RGB* color intensity in a CRT monitor by controlling the intensity of the electron beam.) In reality, this is difficult to achieve with

```
Basic palette on three primaries

Nothing (= white)
C
M
Y
Y,M (= red)
C, Y (= green)
M, C (= blue)
Y,C,M (= black)

Augmented palette on three primaries and two levels of colors

Nothing (= white)
C₁
C₂
M₁
M₂
Y₁
Y₂
(Y₁,Y₂)(M₁,M₂), four combinations
(C₁, C₂)(Y₁, Y₂), four combinations
(M₁,M₂)(C₁, C₂), four combinations
(Y₁,Y₂)(C₁, C₂)(M₁,M₂), eight combinations
```

**Figure 5.2**   Print palette.

most printers because they typically are binary— fully "on," say, in the magenta delivery, or fully "off" in the magenta delivery.

Another method of extending the scope of color is to employ halftoning. With halftoning, colors are placed on the paper as small dots that can vary in density or size. Pure red, for example, requires the highest dot frequency (say, 200 dots per inch), while a desaturated pink is obtained when the dot density is reduced (e.g., to 120 dots per inch). Note that with this technique, the desired hue is effectively obtained as a result of the additive mixture of red and the white of the paper.

Commercial offset lithography uses halftoning to create the appearance of shades of gray with binary printers. Until recently desktop applications were effectively restricted to printing computer-generated graphics rather than richer photographic-quality images because of insufficient quality of halftone images. The quality of color halftone images is determined mainly by the quality of the color reproduction process.[7]

Figure 5.3, top panel, shows one approach to halftoning. Here the size of the printed dot is changed to vary the area coverage of the picture element, thereby creating an optical illusion of gray level to the eye that is receiving an integrated light signal. Figure 5.2, bottom panel, shows the method of digital halftoning. Here each picture element consists of a matrix of fixed dots.

This approach for printing continuous images is subject to a tradeoff between the effective resolution of the printed material and the num-

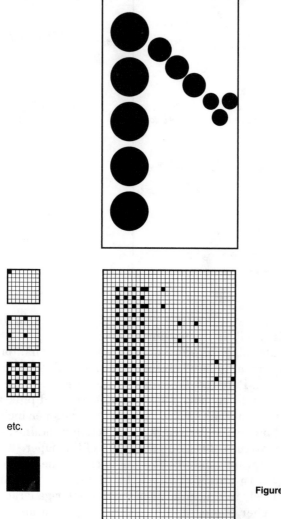

etc.

Figure 5.3  Halftoning.

ber of allowable gray levels. For example, a 300-dpi printer supports 2 bits of gray or 4 = $2^2$ patterns ( a 2 × 2 matrix) at a 150 lines per inch (lpi) screen size (screen size is the basic spacing of the picture elements). A printer with a 1200-dpi resolution allows 6 bits of gray or 64 = $2^6$ patterns (a 8 × 8 matrix) at the same screen size. The requirement for high resolution can be relaxed if each dot can be printed with multiple intensity levels. A 300-dpi printer can print an equivalent image (64 gray levels at 150-lpi screen) if each printer has an "off" state and 16 other equispaced intensity levels for the "on" state; this is called

**Figure 5.4**   Example of moiré effects.

*hybrid digital halftoning*.[2] High-quality text requires sharp contrast and thus benefits from high resolution; on the other hand, color images benefit from a wide range of gray scales. The hybrid approach enables a practical compromise between obtaining a sufficiently high resolution and a controlled level of multiple intensities.

Dot placement accuracy is a stringent requirement for subtractive printing. Dot misregistration often gives rise to a significant color difference. For example, moiré artifacts are due to misregistration of regular patterns in dot-on-dot placement. In commercial halftone printing, the halftone screen for each *CMYK* color is printed at different angles. Since the dots now overlap in a nonperiodic fashion, this approach eliminates the moiré artifacts (*moirés* are patterns created when two or more finer patterns interfere); the angles are specifically chosen to minimize the moiré pattern (see Fig. 5.4).

### 5.1.4   Color coordinates for printing

As discussed in Chap. 2, a color image may be captured in an input color scanner; the information representing the image may be sent to a color editing workstation for adjustment. The information representing the color image is then stored on a file server. Black-and-white printers may be used to obtain quick and inexpensive copies, while one or more (types of) color printers may be used for final production. As it can be deduced, all these disparate systems need to represent color in a consistent manner.

Specifically, one key issue of interest in imaging systems is how to represent an image so that it has high fidelity when displayed on an additive-based (*RGB*) monitor, and at the same time have the same fidelity when printed with a subtractive-based (*CMYK*) printer. Mechanisms to convert from one representation system to the other are required. At this time, many systems utilize a lookup table. This works reasonably well when many ranges of additive hues are mapped into a small subtractive palette (e.g., color copiers and PC color printers still support a small palette); however, as the color printing technology advances, other methods (e.g., computationally based) may be required.

This is actually part of a bigger problem. At the physical level, a generic color system is composed of input elements (cameras, scanners, and graphics software) generating color image information and output elements (monitors, printers, film plotters, and application software) receiving color image information. Linking and supporting these input elements and output elements are accomplished with a variety of file systems, databases, application software, and communication links (local and wide area). The input elements typically comprise one or more hardware units and one or more software modules, all of which may come from a number of different vendors. In many cases, the input elements may not have knowledge of the output element during creation of the image information. The requirement to produce consistent and predictable color in such heterogeneous (open) systems translates into the need for standardization in a number of these areas. Clearly, there must be standardization at the communication level (connectors, speed, protocols, error detection/correction, file formats, etc.) but also at a higher level (e.g., color representations).

Hence, given the wide variety of available technologies the user contemplating color imaging can follow one of two approaches:

- Select a system-printer combination and rely on that closed arrangement

- Select a system where color is described in device-independent (colorimetric) terms (i.e., using chromaticity coordinates)

The closed systems normally use printer-dependent color descriptions. These typically require 16 Mbytes per page of information at 600 dpi, before compression. Fortunately the second approach is now becoming somewhat more common. The open systems now appearing typically utilize a 400-dpi gray scale coupled with a luminance-chrominance description similar to that used in television, where the majority of the chrominance samples can be safely discarded.[8] However, there are many applications where different systems are involved, particularly as imaging evolves from a desktop and local or campus environment to a truly networked environment. Often, at scan time one may not know which specific system elements will be used to edit, process, or print the image. Thus one needs to be able to describe the images in a device-independent manner. Even locally users may need or want to cross boundaries between systems. One example entails the creation and perhaps proofing of color material on a desktop system while then moving to higher-quality systems for output of either presentation slides or hard copy for distribution. Another example may be the interworking of two systems in a campus, say, one used by the engineering and design department and one used by the manufacturing department.

The lack or lack of use of true standards for color data stream representation has a retardant effect on the widespread introduction of the technology in the corporate office. The adoption of a color representation standard by vendors of equipment and materials and the unambiguous translation of color data from one space to another is a fundamentally important issue in achieving device independence. Multivendor environments are very common in end-user computing in general; desktop color systems will likely follow the same avenue. Since end-user computing is within the budget of departmental managers, different departments typically end up buying different equipment. Yet, users soon want to exchange information across the different platforms and achieve interoperability. These issues need to be addressed and resolved before there is widescale interchange of color image files across communication networks. In the immediate past, color systems have tended to remain closed systems, namely, using a specific printing capability linked to a given entry and creation system.

As covered in Chap. 3, there are standards that can be utilized such as the CIE $XYZ$, the normalized $RGB$, the CIE $L*a*b*$ (normally referred to as CIELAB), and the CIE $L*u*v*$ (normally referred to as CIELUV). In printing, the CIELAB $(L*a*b*)$ color coordinate system is increasingly being used to specify the color gamut of the printer. In this system, lightness $L*$ is shown in the $Z$ axis with black (total light absorption) at the bottom and white (total light reflection) at the top; the color hue is represented by the angular position and the saturation by the magnitude of the vector. However, there are several color spaces commercially in use today. For flat colors, the Pantone Matching System 2 (PMS) is a widely used standard. PMS gives unique numbers to hundreds of distinct hues, but it cannot be used for describing scanned images, because most of the colors in the scanned images will fall between the PMS colors.[4] In the prepress and printing industry the well-established method for assigning color is $CMYK$, which is directed toward paper printing. One limitation of $CMYK$ is that it cannot be directly displayed on a monitor. Because color displays use red, green, and blue phosphors, as mentioned in Chap. 3, $CMYK$ images must be converted to $RGB$ before they can be displayed on the PC or workstation monitor. Another limitation is that $CMYK$ lacks standardization in the sense that numbers represented in a $CMYK$ image are not absolute, but are directly tied to the printing parameters—paper, ink, and press, making data interchange between $CMYK$ and $RGB$ ambiguous. $RGB$ is another common color space. The limitation of this color space also arises from the fact that images expressed in *RGB* values may look different when displayed using different monitors, phosphors, or video boards.

Vendors have been slowly adopting variations of the internationally recognized color spaces. Adobe has announced the use of normalized *RGB* as its internal representation for PostScript Level 2 (it also supports input of color in *CMYK* and CIELAB formats). Tektronix is promoting a standardized hue-value-chrominance space (TekHVC) for color monitors and printers. Kodak is using a variant of the normalized *RGB* for the Photo CD product.[4] Having adopted this partial migration to international standards, vendors realize that given specific products, users need to be able to compute exact transformations to and from internationally recognized standard representations, so as to convert to an international standard as an intermediate representation in support of an interchange of image information between a product and another product. Naturally, it would be desirable to minimize the computations required to accomplish the translations between the interchange color space and the native-device-dependent color space, since about nine multiplications and six additions are needed at each pixel— an image of 2000 × 2000-pixel resolution needs millions of computations. (Some examples of translations were given in Chap. 3.) Another important feature is that the space must allow for the representation of the entire visible color gamut.

Effectively one wants to describe how the image looks rather than how to print it. These device-independent color descriptions are based on the CIE international standards for colorimetry. However, the desire for device independence creates a new set of challenges:[8] real scanners are not colorimetric, visual adaptation makes comparison of displays to prints difficult, users lose the freedom to adjust their creations for a specific printer's characteristics, etc.

The CIE color descriptions assume implicitly that if two color samples have the same description (i.e., correspond to the same point in the chromaticity coordinate space), then when viewed in the same surroundings, they will appear to match. If the samples are physical materials, then they probably match only when a specific illuminant (the one specified by the CIE) is used; if another illuminant is used, effectively implying that the two objects are viewed in some available ambient light, they may not actually match. Additionally, the images under comparison may be in two media, that is, one on the PC or workstation monitor and the other in hard copy, making the comparison more difficult.

In practice, full-color printing requires that color separation be done external to the marking process. Therefore, the continuous-tone color image is normally input into electronic form by either a videocamera or a color scanner in *RGB* form. The *RGB* color coordinates must be converted to $CMYK$ before printing. The image processing required to maintain color fidelity between the original, the copy on the display, and the final printed copy involves complex algorithms that must take into account the specific attributes of the output devices.[2] The color reproduction process, often called "color correction," maps an additive $RGB$ color space to an absorptive $CMYK$ printer color space. Different $RGB$ devices produce different $RGB$ color spaces. Similarly, different printers produce different $CMYK$ color spaces. As long as there is no standard for color in computer applications, an individual adaptation is necessary for any device combination. How to map the $RGB$ pixel values to the $CMYK$ values is the key issue of color correction. Some techniques for color correction are (1) mathematically based color correction by using first- or second-order polynomials; (2) division of the color space into subspaces and use of linear transformations with different parameters for each subspace; and (3) use of a masking matrix in combination with input and output gamma tables. In many cases reproduction quality is limited because laws of colorimetry are not adequately taken into consideration by the algorithms used.[7] Color printing also requires the handling of substantially more data than does monochrome printing.

## 5.2   Printer Technology

Three key concepts related to hard copy are addressability, resolution, and registration.[6] *Addressability* refers to the number of positions per linear measure to which the printhead mechanism can be guided. *Resolution* refers to the number of distinguishable dots per linear measure and is related to the size of the dot formed on the printing material (typically paper). The dot size is influenced primarily by the ink-paper relationship. *Registration* refers to the precision with which a dot can be placed on a given spot; this is critical to support superimposing colors to form composite colors using subtractive dyes.

In black-and-white printing, the typical resolution has been 300 dpi for a number of years; the binary output is carried in the system as either a page description language or binary raster data. Typically, the content consists of text or synthesized graphics; occasionally one finds scanned information. Most printers have sufficiently similar characteristics that binary description normally gives adequate quality.[8] Color will see increased introduction in the next few years, as discussed earlier. Technological improvements in color printing are occurring in two main areas:

1. *Print quality.*   Quality depends on higher resolution, broader color gamut, and more fully saturated colors.

2. *Print speed.* At this time, technologies offering quick reproduction time include ink-jet, laser, and electrostatic copiers.

The early office systems supporting color utilized, by and large, the wire (dot) matrix or the pen plotter technologies. The wire matrix is a serial device that moves the printhead across the paper. Color printing is achieved in one of two ways: (1) by advancing a ribbon parallel to the direction of printhead motion to expose different color zones or (2) by shifting a ribbon in the perpendicular direction in order to expose different color bands. A *plotter* is a vector-based data device in which a color pen is directed to various coordinate locations to produce a drawing on the paper. The various color pens reside in a pen repository and are picked up as needed. The pen plotter has been used for color business graphics, being fairly adequate for line graphics applications; however, it is too slow for other applications, particularly high-resolution graphics. Therefore, other printing technologies are sought. There are several available technologies for color printers, as seen in Table 5.1. About 51 percent of the deployed printers are dot-matrix; 28 percent, ink-jet; 14 percent, pen plotters; 3 percent, thermal transfer; and the balance, 4 percent, all other technologies.[3] There is a trend for moving to raster-type output and away vector-type output (typical of pen plotters).

Most of these systems operate sequentially to form a color image on paper. The simplest printing methods require either electromechanical or thermal action; they are reliable, but are generally slow and energy-inefficient. In contrast, the optically triggered processes (e.g., EP) are faster and are more energy-efficient; this, however, is achieved at the cost of

**TABLE 5.1    Color Printer Technologies**

Continuous ink jet (CIJ)

Cycolor

Drop-on-demand (DOD) ink jet*
    Piezoelectric (PZT)
    Bubble jet (BJ)

Dry-silver technology

Dye-diffusion thermal transfer (D2T2)

Electrographic (EG)

Electrophotographic (EP)*

Pen plotters (PP)

Photographic (PG)

Thermal transfer (TT)*

Wire (dot) matrix (WM)*

*Most common systems.

being more complicated and may require multiple printing steps. The discussion that follows covers only the more widely deployed systems.

### 5.2.1 Dot-matrix systems

Dot-matrix (also known as *wire-matrix*) impact printers are similar to the monochrome matrix line printer, but use color ribbons instead. The color system utilizes the same technique as that of black-and-white printers in that a ribbon is placed between the printing surface and the small wires or hammers in the printhead. The majority of the matrix printers available today use a 9-wire printhead and produce output with a resolution of 50 to 100 dots per inch.

### 5.2.2 Ink-jet technology

Ink-jet printing is the most direct method of printing by creating individual drops of ink that are transferred to the paper. There is no intermediate medium, e.g., ribbon. There are two basic categories of ink-jet systems: continuous jet and drop-on-demand jet. The drop-on-demand category comprises two subcategories in terms of the printhead actuator: piezoelectric (PZT) and bubble jet (BJ).

**Continuous jet systems.**    These printers are complex and expensive and are usually employed in high-end applications. The printheads of these systems utilize a pressurized ink supply. The ink is fed to a nozzle where ink drops are generated and directed to the paper; the drops are generated in a continuous stream. Figure 5.5 shows a simplified example. A voltage charge is used to deflect unwanted droplets into a waste area, while the undeflected drops go directly to paper positioned on a large rotating drum. For color printing, separate nozzles are used for each of the four *CMYK* colors.

**Drop-on-demand jet technology.**    In this configuration, the ink is ejected from the nozzle only when a electrical signal is applied to the print-

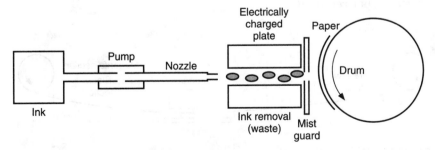

**Figure 5.5**    Continuous ink-jet system.

head. Again, the printhead has multiple nozzles, one for each ink color. This system is a relatively simple design and is often found in office applications.

### 5.2.3 Thermal transfer systems

The thermal transfer printing system consists of discrete elements that are thermally activated by electrical pulses (they become hot, based on resistive principles) to selectively transfer ink to paper. The thermal printhead operates on a ribbon coated with a transfer (waxy) ink, which, given the uniform contact with the paper, affects the ink transfer. The dimensional pitch of the heater elements determines the addressability of the printhead, which is usually 150 to 300 dpi, but occasionally can be as high as 400 dpi. Figure 5.6 depicts the process required for color thermal transfer printing. Sections of the ribbon sheet are coated with cyan, magenta, yellow, and black inks. Each individual color is printed as the ribbon passes under the printhead. After printing a color, the paper is reversed and repositioned, and the color ribbon advances to the next color. The color quality obtained with this type of printer is good; these printers are used in DISs, EISs, and SISs (CAD/CAM/CAE applications, in particular), although the cost per printed page is high because of the expensive ribbon required.

The dye-diffusion thermal transfer technology is a variant of thermal transfer printing. This system uses a ribbon coated with a dye binder layer instead of a waxy ink. The advantage of this approach is that instead of binary ink transfer (say, fully "on" in the magenta delivery, or fully "off" in the magenta delivery), the quantity of colored dye transferred to the receiving media is (nearly) a linear function of the activation pulse to the printhead element. This linear response allows controlled variation of optical density, thereby enabling the generation of up to 256 gray levels per color per pixel. The printing medium is a special paper with a top dye-receiving surface. Usually it takes about 2 min to print a page. This printing technology allows a fairly good image quality, but it has a higher per-page cost due to the higher cost of the special paper required.

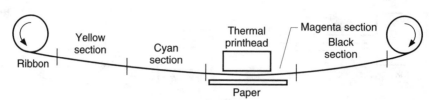

**Figure 5.6**  *CMYK* thermal printing principles.

**Electrophotography systems.** Electrophotography (EP) is the basic process used in paper copiers and printers. In a copier, a light source within the machine illuminates the document and projects the image on the photoconductor. In a printer, the light source in the imaging printhead is electronically generated. (Copiers where the image is captured by an electronic scanner also use the same approach.) The printhead used to form the image may be a light-emitting diode, a liquid-crystal shutter, or, more commonly, a laser scanner. There are six key steps in this printing process:[2] charge, expose, develop, transfer, fuse, and clean. EP technology is pervasive in black-and-white nonimpact printing because of (1) the excellent print quality on plain paper, (2) relatively low supplies cost, and (3) the ability to achieve high throughput. However, it is more difficult to support color with this technology, but there is ongoing research to develop further. A color machine must use multiple passes (each covering most or all of the six steps listed above), since the process must be undertaken for each *CMYK* color. As already indicated, subtractive color imaging imposes tight tolerance control of spot size across the length of the scan; there is also a rotating polygon mirror that has to spin relatively fast in order to support multiple passes. Both these factors must be dealt with to increase the resolution of the machine. Most high-quality systems (400 dpi) print only a few pages per minute (see Fig. 5.7).

Several approaches are used for toning the electrostatic image. Some systems use liquid development, while others utilize dry powder devel-

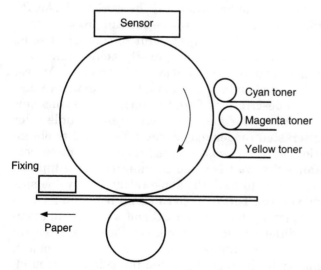

**Figure 5.7**    Basic elements of an electrophotographic color printer.

opment. Liquid toning entails suspending small toner particles in a liquid; this provides the best image quality, but there are problems associated with the release of the liquid inside of the printer mechanism. Most office printers utilize the dry powder EP development. Another choice is between dual-component versus single-component development. In the dual-component method the toner is transported on magnetic carrier beads, thus forming a rotating brush. The single-component method does not use the carrier beads; it transports the toner electrostatically on a rotating developer roller.

## 5.3  Interworking among Color Systems

The need for open color representation systems was identified above, in order to facilitate a transition to distributed BISs, EISs, DISs, and SISs. The solution, as discussed earlier, is to use colorimetric methods. Calibration allows each element in the system to be referenced to the input CIE-based description. Even when using these methods, however, one needs to perform some level of end-to-end calibration, which is not easy.

As discussed in Chap. 4, color scanners generate color separations that do not often not correspond to what one sees. The transformation between what the scanner "sees" and what we see depends on the spectral reflectance curve of the input image. Thus, in calibrating a low-end scanner one must be cognizant of whether the input is photographic film, printed material, or some other source.

The next step in a typical imaging system is the workstation or PC display. One would want a color system where one can proof the color images on the display, then print at that point in time or at some future point in time. This is not, in fact, easily achievable. It is expected that calibrated displays will alleviate this problem. At best the problem can be alleviated and not eliminated. Tristimulus values, as used in color system descriptions found in imaging systems now being introduced, describe color matching but do not handle color appearance. (The interested reader may consult Table 3.2 to obtain additional information on these two concepts.) As already discussed, even when two "samples" have the same chromaticity coordinates, they will match (i.e., appear to have the same color) in only one specific illuminant (light source). This in itself can limit how well an original page and its copy match. However, for PC and workstation monitors, there is also the difference in surroundings. Paper samples are viewed in lighted rooms where the paper is not the brightest object; the eye adapts primarily to the room light and immediate surroundings. Monitors are typically viewed in dimmer rooms, often making them the dominant control of the viewer's adaptation mechanism. One result is that one must increase the contrast on the monitor relative to the print to obtain a similar appearance.[8]

Then there are the printers. Traditionally one utilized a closed system; the individual developing a color image was familiar with the response and idiosyncrasies of the printer and could therefore optimize the quality of the final output by using device-dependent color descriptions in conjunction with this acquired knowledge. In this environment, the novice user usually would not be able to obtain reasonable-looking color. As mentioned above, a number of PDLs describe color by CIE-based, device-independent means. For example, Adobe's PostScript Level 2, Tektronix's TekHVC, Xerox's Interpress and Color Encoding Standard, and the International Organization for Standardization's Standard 8613: 1989 Addendum 2 (Color Support in Office Document Architecture) follow this approach. The PostScript PDL was introduced in 1984, and is now a de facto standard.

As long as the color to be printed is physically realizable (i.e., is within the printer gamut), a calibration can be found which facilitates the generation of the correct color on hard copy, regardless of how nonlinear the response of the printer may be, as long as the printer is stable (repeatable); stability enables the user to establish a calibration that makes the printer CIE-compatible. These PDLs now enable the novice user to get much better color hard copy, almost equaling that produced by the professional printer. For optimization some of these systems allow both device-dependent and device-independent descriptions.

Another important issue in printing is related to halftoning and potential artifacts generated by this process. As noted earlier, the practical approach to achieving many colors on a three- or four-color binary printer (where only one color level is possible) is to use halftone methods. Because the colorants are imperfect, the overlaid halftone patterns create intercolor moirés. In traditional, nondigital color printing, the three or four halftone patterns are laid down at different orientations, in order to achieve a high frequency. This orientation approach results in a frequency that is about 50 percent that of the halftone pattern, implying that with high enough halftone frequencies (about 150 dpi) the moirés are not visually objectionable. To achieve the same appearance on a digital printer requires about 600 dpi or more.

## 5.4    Merging of the Publishing and Printing Processes

Until recently, almost all the original graphics arts have been produced with film-based photography; the color tints used in printing are prepared with exposing film through different filters. Scanning of the original art and exposure of the color-separated halftone films have been accomplished through electronic drum scanners and laser plotters. These and other related methods are as follow:

1. *Analog.* Analog optical modulation of light; not done with computers at this stage of the process

2. *Physical.* Manual intervention needed in several steps (e.g., create the film)

3. *Chemical-based.* Harmful products needed in the process

The shift, however, is now toward digital techniques for preparing the printed page, making the process digital, computer-based (mechanized, without physical film), and electronic (rather than chemical). This transition has been driven by two technologies that have appeared in the 1980s: (1) digital color prepresses and (2) PostScript PDL.

**Color prepresses.** Color prepress systems support a gamut of capabilities for manipulating digital images to produce high-quality hard copy. These capabilities include design-related functions such as changing the content of the image (color changes, crops, drop shadows, clones, etc.) and print-related functions such as color corrections, gray-component replacement, undercolor removal, and unsharp masking.[4]

**PostScript.** PostScript provides a way of handling the various elements on a page digitally, including text, graphics, and some images. The use of PostScript in either desktop publishing or custom publishing systems has become common in many corporate publishing tasks such as communications, newsletters, technical documentation, magazines, books, and directories. The acceptance of PostScript as a de facto standard has resulted, at the practical level, in the ability of constructing a digital page that contains all text, line art, tints, and rules in position, and then either sending this information to a prepress system or to film.

The impact of these technological shifts toward a "filmless environment" has been the fact that publishers are increasingly preparing their material in a ready-to-print format, thereby taking additional responsibility and control of the overall process, in contrast with the traditional approach where the printing organization, the "printer," took such responsibility. In addition, an electronic link between publishers and printers has been instituted. With this approach, the publisher makes up pages with all text, graphics, rules, and tint; translates that to a PostScript file; and then sends the PostScript file to the printing organization. The printer takes the PostScript file and sets the image on a high-quality, high-speed image setter to produce color-separated halftone films. The continuous-tone image is scanned with a drum scanner and separated, and the halftones are plotted on a second set of films.[4] The two sets of films are manually stripped together to make up one complete set of films for the page.

This process is the most common method for publishers to send electronic files to a printer organization, as it makes optimal use of resources: electronic publishing for composition, graphics, and page makeup; and drum scanning for high-quality image reproduction. However, this approach has some disadvantages, including the requirement for manual stripping, the need for handling two sets of films, the difficulty of making revisions once the final set of films has been made up, and the fact that for archiving purposes either the final set of films has to be saved or the incomplete digital data has to be archived.

An alternative method for publishers to send electronic files to a printer organization exists. The publisher sends the PostScript file to the printer, but instead of directly plotting films with the file, the printer may interpret the PostScript code with a software raster image processor and take the resulting image into a prepress system. The prepress system then combines the scanned image with the balance of the page received in the PostScript file, to generate a completely digital page.

**Digital proofing of color images.**    This is necessary in a filmless environment. There are a number of views as to the exact scope of digital proofing. There is general agreement that the primary purpose of a proof is to provide the customer with an idea of what the final printer product is going to look like, but there are some differences in nuances within the industry as to the exact set of requirements for a digital proofing system. Several vendors supply products in this arena, with many entering the market in the recent past. With the advent of digital proofing the concept of remote proofing is beginning to take hold. With digital compression products just becoming available, supporting compression in the range of 20:1 with no visible loss in quality (some of which are discussed in Chap. 6), and with faster digital communication networks also becoming available (discussed in Chap. 9), it is possible to transmit the digital color image data to a remote proofer sitting at a customer's site for inspection and proofing.

**Direct-to-press capability.**    The truly filmless environment requires a *direct-to-press* capability, namely, the ability to directly manipulate the image carrier in the press with digital means. This helps eliminate any errors and variations introduced in first going to a set of halftone films and then producing the printing image carrier from this. For volume offset printing, this translates to direct-to-plate techniques and for volume rotogravure printing, this means engraving the cylinders from the digital information.[4] Plates and the equivalent are used in the printing industry when large print runs (100,000 or more) are needed. However, now one also sees more focused dissemination of information and marketing through customization of a publication (e.g., magazines, catalogs, multiple versions of a printed product). Also, there is a requirement for shortening the time in which the material has to reach the market. Systems supporting electronic printing (i.e., filmless and plateless) in a cost-effective manner have emerged in the past 5 years. These systems targeted toward demand and custom printing are based on the principle of xerography—putting dry toner particles on paper. Some of these products, at the high end of this category, can print as many as 100 pages a minute using four-color methods (continuous tone) at 300 dpi. Other products, at the low end of this category, in support of desktop color, are used as desktop peripherals of PCs and workstations, utilizing some of the printer equipment discussed earlier in the chapter.

## References

1.  D. B. Dove, *Printing Technologies for Images, Gray Scale, and Color,* SPIE Proceedings, February 26–28, 1991, San Jose, CA, Vol. 1458, SPIE Press, Bellingham, WA, 1991.
2.  O. Sahni, "Color Printing Technologies," in *Printing Technologies for Images, Gray Scale, and Color,* SPIE Proceedings, February 26–28, 1991, San Jose, CA, Vol. 1458, SPIE Press, Bellingham, WA, 1991.
3.  P. Testan, "Trends in Color Hard Copy," in *Printing Technologies for Images, Gray Scale, and Color,* SPIE Proceedings, February 26–28, 1991, San Jose, CA, Vol. 1458, SPIE Press, Bellingham, WA, 1991.
4.  N. R. Sarker, "Images: From a Printer's Perspective," in *Printing Technologies for Images, Gray Scale, and Color,* SPIE Proceedings, February 26–28, 1991, San Jose, CA, Vol. 1458, SPIE Press, Bellingham, WA, 1991.
5.  E. J. Giorgiani, "Physics and Psychophysics of Color Reproduction," in *Printing Technologies for Images, Gray Scale, and Color,* SPIE Proceedings, February 26–28, 1991, San Jose, CA, Vol. 1458, SPIE Press, Bellingham, WA, 1991.
6.  J. Durrett, *Color and the Computer,* Academic Press, San Diego, 1987.
7.  B. Petschik, "Color Hard Copy—a Self Color Correction Algorithm Based on a Colorimetric Model," in *Printing Technologies for Images, Gray Scale, and Color,* SPIE Proceedings, February 26–28, 1991, San Jose, CA, Vol. 1458, SPIE Press, Bellingham, WA, 1991.
8.  P. G. Roetling, "System Considerations in Color Printing," in *Printing Technologies for Images, Gray Scale, and Color,* SPIE Proceedings, February 26–28, 1991, San Jose, CA, Vol. 1458, SPIE Press, Bellingham, WA, 1991.

# 6

# Compression and Storage Techniques and Standards

The need for handling digital images is increasing in the business, publishing, medical, and scientific areas, as already discussed in other sections of this text. Not only is the conversion of photographs, documents, and other media into digital form possible and desirable, but the direct acquisition of digital images (as with electronic still cameras discussed in Chap. 4) is also becoming more common, as capturing hardware and related electronics improve. However, as is clear from the previous chapters, images involve large amounts of digital information, particularly for DISs and SISs; hence, compression is a very important element of any imaging system. For example, scanning a 24 × 36-mm (35-mm) color negative at 12-μm pixels (as is done in the Kodak Photo CD system discussed in Chap. 4) generates approximately 144 Mb (18 MB—less if the pixel size is larger). It follows that a typical PC hard disk can store only two to four images of this size, say, for image-editing purposes, and magnetic tape does not do much better; this has driven image storage systems to optical media. As another example, the transmission of a single 512 × 512-pixel frame (approximately equivalent to TV-quality video image) over dial-up telephone lines using even the fastest modems at 57.6 kbps takes over 2 min; most modems on a PC operate at 9.6 kbps, increasing the transmission time sixfold.

The field of image coding deals with efficient ways of representing images for transmission and storage purposes. Research in this field started over 40 years ago.[1] Various terms have been used, including *image compression, bandwidth reduction,* and *redundancy reduction.* The goal of an image coding algorithm is to remove redundant information and greatly reduce the amount of digital information that needs to be stored and transmitted. Once an image is digitized it becomes a bit stream and can therefore be transmitted at any channel rate. Naturally, for real-time applications, the transmission channel speed must equal the data rate of the specific implementation of the algorithm; however, for applications such as messaging, the transmission channel speed can be lower (or higher, for that matter) than the algorithm's data rate. Compressed image and video signals are highly sensitive to transmission impairments such as bit inversion or dropout, and block, frame, or cell loss; this requirement translates itself into a stringent set of quality-of-service goals for networks (LANs and WANs) supporting image and video applications.

This chapter provides a (relatively short) overview of some of the available compression techniques, and then focuses on one of the more important encoding and compression standards for imaging at the practical commercial level, the JPEG (Joint Photographic Expert Group) ITU-T/ISO standard.

## 6.1 Overview

The past decade has seen advances in many aspects of digital technology in areas such as image acquisition, data storage, and bitmapped printing and display (black-and-white as well as color). These advances have enabled a variety of new applications. However, compared with textual information image material requires a large amount of communication bandwidth and storage space. Fortunately, images typically contain a substantial amount of intrinsic redundancy, so that compression can be undertaken prior to storage or transmission; additionally, the data that composes a digital image (or a sequence of images) is often relatively irrelevant, as described in Table 6.1. Recent advances in VLSI (very-large-scale integrated circuit technology) make image compression possible in a cost-effective manner. For many applications, the eye will not detect a compression of 10:1 on displayed material, and a compression of 25:1 on printed material. (Note that at 25:1 compression, 96 percent of the original data is discarded.) For example, simple run-length encoding (e.g., ITU-T Group 3 standard for bilevel facsimile) utilizes any pixel-to-pixel correlation in the image to eliminate data storage and transmission redundancies. Typically run-length data is recoded into digital codes of varying length, with shorter codes assigned to the (original) run sequences that occur most often. Image compression techniques aim at removing redundant and irrelevant information and then efficiently encoding the information left over. In practice, it often is necessary to throw away both nonredundant and relevant information to achieve the necessary degree of compression.[2] As image coding techniques advance into practical applica-

TABLE 6.1    Redundancy of Image Data*

| Redundancy | Relates to the statistical properties of images | Spatial redundancy: due to correlation between neighboring pixels in an image |
| --- | --- | --- |
| | | Spectral redundancy: due to correlation between color planes or spectral bands |
| | | Temporal redundancy: due to correlation between neighboring frames in a sequence of images (not generally applicable to imaging applications) |
| Irrelevancy | Relates to the observer's view of the image | Spatial |
| | | Spectral |
| | | Temporal |
| | | Physiological and perceptual: limitations and variations of the human visual system when presented with certain stimuli under various viewing conditions |

*Based partially on Ref. 6.

tions, aspects such as implementability, computational complexity, and error sensitivity of proposed algorithms will receive increased attention.[1]

Image coding can be classified into four major groups: pulse-code modulation (PCM), predictive coding, transform coding, and interpolative/extrapolative coding; each of these classes can be further divided according to whether the parameters of the coder are fixed or whether they adaptively change as a function of the type of data that is being coded.[3] Additionally, there are other schemes that do not fall into any of these four classes, but which are tailored for certain types of images. These fall into two classes: statistical coding (e.g., Huffman coding, arithmetic coding) and other coding (e.g., vector quantization, run length).

Compression schemes that are able to reduce the raw bits by a factor of 100 or 200 are sought, and are indeed technically possible. Some have even claimed compression ratios of 1:2500 using *fractal* methods. Fractal geometry was introduced into natural sciences (and engineering) less than two decades ago. In a rather short time, the fractal concept has turned from an esoteric mathematical idea into a useful tool in a number of branches of pure and applied science. The interested reader may refer to Refs. 4 and 5.

## 6.2 Compression and Encoding Methodologies

### 6.2.1 Lossless versus lossy compression

There are two classes of compression and encoding algorithms as seen in Table 6.2: "lossless" algorithms and "lossy" algorithms. Lossless compression is one where the entire information contained in the uncompressed message can be faithfully recovered by the decompressor. For example, instead of sending a 100-bit message 0111111111...111111, one could compress it as $x0y1$, where $x$ and $y$ are octets that take values 0 (base 10) to 255 (base 10). In this case, one would send (00000001)0(01100011)1, which is only 18 bits long, and yet the receiver is still be able to recover the message exactly. Lossless compression algorithms are symmetrical; namely, either the sender or receiver can perform the compression and decompression with the same level of computational complexity and without loss of data integrity. Compression of *data* material, for either transmission or storage, clearly requires lossless methods.

Huffman codes provide a method for generating minimum-redundancy codes, namely, codes that have the smallest average length per source symbol for a given symbol set and symbol probabilities. These codes are used extensively in image compression. Huffman coding is a "block-to-variable" code. There are also variations of the basic algorithm. One approach is to modify the basic Huffman code to save memory at the expense of a small loss in efficiency. Huffman codes assume that the source symbol probabilities are known a priori. In many practical situations this assumption does not hold; in such cases, the coding process needs to be integrated with a dynamic learning process to accommodate the changing source characteristics. In this dynamic Huffman coding, the codewords are updated as more source symbols are encoded.

There are "variable-to-block" codes, where a variable number of source symbols are mapped into a fixed-length codeword. One of the

TABLE 6.2    Basic Compression Methodologies

| | |
|---|---|
| Lossless compression (also known as *bit preserving* or *reversible compression*) | The reconstructed image is numerically identical to the original image on a pixel-by-pixel basis |
| Lossy compression (also known as *irreversible compression*) | The reconstructed image contains degradations compared to the original; in some circumstances these degradations may not be visually apparent (this last condition is called *visually lossless compression*) |

more well-known examples in this category is the Lempel-Ziv-Welch (LZW) method. LZW coding is applicable for coding one-dimensional data, i.e., text or computer source code, where repetitions of some symbol strings are frequent.

In both Huffman and LZW coding, there is a one-to-one correspondence between the codeword blocks and the source sequence blocks; there also are "nonblock codes," such as arithmetic codes, where a codeword is assigned to an entire sequence of source symbols.[6] The Q-coder is an example of a dynamic binary arithmetic coder (developed by IBM) where source symbol probabilities are estimated as an inherent part of the arithmetic coding process.

Many hardware and software products implement lossless compression. They typically double the storage capacity on a disk (i.e., have a compression ratio of about 2:1), or double the apparent speed of a communication line. These algorithms can also be applied to files that represent voice or image information. Because the redundancy is higher, the compression ratios can be as much as 10:1. However, this is both (1) less effective than the compression obtained with specialized "lossy" techniques and (2) less than the information bandwidth reduction that is sought (typically 100:1 or even 200:1). In addition to the direct disk storage applications just mentioned, lossless compression is used for satellite data interpretation or storage and for medical imaging.

Bilevel images have been discussed in earlier chapters; examples include text, graphics, and digital halftones. Because of the particular nature of binary images, the algorithms used for their encoding may significantly differ from those used for the encoding of continuous-tone gray-scale and/or color images. Section 6.6 discusses some aspects of Group 3 and Group 4 encoding. The ITU-T/ISO standard advanced by the Joint Bi-level Image Expert Group (JBIG) is another relevant example of lossless compression for binary (1-bit per pixel) images. JBIG may replace the current but less effective facsimile Group 3 and Group 4 algorithms.

Lossless compression of continuous-tone images only achieves modest compression ratios and, hence, it is not often used in low-end applications where storage and transmission costs are a key factor. However, there are certain applications, such as medical imaging, where the image quality is of utmost importance, and lossless compression is often a requirement. In cases such as this one, an important issue is the maximum compression that can be attained with lossless encoding. It can be proved with information theory principles that an image can be compressed to bit rates arbitrarily close to its entropy. Unfortunately, determining the entropy of natural images is a difficult task.

Lossy compression algorithms do not aim at retaining the entire information, but (just) enough to be adequate for the task at hand. In practice, lossy compression techniques work well with audio and video, even though they give rise to (slightly) degraded pictures.

### 6.2.2 Entropy versus source coding

Another way of classifying compression algorithms is as "source" coding and "entropy" coding. Entropy coding achieves compression by using statistical properties of the coded signal, and is, in theory, lossless. Source coding, on the other hand, deals with *features* of the source material, and encompasses lossy algorithms. For example, in a video context, source coding can use intraframe or interframe coding. Intraframe coding is used for the first picture of a sequence and for downstream pictures after some major change of scenery. Intraframe coding is used for sequences of similar pictures (even for those including moving objects). Intraframe coding removes only the spatial redundancy within a picture; interframe coding also removes the temporal redundancy between pictures.

### 6.2.3 Stages of compression

Compression schemes used in image compression utilize, at the conceptual level, three stages: image decomposition or transformation, quantization, and symbol encoding, as shown in Fig. 6.1. The first stage, image decomposition or transformation, entails a reversible operation used to reduce the dynamic range of the signal, eliminate redundant information, or provide a representation that is better suited to efficient coding. Examples include the discrete cosine transform (DCT) used in JPEG (discussed later), and the formation of the

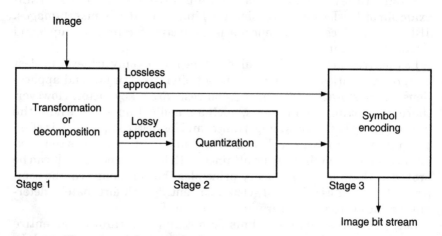

**Figure 6.1**  Three stages of compression.

prediction error values in differential pulse-code modulation (also discussed later).

The second stage, quantization, embodies the primary difference between lossless and lossy compression techniques. Effectively, quantization is a many-to-one mapping; as such, it results in a reduction of the number of possible output values (also called *symbols*), but at the expense of information loss and quality degradation. The type of quantization and related parameters determine to a large degree the bit rate of the image and the associated quality. Examples include vector quantization and uniform or nonuniform scalar quantization based on the optimization of certain specified criteria. A quantizer implements a staircase function that maps a range of continuous input signal values into a finite number of output values, reducing the number of symbols that need to be encoded, but at the same time introducing quantization error. Quantizers are typically designed on the basis of statistical criteria, although other criteria also exist. For statistical design, the most practical distortion criterion is mean-squared error. It should be noted that in situations where the quantizer output levels are variable-length-encoded, the final bit rate is affected by the entropy of the quantizer output rather than the number of quantizer output levels; this leads to another approach for quantizer design where the quantization error is minimized subject to an entropy constraint.[6]

The third stage, symbol encoding, provides a method for mapping the values (symbols) generated by the decomposition or quantization stages into codewords suitable for transmission or storage. Symbol encoding may utilize a simple fixed-length binary codeword mechanism, or may utilize either memoryless or conditional variable-length codewords. The more complex procedures aim at achieving rates closer to the entropy of the data being encoded. Examples of variable-length coding include Huffman coding, Lempel-Ziv coding, and arithmetic coding.

## 6.3    Summary of Available Methods

### 6.3.1    Pulse-code modulation

In PCM, a time-discrete, amplitude-discrete representation of a pixel is created without removing much statistical or perceptual redundancy from the signal. The time discreteness is provided by sampling at the Nyquist rate; the amplitude discreteness is provided by using a sufficient number of quantization levels (e.g., $2^8 = 256$) so that degradation due to quantization errors is acceptable. PCM has been used for several decades as a video digitizing scheme for storage and transmission; it is also for digitizing a signal prior to using a more sophisticated coding. This method entails sampling a one-dimensional raster-scanned waveform at the Nyquist rate (i.e., twice the bandwidth of the signal), and quantizing each sample using $2^N$ levels. (The number and placement of the levels are based on psychovisual criteria.) In a typical arrangement, uniform PCM on a gamma-corrected camera signal is used. PCM coding systems for monochrome video needs 128 to 256 levels per pixel. For monochrome television with a sampling rate of 8 MHz, this generates 56 to 64 Mbps. For still frames images 64 or 128 levels per pixel may be sufficient. If the number of quantization levels is too low, quantization error is perceived as contouring, i.e., as false contours in the image.

A color camera usually generates $R$, $G$, and $B$ tristimulus values for each pixel, as discussed in Chap. 3. These values can be used in the PCM procedure. It is not necessary to quantize each of them with the same accuracy, since quantization noise is not equally visible in each of these components; fewer bits can be used for quantization of the red and blue signals compared to the green signal. PCM encoding does not always utilize the $R$, $G$, and $B$ signals; these values may be transformed to another color space before digitization, e.g., $Y$, $I$, and $Q$ (luminance and chrominance). There also are other approaches. Signal components can be converted by a nonlinear transformation to a new three-dimensional space that approximates a uniform chromaticity space discussed in Chap. 3. In this space, uniform quantization is accomplished by subdividing the space into cubes and giving each cube an output value. Or, a perceptually uniform space is chosen first, for example, the 1976 $L^*u^*v^*$ space, and uniform quantization of this space is mapped back to the original chrominance signal space for digitization. (Therefore, instead of a nonlinear mapping of the chrominance signals followed by uniform quantization, nonlinear quantization is performed directly on the chrominance signals.[3])

In some applications, the pictures may inherently have a limited number of colors; here it is necessary to map the space of colors into a small number of representative colors. If 8 bits are used for each color component before mapping, then the color space has $2^{24}$ coding values. However, if only a small number (say, 128) of colors are to be used to represent this space, then a mapping is necessary from $2^{24}$ to 128 colors.

### 6.3.2 Differential pulse-code modulation

There has been considerable research in lossy compression schemes known as *predictive coding*, also referred to as *differential pulse-code modulation* (DPCM). In predictive coding, each pixel value is predicted on the basis of pixel values in a neighborhood of the pixel in question. There is a high correlation between adjacent pixels that are spatially close to each other. Predictive coding exploits this correlation. In a basic predictive coding system, an approximate prediction of the sample to be encoded is made from previously coded information that has been derived. The error (or differential signal) resulting from the subtraction of the prediction from the actual value of the pixel is quantized into a set of discrete amplitude levels. These levels are then represented as binary words of fixed or variable word lengths.

In predictive coding an effort is made to predict the pixel to be encoded. The prediction is made using the encoded values of the "previously" transmitted pixels (or already encoded pixels), and only the prediction error (differential signal) is quantized for transmission. The prediction may be either a linear or a nonlinear function of the pixels in the neighborhood. In a DPCM system, both the prediction and/or the quantizer may be adaptive or nonadaptive. Predictive coding can be made adaptive by one or more of the following techniques:[3]

- Adaptively changing the algorithm's parameters on the basis of local picture statistics

- Varying the coarseness of the quantizer on the basis of visual criteria

- Suspending the transmission of the prediction error whenever it is below a certain threshold

- Delaying the encoding of a pixel until the "future trend" of the signal can be observed, and then coding to take advantage of this trend

### 6.3.3  Transform coding

There is a class of important lossy compression schemes that belong to the transform coding family. A transform coding technique involves subdividing an image into smaller blocks, typically including 8 × 8 pixels; then each block undergoes a reversible linear transformation. (As noted earlier, this is followed by quantization and coding.) The objective of the transformation is to decorrelate the original block of pixels; this transformation usually results in the block energy being redistributed among a small set of transform coefficients, enabling many coefficients to be discarded after quantization and prior to encoding. Therefore, in transform coding, instead of coding the images as discrete intensity values, an alternative representation is made first by linearly transforming blocks of pixels into blocks of data (called *coefficients*) and then quantizing the coefficients.

The discrete cosine transform is one of the most widely used transforms for image compression. It was introduced by Ahmed, Natarajan, and Rao in 1974. DCT has become common because it appears to be well matched to the statistics of the picture signal. In many image compression schemes employing the DCT, the transform coefficients are weighted (prior to quantization) according to their perceptual importance. A major issue associated with DCT-based compression schemes is the generation of artifacts at low data rates. One-, two-, and three-dimensional blocks (i.e., two spatial dimensions and one time dimension) have been used for transformation. Adaptation of transform coders is possible by changing the transformation in order to match picture statistics or by changing the criteria for selection and quantization of the coefficients in order to match the subjective quality requirements.

### 6.3.4 Other

Interpolative and extrapolative coding techniques attempt to send a subset of the pixels to the receiver, which then either extrapolates or interpolates to obtain the unsent pixels. These techniques are better suited to full-motion video than to imaging.

Subband coding has become a commonly used technique for image compression. Subband coding can be considered as a transformation followed by a particular ordering of the resulting data. This approach utilizes two stages: first, an image is filtered to generate a set of images (called *subbands*), each containing a limited range of spatial frequencies; second, the subbands are downsampled because of their limited bandwidth. As with other schemes, the resulting images are quantized and encoded. The decoder uses a set of interpolation filters to reconstruct the subbands and combine them to create an approximation of the original image.

Another compression scheme is hierarchical coding. Here, image information is encoded in such a way that it is possible to access an image at different quality levels or resolutions. An application that can utilize this technique is in image database browsing. Here hierarchical coding allows the user to start out by accessing a low-quality version of an image (this requires a low bit rate), in order to determine if the image is the desired one. Additional details can then be transmitted in stages to further refine the image. (This approach is also called *progressive transmission.*)

Other coding techniques include[3,6,7] wavelet transforms, block truncation coding, contour coding, and vector-quantization (VQ)-based compression.

### 6.4 JPEG

The standard* produced by Joint Photographic Experts Group (JPEG) is the first international digital image compression standard for multilevel continuous-tone still images (both gray-scale and color). Some

---

*This discussion is based partially on Ref. 8.

applications to which JPEG addresses itself include photovideotex, color facsimile, quality newspaper wirephoto transmission, desktop publishing, graphic arts, and medical imaging. The Joint Photographic Experts Group started working on a still-image color compression standard in 1986. This work has its origin in Working Group 8 (WG8) of ISO/IECJTC1/SC2 (Coded Representation of Picture and Audio Information), which was established in 1982. The JPEG standard has been developed jointly by both ISO and ITU-T (hence the nomenclature "joint"), for compression of still images. It can compress typical images from one-tenth to one-fiftieth of their uncompressed bit size without visibly affecting image quality.

JPEG utilizes a methodology based on DCT. It is a symmetrical process, with the same complexity for coding and for decoding. JPEG will be an important image technology compression standard for the foreseeable future since it works relatively well and is already available in the marketplace, as evinced by vendor support. JPEG is also part of the PostScript Level 2 standard, to enable faster printing of documents that include complex images. Digital videocameras, fax machines, copiers, and scanners will likely include JPEG chips starting in 1993 or 1994.

During 1987 JPEG undertook a selection process based on assessment of subjective picture quality, narrowing 12 proposed methods down to 3. In 1988, a second, more detailed selection process led to a proposal based on the $8 \times 8$ DCT, which is now one of the key coding methods in the standard. From 1988 through 1990, JPEG undertook the task of defining, documenting, simulating, testing, validating, and specifying the details necessary for actual implementation and multivendor interoperability. Table 6.3 provides some highlights of JPEG.

**TABLE 6.3    Highlights of JPEG**

Specifies two classes of coding processes: lossy and lossless

Lossy processes based on the discrete cosine transform; lossless are based on a predictive technique

Predicted value of each pixel position is calculated from the three nearest neighbors above and to the left, and the difference between the predicted value and the actual value is entropy-encoded losslessly; sample precisions from 2 bits per sample to 16 bits per sample are allowed

Four modes of operation: the sequential DCT-based mode, the progressive DCT-based mode, the sequential lossless mode, and the hierarchical mode

All decoders that include any DCT-based mode of operations must provide a default decoding capability, referred to as the *baseline sequential DCT process*

In the hierarchical mode, an image (or image component) is transmitted with increasing spatial resolution between progressive stages

The JPEG algorithm aims at meeting the following requirements:[9]

- Be at or near the state of the art with regard to compression rate and image fidelity, over a wide range of "originals" ratings, but particularly for good "originals"

- Be applicable to any kind of continuous-tone digital source image (e.g., not be restricted to images of certain dimensions, color, aspect ratios, scene content, complexity)

- Have moderate computational complexity so as to permit software implementations with viable performance on a range of processors (PCs, workstations, etc.), as well as hardware implementations at reasonable cost

- Support the following four modes of operation:
  1. *Sequential encoding.* The image is encoded in a single left-to-right, top-to-bottom scan.
  2. *Progressive encoding.* The image is encoded in multiple scans for applications in which transmission bandwidth is low and, hence, the transmission time may be long. (The viewer can watch the image build up in multiple coarse-to-fine passes.)
  3. *Lossless encoding.* The image is encoded to guarantee exact recovery of every source image sample value (although this results in lower compression efficiency compared to lossy methods).
  4. *Hierarchical encoding.* The image is encoded at multiple resolutions, so that lower-resolution displays may be accessed without having to decompress the image at full resolution.

For each JPEG mode, one or more codecs are specified in the standard. These modes of operation originated from JPEG's goal of wanting to be generic and to specify a flexible and comprehensive encoding family that can span a gamut of continuous-tone image applications. It is unlikely that low-end implementations will incorporate each and every coding mode listed in the standard; in fact, most of the implementations now on the market have implemented only the sequential codec. The sequential codec is a sophisticated compression method that will be sufficient for many image technology applications of the first half of this decade. In practical terms, JPEG's mathematical processing makes it a challenge for real-time software-driven implementation on a PC. JPEG-specific chips are now becoming available. Typically, 10-MHz chips can compress a full-page 24-bit-color, 300-dpi image from 25 to 1 MB in about 1 s, or can compress a $640 \times 480$-pixel image, with 24-bit "true color," by a factor of 10 in 0.1 s. There are 25-MHz chips that can do the same job in 0.03 s. These chips cost around \$150–\$250 in quantities of 1000 or more.

The discussion that follows starts with single-component continuous-tone image compression. (*Single-component* refers to a single shade of color, say, gray.) Then attention is shifted briefly to color (i.e., multiple-component) images. Color image compression can be viewed as compression of multiple gray-scale images that are either compressed entirely one at a time or are compressed by alternately interleaving $8 \times 8$ sample blocks from each in turn.[9]

### 6.4.1  Single-component compression

Figure 6.2 depicts the key processing steps that are embodied in the DCT-based operation for the case of a single-component image sequential codec. Notice a forward DCT (FDCT) function and an inverse DCT (IDCT) function. The DCT comes closest to the Karhunen-Loeve (K-L) transform (mentioned in Chap. 3) in energy compaction, that is, the packing of most of the energy of a block of data into a few uncorrelated coefficients. The K-L transform, however, requires intensive computation and the transmission of the transform basis functions for each frame. The DCT is fixed transform, known to both transmitter and receiver, and performs almost as well as the K-L transform.[10]

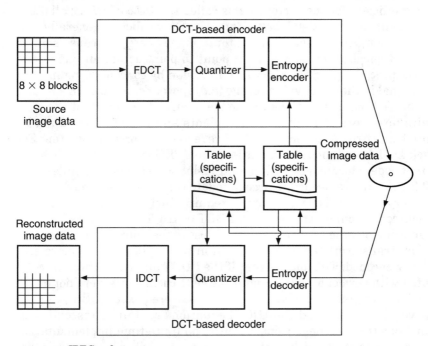

**Figure 6.2**  JPEG codec.

For this discussion, one can think of DCT-based compression as compression of a stream of $8 \times 8$ blocks of gray-scale image samples. Each $8 \times 8$ block [represented by 64 point values known as $f(x,y)$, $0 \le x \le 7$, $0 \le y \le 7$] makes its way through each processing stage, yielding output in compressed form. For progressive-mode codecs, an image buffer is placed between the quantizer and the entropy coding module; this allows the image to be stored and then sent out in multiple scans with follow-up information aimed at successively improving the quality of the received image.

Each $8 \times 8$ block of source image samples can be viewed as a 64-point discrete signal that is a function of the two spatial dimensions $x$ and $y$. At the input to the encoder, these 64 source image samples are cranked through the following equation. For $0 \le u \le 7$, $0 \le v \le 7$ calculate the following 64 values:

$$F(u,v) = 0.25\, C(u)\, C(v) \left[ \sum_{x=0}^{7} \sum_{y=0}^{7} f(x,y) \cos \frac{(2x + 1)\, u\pi}{16} \cos \frac{(2y + 1)v\pi}{16} \right]$$

where $C(u) = C(v) = 1\sqrt{2}$ for $u,v = 0$ and $C(u) = C(v) = 1$ otherwise.

Mathematically, the FDCT takes the input signal and decomposes it into 64 orthogonal basis vector signals. The output of the FDCT is the set of 64 basis signal amplitudes that are known as *DCT coefficients*. The coefficient for the vector $(0,0)$ is called the *DC coefficient*; all other coefficients are called *AC coefficients*. The DC coefficient generally contains a significant fraction of the total image energy. Because sample values typically vary slowly from point to point across an image, the FDCT processing achieves data compression by concentrating most of the signal in the lower values of the $(u,v)$ space. For a typical $8 \times 8$ sample block from a typical source image, many, if not most, of the $(u,v)$ pairs have zero or near-zero coefficients and therefore need not be encoded. At the decoder, the IDCT reverses this processing step. For each DCT-based mode of operation, the JPEG standard specifies different codecs for images with 8- and 12-bit source image samples. The 12-bit codecs are needed to accommodate certain types of medical and military images. These, however, require fairly large computational resources to achieve the required FDCT or IDCT calculations.

In principle, the DCT introduces no loss to the source image samples; it just transforms them to a domain in which they can be more efficiently encoded. This means that if the FDCT and IDCT could be computed with perfect accuracy and if the DCT coefficients were not quantized, the original $8 \times 8$ block could be recovered exactly. But, as seen above, the FDCT (and the IDCT) equations contain transcendental functions (i.e., cosines). Consequently, no finite-time implementation can compute them with perfect accuracy. In fact, a *number* of algorithms have been proposed to compute these values approximately. No single algorithm is found to be optimal for all implementations: an algorithm that runs optimally in software usually does not operate optimally in firmware (say, for a programmable DSP), or in hardware.

Given the finite precision of the DCT inputs and outputs, an interworking challenge arises: coefficients calculated by two different algorithms (say, one in the sender and one in the receiver), or even by independently designed implementations of the same FDCT or IDCT algorithm (that differ only minutely in the precision of the cosine terms or intermediate results), will result in slightly different outputs from identical inputs. Two JPEG-compliant encoders (or decoders) generally will not produce identical outputs given identical inputs. Multiple encodings and decodings will also aggravate the problem. Also, the issue becomes more pressing for a 12-bit codec. To enable innovation and customization, JPEG has chosen not to specify a unique FDCT/IDCT algorithm; however, the JPEG standard addresses the quality issue by specifying an accuracy test to ensure against largely inaccurate coefficients that degrade image quality.

Each of the 64 DCT coefficients obtained at the output of the FDCT is then uniformly quantized by utilizing a 64-element quantization table, which must be specified by the application (or user). Each element can take an integer value from 1 to 255 (or 1023) that specifies the step size of the quantizer for its corresponding DCT coefficient. The purpose of quantization is to achieve further compression by discarding information that is not visually significant. Quantization is a lossy process and is the principal source of lossiness in DCT-based encoders.

When the aim is to compress the image as much as possible but without visible artifacts, each step size is chosen to be the perceptual threshold of human vision. These thresholds are functions of the source image characteristics, display characteristics, and viewing distance. Psychovisual experiments can be performed to determine the best threshold.

After the quantization process, the DC coefficient, representing a sort of average of the value of the 64 image samples, is handled separately. Since there is usually high correlation between the DC coefficients of adjacent 8 × 8 blocks, the quantized DC coefficient is encoded differentially, namely, as the difference between the current value and the previous value. In order to facilitate entropy coding, the quantized AC coefficients are ordered into the "zigzag" sequence shown in Fig. 6.3. This ordering helps the entropy coding process by placing low-coordinate coefficients (that are more likely to be nonzero) before high-coordinate coefficients.

The last step for DCT-based encoding is entropy coding itself. This step achieves additional lossless compression by encoding the quan-

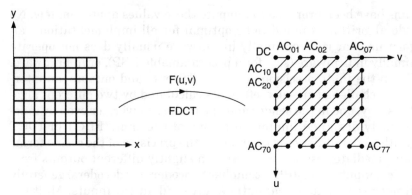

**Figure 6.3**    Ordering of quantized samples for entropy encoding.

tized DCT coefficients more compactly, on the basis of their statistical characteristics. Entropy coding can be viewed as a two-step process. The first step converts the sequence of quantized coefficients (ordered as discussed above) into an intermediate sequence. The second step converts the symbols to a stream in which the symbols no longer have externally identifiable boundaries.

The JPEG proposal specifies two entropy coding methods: Huffman coding and arithmetic coding. The sequential codec uses Huffman coding, but codecs with both methods are specified for all modes of operation. Arithmetic coding produces about 10 percent better compression than Huffman; however, it is more complex. Huffman coding requires that one or more sets of code tables be specified. The same tables used to compress an image are needed to decompress it. Huffman tables may be predefined and used within an application as defaults, or developed specifically for a given image in an initial statistics-gathering pass prior to actual compression. The arithmetic coding method specified in the JPEG proposal requires no tables because it adapts to the image statistics as it encodes the image. Entropy coding differences between codecs means that there may be a need to perform transcoding to enable display of a received image or picture.

### 6.4.2    Lossless encoding and decoding

As implied earlier, a DCT-based lossless mode is difficult to define as a practical standard, using which encoders and decoders can be independently implemented, unless one is willing to dictate severe constraints on both encoder and decoder implementations. Hence, to meet its requirement for a lossless mode of operation, JPEG has chosen a simple predictive method that is completely independent of the DCT processing described above. This predictive method produces results

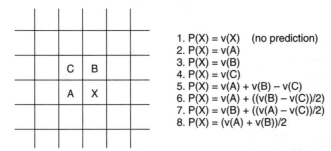

1. P(X) = v(X)    (no prediction)
2. P(X) = v(A)
3. P(X) = v(B)
4. P(X) = v(C)
5. P(X) = v(A) + v(B) – v(C)
6. P(X) = v(A) + ((v(B) – v(C))/2)
7. P(X) = v(B) + ((v(A) – v(C))/2)
8. P(X) = (v(A) + v(B))/2

**Figure 6.4**  Lossless predictor. P(X): predicted value for sample X.
v (A), etc.: value of sample A, etc.

that, considering its simplicity, are close to the state of the art for loss-less continuous-tone compression. These codecs typically produce a compression of 2:1 for color images with moderately complex scenes.

For a single-component image, source information is run through a predictor and then through an entropy encoder. The encoders can handle any source image precision from 2 to 16 bits per sample. To develop a prediction of the sample indicated by X in Fig. 6.4, the predictor combines the values of up to three neighboring samples (A, B, and C). This prediction is then subtracted from the actual value of sample X, and the difference is encoded losslessly by Huffman or arithmetic entropy methods (i.e., two codecs are available).

Any one of the eight predictors shown in the figure can be used. Selection value 1 can be used only for differential coding in the hierarchical mode of operation. Selection values 2, 3, and 4 are one-dimensional predictors, while selection values 5, 6, 7, and 8 are two-dimensional predictors. A family of encoders then arises, since an encoder can use any of the predictors except selection value 1.

### 6.4.3  Multiple-component images

The JPEG proposal also addresses the handling of images with multiple components. It must be noted, however, that the JPEG compressed data format does not encode enough information to serve as a complete image representation; for example, JPEG does not specify or encode any information on pixel aspect ratio, color space, or image acquisition characteristics.[9]

Figure 6.5 depicts the JPEG source image model. A source image can contain 1 to 255 image components (also called *colors, spectral bands,* or *channels*). Each component consists of an array of samples. A sample is expressed as an integer with precision $P$ bits with values in the range $[0, 2^P - 1]$; all samples of all components within the same source

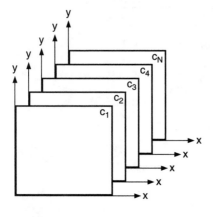

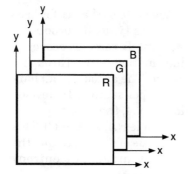

**Figure 6.5** Multiple components (logical view). Top: general model. Bottom: *RGB* example.

image must have the same precision. $P$ can be 8 or 12 for DCT-based codecs, and 2 to 16 for predictive codecs. Image components may be sampled at different rates compared to each other; in other words, components can have different dimensions, where the $i$th component has sample dimensions $x_i \times y_i$.

Many systems need to pipeline the process of displaying images with the process of decompression itself. This is generally done by interleaving components within the compressed stream. To make the same interleaving process applicable to both DCT-based and predictive codecs, the JPEG standard uses the concept of "data unit," which is a sample in predictive codecs and an $8 \times 8$ block of samples in DCT-based codecs. Without any interleaving (i.e., compression without being interleaved with other components), data units are ordered from left to right and top to bottom, as shown in Fig. 6.6(*a*), which shows a pure raster scan. When two or more components are interleaved, each component $C_j$ is partitioned into rectangular regions of $H_j \times V_j$ data units, as shown in Fig. 6.6(*b*), depicting some illustrative examples. Within a region, data units are ordered from left to right and top to bottom. Regions themselves are ordered within a component from left to right and top

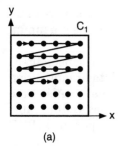

(a)

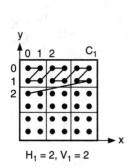

$H_1 = 2, V_1 = 2$

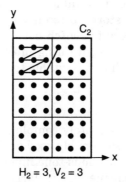

$H_2 = 3, V_2 = 3$

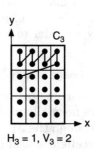

$H_3 = 1, V_3 = 2$

$MCU_1 = (d(C_1, 0, 0), d(C_1, 0, 1), d(C_1, 1, 0), d(C_1, 1, 1), d(C_2, 0, 0), d(C_2, 0, 1), d(C_2, 0, 2),$
$\quad d(C_2, 1, 0), d(C_2, 1, 1), d(C_2, 1, 2), d(C_2, 2, 0), d(C_2, 2, 1), d(C_2, 2, 2), d(C_3, 0, 0),$
$\quad d(C_3, 1, 0))$

$MCU_2 = (d(C_1, 0, 2), d(C_1, 0, 3), d(C_1, 1, 2), d(C_1, 1, 3), d(C_2, 0, 3), d(C_2, 0, 4), d(C_2, 0, 5),$
$\quad d(C_2, 1, 3), d(C_2, 1, 4), d(C_2, 1, 5), d(C_2, 2, 3), d(C_2, 2, 4), d(C_2, 2, 5), d(C_3, 0, 1),$
$\quad d(C_3, 1, 1))$

etc.

(b)

**Figure 6.6**  Interleaving of minimum coded unit.

to bottom. The JPEG standard defines the term *minimum coded unit* (MCU) to be the smallest group of interleaved data units. For example, $MCU_1$ in Fig. 6.6(*b*) consists of data units taken first from the top left-most region of $C_1$ followed by data units from the same region of $C_2$ and likewise for $C_3$; $MCU_2$ continues the pattern in a similar manner.

Interleaved data is an ordered sequence of MCUs, and the number of data units contained in an MCU is determined by the number of components interleaved and their relative sampling factors. (Note that the JPEG standard allows some components to be interleaved and some to be noninterleaved within the same compressed image.) The maximum number of components that can be interleaved is 4, and the maximum number of data units in an MCU is 10.

The interleaving process adds complexity in another sense: JPEG codecs must assure applications of the proper table data (quantization table and entropy coding table) to the proper component. (Also note that the same quantization table and the same entropy coding table must be used to encode all samples within a specific component.) JPEG decoders can store up to four different quantization tables and up to four different entropy coding tables simultaneously. (The baseline sequential decoder can store up to only two sets of entropy tables.) Thus, it may be necessary to switch between different tables during decompression of a signal containing multiple (interleaved) components, in order to apply the proper table to the proper component.

### 6.4.4  Image quality

For color images with moderately complex scenes, the various JPEG codecs normally produce reasonably good quality as shown in Table 6.4.

Although the JPEG continuous-tone image compression standard is an excellent encoding scheme, particularly for still images, it is not a panacea that will solve all issues that must be addressed before digital images will be fully integrated within all the applications that will ultimately benefit from them; for example, if two applications cannot exchange uncompressed images because they use incompatible color spaces, aspect ratios, dimensions, etc., then a common compression method will not help.[9]

TABLE 6.4    Quality of Compressed Image

| Ratio of number of bits in the compressed image to the number of samples in the luminance component* | Quality |
| --- | --- |
| 0.25–0.5 | Moderate to good quality, sufficient for some applications |
| 0.5–0.75 | Good to very good quality, sufficient for many applications |
| 0.75–1.5 | Excellent quality, sufficient for most applications |
| 1.5–2.0 | Effectively indistinguishable from originals, sufficient for the most demanding applications |

*Loosely known as "bits per pixel."

Intercolor-based redundancies cannot be eliminated by the JPEG algorithm, since it is independent of a particular color space or model; namely, it handles colors as separate components. There are advantages in this, however, since it can compress data from any color model such as *RGB* or *CMYK*.

Accelerated JPEG PC boards (boards containing processors that speed up operation beyond what the basic host machine can provide) can be purchased for $800 to $2000.[11] A partial list of products for Macintosh computers includes SuperMac Technology's ThunderStorm board, Spectral Innovations' Lightning Effects board, and Newer Technology's Image Magic board.[12] As discussed elsewhere, some users have opted for software decoding, although performance is generally affected.

## 6.5  Facsimile Standards

### 6.5.1  Group 3 and Group 4

This section briefly reviews aspects of Group 3 and Group 4 techniques, since some imaging systems (particularly BIS) currently use this technology to transmit images remotely. The ITU-T produced the first international facsimile standard in 1968. This standard, known as Group 1 facsimile (Recommendation T.2), supported a transmission of a $210 \times 297$-mm page at a scanning density of 3.85 lines/mm. It required a transmission time of 6 min. The Group 2 standard followed in 1976. It transmitted a page in half the time of a Group 1 machine with about the same quality. Both of these systems were analog and did not use image compression methods. In 1980 the Group 3 standards (Recommendations T.4 and T.30) were published. Group 3 provided better quality and shorter transmission time than Group 2. This was accomplished using digital image compression. The Group 4 standard (Recommendation T.6) was published in 1984. The goal of the Group 4 standard was to provide twice the resolution of Group 3 while using higher-speed digital networks. Since 1984 work has continued on both the Group 3 and Group 4 standards.

In order to support interoperability, the compression algorithm of a Group 3 machine was standardized in 1980. The selection was a one-dimensional coding technique known as *modified Huffman code*. This technique is relatively simple to implement. Recommendation T.4 covered the compression algorithm and modulation specifications, and Recommendation T.30 described the protocol. Group 3 was designed to operate on the switched telephone network in a half-duplex mode. The protocol specifies a basic operation that all Group 3 terminals must provide, plus a number of options. All Group 3 machines must provide the following set of capabilities: a pixel density of 204 pixels/in horizontally and 98* pixels/in vertically; one-dimensional compression using the modified Huffman code; a transmission speed of 9600 bps with a fallback to 4800 or 2400 bps; a minimum time per coded scan line of 20 ms, to allow real-time printer operation without extensive buffering; and a mechanism to escape the standard protocol.[10] Early in 1991 the ITU-T approved a new modulation technique, V.17, for use with Group 3 facsimile. In addition to the existing data rates of 9.6 kbps, 12.0 and 14.4 kbps were added. V.17 operates in half-duplex mode and is intended only for facsimile.

The Group 3 facsimile recommendations originally were directed toward facsimile terminals and paper-to-paper transmission. Today, an increasing number of facsimile terminals are integrated with PCs. Along with the standard facsimile functions, these new devices offer additional capabilities inherent with PCs. Examples of these new features are higher-resolution scanners and printers, color, large memories for buffering and storage, scheduling and distribution, and confidential reception.[10] The binary file transfer (BFT) has been developed to enhance the use of these new features by providing a general method to transmit files from one computer to another.

Group 4 terminals were developed to be capable of sending both characters and raster graphics (facsimile). The Open Systems Interconnection seven-layer model was employed to support error-controlled communication and to allow the use of a two-dimensional compression algorithm (to support higher compression). A transmission speed of 56 or 64 kbps allows an image scanned at 400 pixels/in to be transmitted in approximately 5 s. In 1984, the application layer was specified by just two recommendations, T.5 and T.73. Since 1984 there have been a number of changes; in particular, document transfer and manipulation recommendations have been expanded. This set of recommendations provides for transfer of processable or formatted documents containing any combination of character, raster graphics, or geometric graphics content.

The Group 4 bilevel image compression algorithm, described in ITU-T Recommendation T.6, is similar to that of Group 3. The algorithm was changed slightly to accommodate the higher number of pixels per line resulting from the 400 pixels/in. The 1984 recommendations applied to bilevel images only; gray scale and color were for further study at that time.

The resolution of the scanners and printers used in facsimile has a direct effect on the output image quality. The highest resolution specified for Group 3 is $204 \times 196$ pixels per 25.4 mm. (Note that the resolutions specified for Group 3 are "unsquare," that is, not equal horizon-

---

*Most systems support 196 pixels/in.

tally and vertically.) Many of the scanners and printers being installed at this time are capable of higher resolutions (see Chaps. 4 and 5). The Group 4 recommendations support the following standard and optional resolutions: $200 \times 200$, $240 \times 240$, $300 \times 300$, and $400 \times 400$ pixels per 25.4 mm. Note that Group 4 resolutions are "square." This difference causes a compatibility problem. If the Group 3 resolutions are extended in multiples of the base resolutions, for example, to $408 \times 392$, then a distortion of approximately 2 percent horizontally and vertically occurs when communicating with a $400 \times 400$ square machine. The U.S. position has been to accept this distortion and encourage a gradual migration to the square resolutions. The ITU-T has agreed in principle to enhance Group 3 to include higher resolution for both multiples of current Group 3 resolutions and square resolutions. Specifically, optional Group 3 resolutions of $408 \times 196$, $408 \times 392$, $200 \times 200$, $300 \times 300$, and $400 \times 400$ pixels per 25.4 mm have been agreed to. The discussion in the standards bodies has centered on the "square" versus "unsquare" compatibility issue and how to handle distortion.

### 6.5.2  Color facsimile

An ad hoc group was created early in 1990 to address color facsimile under then ITU-T Study Group VIII. JPEG has been the leading candidate for continuous-tone color facsimile compression. Two issues addressed by the standardization group requiring agreements for interoperability are (1) a color model must be selected, and (2) parameters must be appropriately selected.

Two types of color spaces have been discussed: color spaces such as *RGB, CYM,* or *CYMK*; and luminance-chromaticity color spaces such as CCIR 601 and CIELAB. The *RGB* and *CYM* spaces are associated with scanners and printers, as covered in Chaps. 4 and 5, while the luminance-chromaticity spaces offer gray-scale compatibility and higher compression. The chrominance components $C_b$ and $C_r$ are subsampled horizontally. Much of the JPEG research and quantization matrix optimization has been based on the $YC_bC_r$ color model. The eye is more sensitive to luminance than chrominance; therefore, it is easier to optimize the quantization matrix where luminance and chrominance are specific separate components. (This is not the case in the *RGB* or *CYMK* color systems.) Subsampling the chrominance components provides further compression; one can subsample the chrominance just horizontally, or horizontally and vertically.

Parameters to be agreed to include the resolution or pixel density of the image and data precision. For bilevel images, Group 3 and Group 4 cover the range of 200 pixels/in horizontally $\times$ 100 pixels/in vertically, to $400 \times 400$ pixels/in. As discussed above, at $200 \times 200$ pixels/in (the standard resolution for Group 4), a color photograph compressed to 1 bit per pixel and transmitted at 64 kbps would require about 1 min to transmit. Higher resolutions may be required. For quantization precision, 8- or 12-bit data precision is possible.

### 6.5.3 JBIG

It is difficult to produce an algorithm that works well on both continuous-tone and bilevel images; therefore, the decision was made for JPEG to concentrate on continuous-tone image compression, while JBIG would select and develop a compression technique for bilevel images.[10] The goals of JBIG were similar to those of JPEG: the compression technique should support a range of services and applications including facsimile, audiographic teleconferencing, and image databases; and, the technique should be adaptable to a wide range of image resolutions and to varying image quality. To accomplish these goals, a progressive bilevel technique is employed.

JBIG models the redundancy in the image as the correlations of the pixel currently being coded with a set of nearby pixels, which are called the *template*. Usually these pixels have already been processed by the scanner (e.g., 2 pixels on the same line preceding the pixel under study and the 5 pixels centered above the pixel under study on the previous line). The current pixel is arithmetically coded based on the 8-bit state thus formed. The arithmetic coder and the probability estimator is the patented IBM Q-coder mentioned above. The Q-coder uses low precision, rapidly adaptable probability estimation combined with a "multiply-less" arithmetic coder.[13]

The progressive bilevel coding technique aims at repeatedly reducing the resolution of a bilevel image $R_0$, creating images $R_1, R_2, ..., R_n$, where image $R_i$ has one-half the number of pixels per line and one-half the number of lines of image $R_{i-1}$. The lowest-resolution image, $R_n$, called the *base layer,* is transmitted losslessly (free of distortion) by binary arithmetic coding. Next, image $R_{n-1}$ is transmitted losslessly, using pixels in $R_n$ and previously transmitted pixels in $R_{n-1}$ as predictors in an attempt to predict the next $R_{n-1}$ pixel to be transmitted. If prediction is supported by the remote machine, the predicted pixel value is not transmitted. This progressive buildup is repeated until image $R_0$ has been losslessly transmitted (or the process stopped at the receiver's request).

A sequential mode of transmission also exists. It consists of performing the entire progressive transmission on successive horizontal stripes of the original image. The algorithm performs image reduction, typical prediction, deterministic prediction, and binary arithmetic encoding and decoding, highlighted in Table 6.5.

**TABLE 6.5     JBIG Sequential Mode Functions**

| | |
|---|---|
| Image reduction | The reduction algorithm aims at preserving as much detail as possible in the low-resolution image under the constraint that the latter be half as wide and high as the high-resolution image. Each low-resolution pixel is determined by the values of several high-resolution pixels and low-resolution pixels that have already been determined. (JBIG recommends a reduction algorithm that produces good results; however, any algorithm can be used.) |
| Prediction | When a difference layer is being encoded (or decoded), the compression is achieved by predicting new pixel values from the values of pixels in a predictor template. The predictor template contains pixels from the reference layer and pixels already predicted or encoded from the difference layer. When the predictor state is such that the prediction is known to be correct, the predicted pixel value need not be encoded or decoded. JBIG employs two types of prediction: (1) *typical prediction,* referring to prediction in which the predicted value is almost always, but not necessarily always, correct; and (2) *deterministic prediction,* referring to prediction in which the predicted value is always correct. |
| Binary arithmetic coding | Data compression is best when the probabilities of the two symbols are near 1 and 0, and worst when they are near 0.5. The best compression is achieved by keeping separate probability estimates for those conditions under which the encoded symbol probabilities are the most strongly skewed. These conditions are called *contexts.* |
| Adaptive context templates | The purpose of adaptive context templates is to take advantage of horizontal periodicity, which often occurs in halftone and dithered images. Data compression is best if at least one of the pixels in a context template is a good predictor of the pixel being encoded. An adaptive context template contains a "floating" pixel; all other pixels in the template are fixed in position relative to the encoded pixel. |

## 6.6   Other Types of Image Processing

For the sake of completeness, this section identifies some of the common types of image processing and analysis. Inclusion of this material in this chapter is simply motivated by the fact that usually a complex level of computation and/or transformation is required, at least as demanding as image compression; in fact, one could classify image compression as an example of image analysis. This section is loosely

TABLE 6.6    Key Techniques for Image Restoration

| | |
|---|---|
| Spatial methods | Continuous image spatial filtering |
| | Pseudoinverse spatial techniques |
| | Statistical estimation |
| | Constrained image restoration techniques |
| | Blind image restoration |
| Point and spectral methods | Sensor and display point nonlinearity correction |
| | Spectral radiance estimation |
| | Sensor and display spectral response correction |
| | Color film exposure estimation |
| | Color image display compensation |

based on Ref. 14, to which the reader is referred for a highly technical treatment.

One type of processing is image improvement. This includes the following aspects: contrast manipulation, histogram modification, noise cleaning, edge crispening, color image enhancement, and multispectral image enhancement. Another type of image analysis is image restoration. Two classes of techniques can be used: (1) spatial image restoration and (2) point and spectral image restoration. Table 6.6 depicts some of the facets of these restoration techniques. Another set of image processing techniques deals with geometric image modification; these include translation, minification, magnification, rotation, spatial warping, perspective transformation, and geometric image resampling. All these processing tasks are well developed at the analytical level, and can be achieved on a computer of adequate computational power.[14]

Image analysis proper covers areas such as

- Morphological image processing (e.g., image connectivity, shrinking, thinning, skeletonizing, thickening, dilation, erosion).

- Edge detection (e.g., edge, line, and spot modeling; edge fitting; luminance and color edge detection).

- Image feature extraction.

- Image segmentation (amplitude, clustering, and region segmentation methods).

- Shape analysis (including distance, perimeter, area, and orientation issues).

- Image detection and recognition (registration).

All these analysis tasks are somewhat developed at the analytical level, and can be undertaken to various degrees on a computer of adequate computational power.[14]

# References

1. R. Forchheimer and T. Kronander, "Image Coding—from Waveforms to Animation," *IEEE Transactions on Acoustics, Speech, and Signal Processing*, December 1989, pp. 2008–2033.
2. G. S. Kimbal, "Color Fundamentals—Part 2: Color Scanning and Data Compression," *Document Image Automation*, May–June 1991, pp. 156 ff.
3. A. N. Netravali and B. G. Haskell, *Digital Pictures—Representation and Compression*, Plenum, New York, 1988.
4. S. H. Liu, "Formation and Anomalous Properties of Fractals," *IEEE Engineering in Medicine and Biology*, June 1992, pp. 28 ff.
5. B. Mandelbrot, *The Fractal Geometry of Nature*, Freeman, New York, 1977.
6. M. Rabbani, *Selected Papers on Image Coding and Compression*, SPIE Milestone Series, Vol. MS 48, Bellingham, WA, 1992.
7. M. Rabbani and P. W. Jones, *Digital Image Compression Techniques*, SPIE Milestone Series, Vol. TT 7, Bellingham, WA, 1992.
8. D. Minoli and B. Keinath, *Distributed Multimedia Through Broadband Communication Services*, Artech House, Norwood, MA, 1994.
9. G. K. Wallace, "The JPEG Still Picture Compression Standard," *Communications of the ACM*, April 1991, Vol. 34, No. 4, pp. 30 ff.
10. S. J. Urban, "Review of Standards for Electronic Imaging for Facsimile Systems," *Journal of Electronic Imaging*, 1992, pp. 5–21.
11. T. Williams, "The Next Stage in the Evolution of Digital Multimedia," *Computer Technology Review*, February 1993, pp. 19 ff.
12. C. Seiter, "24-Bit Color Graphics," *MacWorld*, February 1993, pp. 153 ff.
13. C. Adie, *A Survey of Distributed Multimedia Research, Standards, and Products*, 1st ed., Edinburg University Computing Service, Great Britain, RARE (Reseaux Associes pour la Recherche Europeenne), January 1993.
14. W. K. Pratt, *Digital Image Processing*, 2d ed., Wiley-Interscience, New York, 1991.

# Chapter

# 7

# Storage Technology

The purpose of this chapter is to survey a variety of image storage systems. CD-ROMs, WORMs, recordable CDs, and magnetooptic (MO) storage are examined, among other systems.[1-4] Several formats are now on the market. The 1991 characterization that the current combination of noncompatible hardware and proprietary software made "CD-ROMs on a PC one giant headache" is changing only slowly.

CD-ROMs are now faster and cheaper than just a couple of years ago. The U.S. installed base of CD-ROM drives is about 5 million; this means that about 1 PC in 10 is already equipped with it. The installed base has been doubling every year for the past few years (see Table 7.1). By 1995 more that half the office PCs will have a CD-ROM drive, and by the turn of the century nearly all office PCs will have a drive.[5] At present, 300,000 pages of text (50 ft of two-sided paper) can fit into a single CD-ROM (when stored as text—not so when stored as image).[6] The cost of CD-ROM hardware and software has decreased to one-fourth the original cost in the past decade.

Optical storage media are entering the market at a rapid rate. For example, in 1992 WORM media demand was outstripping supply. As

**TABLE 7.1  CD-ROM Deployment**

| Year | CD-ROM players installed | CD-ROM titles |
|------|--------------------------|---------------|
| 1986 | 9,000 | 100 |
| 1988 | 168,000 | 625 |
| 1990 | 1,200,000 | 2,500 |
| 1992 | 5,300,000 | 5,000 |
| 1994 (estimated*) | 20,000,000 | 10,000 |

*Assumes that the historical trend continues.

discussed in Chap. 4, Kodak's Photo CD system establishes CD-ROMs as a key element of digital photography. In 1992 Sony shipped its 10 millionth audio disk, and was reaching production levels of one million CDs a month.[7] However, one of the challenges faced by the prospective user is that the proliferation of CD standards makes it difficult to decide which CD-ROM drive should be purchased for desktop applications; relatively new formats include the multisession Photo CD (Kodak) and the CD-ROM XA.[8]

## 7.1    A Model of Storage Systems

Developers of storage systems have the goal to keep up with the advances in computer processing power, since memory can easily become a bottleneck of any system. For example, magnetic disks have been doubling in storage capacity every 3 years.[9]

Storage has traditionally been viewed as conforming to a hierarchy modeled by a triangle (see, e.g., Ref. 10). In this model, fast storage is found at the pinnacle, while larger, lower-cost, lower-performance storage is encountered as one descends the triangle toward the base. Figure 7.1 depicts this storage hierarchy, mapped to a traditional client-server model discussed in Chap. 2. In the workstation a small amount of semiconductor memory (known as *cache*) is allocated to support fast, but expensive, access to the information. Cache retains data that is likely to be needed in the immediate future; accessing data

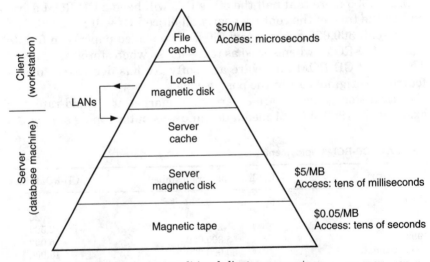

**Figure 7.1**    Storage hierarchy in a traditional client-server system.

**TABLE 7.2  Client-Server Memory Management Techniques**

| | |
|---|---|
| Swapful client | Client allocates virtual memory swap space and temporary files in the local disk; operating system's files and user files are located in the server; network traffic moderate; management simple |
| Dataless client | Client includes the operating system's files in the local disk; network traffic low; more clients supported with a server; management more difficult (e.g., distributing new version of application) |
| Diskful client | Client places all files, except those frequently shared, in the local disk; very low network traffic; most difficult to administer; more expensive since retail memory is more expensive |

across the network, as seen in Fig. 7.1, adds latency. Some of the data can be retained in the local magnetic disk. This is effective if the file is appropriately partitioned between the server and the client. Table 7.2 depicts three ways to accomplish this task.

Figure 7.2 depicts the environment that one can expect in an imaging system of the mid-1990s. In this scenario, conventional disks have been replaced with inexpensive arrays (RAIDs), and optical jukeboxes provide an intermediate level of storage, known as "near-line," that fits between the "on-line mode" and the "off-line mode." (Since the emphasis of this chapter is on optical storage in support of imaging applica-

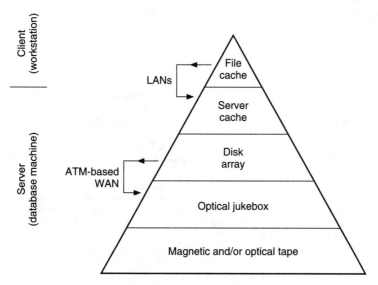

**Figure 7.2**  Memory management in the mid-1990s.

tions, the reader should refer to Refs. 9 and 11 for a discussion of RAIDs.*)

To get a sense of the cost-effectiveness of optical storage at the business level, note that the U.S. Congress Office of Technology Assessment reports that the annual cost of providing the Congressional Record to its repository libraries is $624 on paper, $84 on microfiche, and $10 on CD-ROM.[5] In the mid-1980s the claim was made that optical storage would revamp publishing; about a decade later that promise is closer to reality.

## 7.2 Optical Storage: Developments of the Last Decade

Figure 7.3 depicts the available optical storage technologies. Table 7.3 provides a brief description of each of these "standards."[12,13]

Laser video disks were introduced in the 1970s. About 30 min of analog video (54,000 frames) could be stored on one 12-in platter. The 12-cm Compact-Disk Digital Audio (CD-DA) was introduced by Philips-Sony in 1982. The laser video disk technology was adapted to store up to 72 min of high-quality *digitally encoded* stereophonic audio.

The first optical drives for computer applications appeared in 1982; these were used for large library and database archival functions.[14] CD-ROM drives as PC peripherals appeared in 1984–1985. They provide storage for 600 to 680 MB of prestored information, including text, pictures, databases, and data. CD-ROM drives can now be purchased as PC peripherals for $300–$1000.

---

*Four types of RAID systems are as follows:

- *RAID-0.*   Partitions of a file are written nonredundantly across all drives in the array. This approach, called disk striping, provides an independent array without parity redundancy, thereby achieving the best cost and maximum performance with no redundancy.

- *RAID-1.*   Provides full transparent mirroring: a file is written on two disks in the array. This provides the best reliability with independent support of each drive, with 50 percent usable data availability.

- *RAID-3.*   Provides an array of drives transferring data in parallel. Data is spread across the array and parity information is saved on another disk in the array. Any one drive failure out of $N$ is recoverable. This arrangement is applicable to applications using or generating large data blocks and requiring high speed (this includes scientific, imaging, and multimedia applications).

- *RAID-5.*   Provides an independent array of drives. Data and parity information are written to all drives without an assigned parity drive. Ideal for high I/O and on-line transactions.

A typical redundant tower (disk arrays) consists of 5, 10, 20, 35, or more (some up to 245) palm-sized removable drives, each with capacity from 40 MB to 2 GB. The array capacity can reach 70 GB or more (some systems provide up to 490 GB of on-line storage).

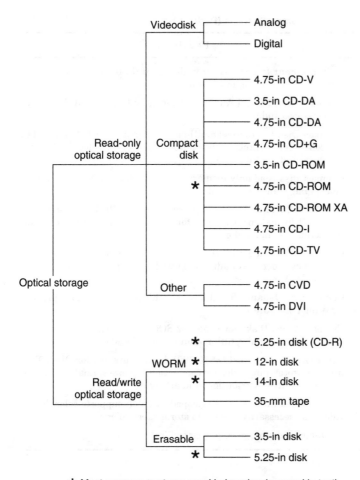

★ Most common systems used in imaging (covered in text).

**Figure 7.3**  Optical storage technologies.

At about the same time, writable optical disks (WORM) became available. These 12-in platters initially stored 1 GB per side of image (and/or video) information; now they can store about 6 GB, and 10-GB systems are expected by 1995. The disk is written by a laser beam; when the beam is turned on, it records the data in the form of pits or bubbles within a specific layer of the disk. The data is read back, as is the case in all optical media, by detecting the variations in reflectivity of the disk surface. One of the limitations of this technology has been its transfer rate of 100 to 200 kBps. New systems (e.g., Kodak's Optical Disk System 6800 Automated Disk Library) have transfer rates of 1 MBps.

TABLE 7.3    Optical Digital Storage Systems (Partial List)

| Technology | Description |
|---|---|
| CD+G | Enhancement to CD-DA: provides digital audio and still-frame graphics for television monitor display |
| CD-DA | Compact Disk Digital Audio: developed by Philips and Sony; consumer stereo audio |
| CD-I | Compact Disk Interactive: multimedia extension of CD-DA aimed at the consumer market; supports text, full-motion video, still video, graphics, and digital audio |
| CD-ROM | Compact-disk read-only memory: contains machine-readable audio, video, image, and textual information |
| CD-ROM XA | CD-ROM Extended Architecture: supports Philips, Sony, and Microsoft format, particularly for consumer market; stores data, text, graphics, and audio |
| CD-V | Compact Disk Video: Philips-Sony technology for consumer market; analog video and audio along with data (players can also utilize CD-DA) |
| CD-TV | Commodore Dynamic Total Vision: multimedia consumer product for Amiga computers |
| CVD | Compact Video Disk: developed by SOCS Research and Interactive Video Systems; analog full-motion video and audio |
| CD-R | CD recordable: low-cost (<$10,000) desktop presses for CD-ROMs; used for prototyping titles for conventional presses, final production disks for limited distribution, and archiving |
| DVI | Digital Video Interactive: developed by Intel; supports color digital video; not necessarily specific to storage technology |
| Optical tape | Digital optical storage on polyester film |

In 1986, specifications for Compact Disk Interactive (CD-I) were being developed for consumer market products supporting video, graphics, images, audio, data, text, and software. CD-I has been developed by Philips, Sony, and Microware. It is a *self-contained multimedia system* aimed principally at the consumer market.

In 1988 erasable (rewritable) optical disks became available. These disks store hundreds of megabytes of information on removable media, enabling the ready (but manual) distribution of digitally encoded imaging information; 5.25-in systems appeared first, followed by 3.5-in systems.

Organizations that need to develop CD-ROM disks for archival material can already do so in a cost-effective manner, using CD recordable (CD-R) technology that has reached the market in the early 1990s. Machines to create CD-ROMs can cost as little as $4000, enabling production of disks for $50 each.[15] Blank writable CDs can be purchased for around $20.

## 7.3  CD-ROMs

Digital data is stored in CD-ROM disks as microscopic pits and spaces. Stored data is read using a laser beam and interpreting the intensity of the light reflected from those pits and spaces as one or zero bits. The physical characteristics of CD-ROM disks were standardized in 1985 by the Sony-Philips *Yellow Book*. The logical file system used on CD-ROM disks follows the High-Sierra file system format (1986) and ISO 9660 (1988) standard. These formats specify file management procedures that compensate for the slow access times of CD-ROM drives. File contents are not specified; several kinds of information (e.g., images, text, audio, video) can be stored on CD-ROM disks.

As seen in Fig. 7.3, CD-ROM disks are available in 4.75- and 3.5-in forms. The 3.5-in CD-ROM disk can store about 180 MB of data, and the 4.75-in CD-ROM disk can store about 680 MB. The 3.5-in form is used in small portable systems such as laptop computers. CD-ROM drives are available as 5.25-in peripheral devices and use SCSIs (small computer system interfaces). Table 7.4 depicts a partial list of CD-ROM products available at press time.

There are a variety of CD-ROM formats not only at the physical level, as just noted, but also in terms of the file layout: the *Red Book* specifies CD-DA; the *Yellow Book* specifies the CD-ROM; the *Green Book* specifies the CD-I; and the *Orange Book* describes the CD-R. The basic specification for imaging applications in a DOS, Microsoft Windows, and OS/2 environment is the ISO 9660 already identified, which is an update of the High-Sierra format.[6] ISO 9660 describes the logical structure and file format for a CD-ROM, while the *Yellow Book* specification describes the manner in which the data is organized on the disk. The other formats are used in the multimedia environment.

**TABLE 7.4    Partial List of CD-ROM Products Selling for $1000 or Less (at Press Time)**

| Vendor and product | Cost,* in $1000 |
|---|---|
| CD Technology, Porta-Drive T3301 | <1 |
| Liberty Systems, 115CD-P | <1 |
| NEC, CDR-73M | <1 |
| Panasonic, LK-MC501S | <1 |
| Pinnacle Micro, PCD-102 | <0.5 |
| PLI, CD ROM 10305 | <1 |
| Procom Technology, MCD ROM650 | <0.5 |
| Sony, System CDU7205 | <1 |
| Texel, DM-5021 | <1 |
| Todd, TCDR-7000 | <1 |
| Toshiba, TXM-3301E | <1 |

*Discounts of 30 to 35 percent are typically achievable.

Philips worked on the extension of the *Yellow Book,* to interleave text, sound, and video for CD-I. The resulting *Green Book* specifies not only the data format but also specific playback requirements. Sony and Microsoft now support a subset of CD-I called CD-ROM-XA, which provides standards for a number of compression modes, allowing continuous audio while textual data is read through, supporting interleaving of text and sound.

There are a number of factors helping CD-ROM technology become part of business systems now being introduced:[6]

- Information in digital format is becoming widely available, driven by advances in desktop publishing. An increasing amount of historical information is now being converted into electronic form, via either imaging or OCR techniques. Additionally, digital audio and video compression techniques are enabling the introduction of CD-ROMs for multimedia-based applications.

- Sophisticated software techniques have been developed to support optimized searches and retrieval of information, in spite of the relatively slower operation of a CD-ROM drive.

- Development software for CD-ROM, including indexing, conversion, authoring, and formatting (per ISO 9660), can now be utilized by nontechnical personnel.

As already discussed, a CD-ROM drive is basically a CD-DA player enhanced with more elaborate data error detection and correction capabilities, data buffers, and SCSIs. CD-ROM applications search for data randomly while CD-DA applications are more sequential in nature; i.e., music in CD-DA players is played from beginning to end. Therefore, the internal components of CD-ROM drives must be more rugged and reliable than those used in CD-DA players. Moreover, an additional loading mechanism is needed in CD-ROM drives to load the caddy that is used to protect the CD-ROM disk. There are two CD-ROM drive designs at the disk-feeder level: (1) Sony-style CD-ROM caddy case and (2) traditional tray- or drawer-configured players based on the CD-DA design. Caddies protect the disks from hand-transferred oils and dust; however, disk loading is more cumbersome (particularly for cases of high exchange activity). Tray designs facilitate CD-ROM handling, but may allow dirt and dust to enter the drive mechanism. Self-cleaning lenses and double doors may be utilized to minimize the influx of foreign particles.

CD-ROMs can store as much as 680 MB of information in a compact, portable optical medium (for comparison, a WORM disk can store 6.55 GB—3.2 GB per side; to read the opposite side, the platter needs to be flipped robotically or manually; otherwise systems with dual-sided

TABLE 7.5   Typical Storage Capacities

| Medium | Size, in | Minimum capacity, MB | Maximum capacity, MB* |
|---|---|---|---|
| CD-ROM† | 4.75 | 128 | 1000 |
| Hard drive | N/A | 20 | 800 |
| Magnetic floppy | 3.5 | 0.7 | 1.4 |
| Magnetic floppy | 5.25 | 0.35 | 1.2 |
| Rewritable and erasable | 3.5 | 128 | 256 |
| Rewritable and erasable | 5.25 | 512 | 1024 |
| WORM | 5.25 | 600 | 6000 |
| WORM | 12 | 4400 | 9000 |
| WORM | 14 | 6800 | 10,200 |

*At press time.
†Typical capacity 650 MB.

readheads can be utilized). The current generation of CD-ROM drives can deliver data at a (maximum) rate of 150 kBps. Table 7.5 depicts typical storage capacities for optical disks; for comparison, magnetic media are also included.[12] The access time of most drives is between 300 and 500 ms, compared with 16 ms on a magnetic hard drive. (Some CD-ROM drives that were on the market in the recent past were rather slow, having an access speed of 850 ms.) Consequently, the access speed is 10 to 30 times slower than that of a hard drive. Improvements are being made; some models now reaching the market have access time in the 200-ms range. While for applications involving only text transfer or low-resolution images (e.g., BISs) the user can utilize a slower, and hence, less expensive unit, multimedia applications involving video and graphics, as well as DIS and SIS imaging applications, require the faster units. These relatively slow access times in CD-ROM drives are the result of having to move the readhead continuously in search of data usually requested in random order and located in non-contiguous areas of a disk's surface. Optical drives with new lighter readhead designs are starting to appear for improved performance characteristics.

CD-ROM data files are laid down sequentially; this implies that sustained transfer rates are generally more important than average access time, particularly when dealing with nontext data. A slow drive can severely impact an imaging application, particularly when there are multiple images in a document or when high-resolution imaging is needed. As noted, progress is being made in developing CD-ROM drives with shorter access time.

SCSI is the channel interface found on PC disk drives, as well as on a variety of peripherals such as tape drives, optical disk drives, and image scanners. SCSI provides a high-level message-based protocol for communication between "initiators" and "targets."[9] This SCSI protocol (now known as *SCSI-1*) has been revised to achieve higher performance. The SCSI-1 uses a 10-MHz clock rate supporting transfers at 5 MBps. The new SCSI interface, SCSI-2 (also known as *fast SCSI*), uses a 20-MHz clock rate to support 10 MBps. Newly announced high-performance disk systems support SCSI-2. There is also a *wide SCSI* supporting transfer of 16-bit words (32 bits when using a second cable) rather than 8-bit words as is customary in SCSI-1; this interface supports transfer rates at 20 MBps. SCSI-2 is an expansion and enhancement of SCSI-1; consequently, a high degree of compatibility exists between the two standards.

SCSI-1 (ANSI X3.131-1986) was developed starting in 1982 and was completed with the publication of the standard in 1986. SCSI was based on a commercially available interface, that had been developed to provide a device-independent peripheral attachment. ANSI X3T9.2 extended the commercial interface in a number of ways: extended the reach to 25 m; added a 4-MBps synchronous transfer option; added an optional extended set for large storage devices; added inquiry commands to allow for self-configuring driver software; and added command sets for magnetic tapes, printers, optical disks, and processors.[17] Examples of commands are Read, Write, Track Select, Rewind, Request Sense, Read Block Limits, Write File Marks, Recover Buffer Data, Release Unit, Copy, Erase, Send Diagnostic, Locate, Read Position, Compare, Copy and Verify, and Read Buffer. Work on SCSI-2 started in 1985, as some vendors sought to increase the functionality of SCSI-1. SCSI-2 added many new options, made several others mandatory, and eliminated obsolete SCSI-1 features. New features and improvements include (in addition to those listed in the previous paragraph): command queueing (up to 256 commands per initiator), high-density connector to improve signal quality, asynchronous event notification, addition of new commands to support CD-ROMs, scanners, WORMs, medium changer, and communication devices.[17] There is also a SCSI-3 effort (the first draft appeared in 1992) to allow operating systems to support both SCSI-1 and SCSI-2 command sets.

Applications are designed to minimize the distances the readhead must travel to access related data. Some new CD-ROM drives come with cache memory, typically 64 kB of RAM, to reduce the access times of frequently requested data even further. These buffers are used also to smooth out the fluctuations in the data transfer rate for better quality and performance when running applications. The standard data transfer rate for CD audio files is 150 kBps. This data transfer rate is relatively slow for handling high-resolution imaging files (and also for multimedia applications where 30 frames per second need to be fetched). If processor overhead is considered, the average data transfer rate in most CD-ROM drives is about 90 to 100 kBps.

Some CD-ROM drives support different data transfer rates for different information types. For instance, some drives support 300-kBps data transfer rates for multimedia files and support the 150-kBps data transfer rate for audio files.

**Server aspects.** Multiworkstation access to CD-ROM drives over the network is not well supported because of the lack of standard client-server computing systems for CD-ROM (see Sec. 7.7). A CD-ROM drive is usually connected to a file server or workstation host that provides network access to one workstation at a time. Additional hardware and/or software are required to support shared multiworkstation access. A typical product used for this purpose is basically a stack of CD-ROM drives arranged in a pedestal configuration.

**Production aspects.** The traditional way to produce a CD-ROM is via the mastering and replication process. CD-ROMs can be mastered for $2000 and replicated for $2 each.[16] Mastering requires the creation of a metal stamp that is then utilized in an injection-molding machine. Replication is the process of injection-molding replicas from the stamp. A specialized environment is required. Steps associated with CD-ROM production are shown in Table 7.6.

Some studies have been undertaken on the costs associated with CD-ROM production. Figure 7.4 depicts the results from one such study. (Consult Ref. 5 for specific assumptions.)

Premastering has traditionally been a costly step in the CD-ROM production phase. Until recently a CD-ROM premastering system cost $100,000; now a PC-based system costs about $10,000, as discussed next.[5]

## 7.4  CD Recordable

CD-Rs are desktop-recordable systems (drives and media) that provide low-cost "printing presses" for three kinds of applications: (1) prototyping titles that eventually may go to a conventional press, (2) final production of disks that have limited distribution (possibly even only one copy), and (3) archiving.[18] The CD-ROM drive is attached to a PC or workstation. CD-R techniques allow a user to produce CD-ROM replicas in low-volume quantities. Once a CD-R disk is produced, it can be used on a traditional CD-ROM drive; data is indexed and organized the same way as it would be on a CD-ROM. The software needed for formatting the data for CD-ROM production is often provided with the CD-R drive. In contrast with the mastering technique discussed briefly above, CD-R blanks can be recorded locally in a single step. The CD-R is immediately usable.

TABLE 7.6    Steps Required for CD-ROM Production

| | |
|---|---|
| Information base creation | This step can, in many situations, be considered to be external to the imaging effort; e.g., it may entail collecting photos of items that may need to be included in a catalog |
| Data preparation, conversion, and verification | This step entails organizing the data in a manner appropriate for storage, including conversion to electronic format, indexing, and verification and editing |
| Premastering | This step involves formatting the information base so that it conforms to the ISO 9660 CD-ROM format; each block of information is formatted; the sector address is determined; error detection and correction codes are added |
| Mastering | This step involves making an original CD-ROM by employing a laser to etch pits into the surface of a glass master disk coated with appropriate substances; the master is used to make metal stampers that are then used to make duplicate copies of the CD-ROM |
| Replication | This step actually generates the duplicate copies of the CD-ROM; replication is based on techniques developed by the audio industry |

CD-R technology provides the benefits of CD-ROM approaches, while improving the economics and rapidity of production and distribution. Users are able to eliminate the mastering costs and expedite the turnaround time compared with traditional CD-ROM production. Because the production is done in-house, security and confidentiality are increased. CD-R systems have been available for a number of years, but were expensive (e.g., $60,000). Now systems are available for $3000–$14,000. Table 7.7 depicts a small selection for illustration purposes.

CD-R media are the same size as CD-ROM and, once installed into a CD-ROM drive, are indistinguishable from a traditional CD-ROM. A

```
Data preparation: $12,000–$24,000
Index and premaster: $6000–$82,000
Master: $2000–$3000
Replicate: $1000–$2000
Total: $21,000–$111,000

Cost per CD-ROM: $42–$222

Assumptions
    Production run: 500 CD-ROMs
    Content: text only (cost for video or image is higher)
```

Figure 7.4    Cost associated with CD-ROM production.

**TABLE 7.7    Small Selection of CD-R Products\* for Illustration Purposes**

| | |
|---|---|
| Philips | CDD 521 ≈ $8000 |
| Sony | CD-900W |
| JVC | Personal RomMaker ≈ $12,500 |
| | Personal Archiver ≈ $10,000 |
| Pinnacle Micro | RCD 202 ≈ $5000 |

\*See Ref. 18 for additional information.

CD-R disk has a gold reflective layer, in contrast with the silver layer used in CD-ROMs. Table 7.8 provides some highlights of the features of CD-R compared to competitive technologies such as WORM and MO.

The first generation of CD-R drives was introduced in the United States in 1989. This generation of equipment was capable of writing the entire disk in one session. (Once a section of a CD-R disk has been written, it cannot be altered.) These devices recorded the disk in real time, requiring over an hour of recording time to write one disk. The second generation of equipment can record at two speeds: real time and twice real time.

Blank CD-R media are available in ether 540 MB or 630 MB; therefore, the CD-R media are not produced at the outer limits of the *Red Book* and *Yellow Book* specifications. Only the best CD-R drives can record the 630-MB media, particularly at twice real time.

With first-generation systems, once the recording of a track on a CD-R disk has started, the entire track must be recorded in one session;

**TABLE 7.8    Comparison of CD-R and Competitive Technologies**

| | |
|---|---|
| CD-R | Standardized format: archived data playable on any CD-ROM drive |
| | Incremental, file-oriented write-update capability not yet implemented (ECMA\* 168 specification); user must "write" a large amount of data at a time |
| | Not fast enough for interactive use |
| | More expensive (≈ $10,000) compared to WORM (≈ $4000) and MO (≈ $4500) |
| WORM | Interchangeability problems |
| | Market being eroded by MO technology (sales of 5 ¼-in systems: 40,000 units in 1992 to 1000 in 1997) |
| | 12-in systems with 6.5-GB capacity (and packageable in jukeboxes[1]) not threatened by CD-R |
| MO | Proprietary aspects (Bernoulli, Syquest) |
| | Increasing market (sales of 5 ¼-in systems: 170,000 units in 1992 to 400,000 in 1997) |
| | Multifunction MO drives (e.g., HP, Sony, Hitachi): standard MO media as well as WORM support |

\*European Computer Manufacturer's Association.

hence, the computer system driving the CD-R drive must be able to sustain the CD-R I/O rate. This rate is 150 kBps for real-time systems and 300 kBps for twice-real-time systems. If the PC, its magnetic media, the PC software and operating system, or the network is not able to sustain the throughput, the CD-R drive will abort the recording and the disk will be useless. (Clearly, this is more of a consideration in the twice-real-time situations.) Some vendors may not guarantee a high rate of success in the recording operation; others precheck the layout of files on magnetic disk and estimate the success rate; still others fully buffer the CD-ROM image in a magnetic disk dedicated to the CD-R operations.[19] First-generation systems cost in the $60,000 range. The newest CD-Rs allow multiple write sessions. Although a section cannot be altered once it is written, these drives allow the user to append information to already (partially) recorded disks. These systems can be purchased in the $3000–$14,000 range. Blank media currently sell for $40 each; the price is projected to fall to $10 by 1996.

## 7.5  Rewritable and Erasable Systems

MO is based on a combination of magnetic and optical recording techniques and supports erasable storage. The disk is composed of a material that becomes more sensitive to magnetic fields at high temperatures. A laser beam is used to heat up the appropriate section of the disk surface; once heated, a magnetic field is used to record on the surface. Optical techniques are used for reading the information off the disk by detecting how the laser beam is deflected by different magnetizations of the disk surface.[9]

First-generation 5 1/4-in *rewritable* optical disk drives cost $4600 in 1991 and $3000 at the end of 1992. In 1991 there was only one second-generation 3 1/2-in rewritable optical disk drive. At the end of 1992 there were over 30 products to choose from, many selling for less that $1500. The 5 1/4-in systems can store as much as 1 GB, with 500 MB per side (650 MB—i.e., 325 MB per side—is more typical, however), while 3 1/2-in systems can store 128 MB (256 MB expected by 1993). They can be rewritten over 100,000 times. Most erasable optical drives use magnetooptical mechanisms; however, systems that do not require magnetization, e.g., phase-change methods, are appearing. Rewritable optical storage can be very cost-effective (e.g., for archiving): $0.13 per MB compared with $1.25 per MB for removable hard drives. About 400,000 3 1/2-in drives were expected to be sold in 1994 worldwide, equating to $260 million, and 700,000 in 1997, equating to $500 million.

The 3 1/2-in drive systems have a much faster access time than do the larger MO drives; the access time is comparable to that of magnetic hard drives. For example, the 256-MB systems have average seek time of 35 ms and an average access time of 45 ms. The recording process is as follows.[14] The disk utilized in MO recording has a thin film of magnetic material that responds to a biased magnetic field when heated to its Curie point (200°C) by a focused laser beam. Recording is performed in two stages: (1) erasing an area and (2) writing information into that area. Erasing of data occurs when the bias magnet is turned on in the erase direction, and a continuous laser beam heats the magnetic layer of the medium to its Curie point. Writing into an erased area occurs when the bias magnet is polarized from the erase direction to the write direction. A data bit is formed when the laser emits a high-energy burst at a selected spot within the erased area. As the laser heats the spot, the magnetic properties held within the thin film of the magnetic material are altered; these alterations create a different light reflection when read by the laser, and are interpreted as 1 bits (unchanged selected spots are read as 0 bits). Once the data has been written, it stays there permanently until a strong magnetic field and high localized heat is applied. Retrieval of data in MO recording is similar to the process of reading data from a CD-ROM.

High-end writable videodisk recorders can cost in the $40,000 range. Some systems aimed at the broadcast industry can store 58,000 frames per side or 32 min of full-motion video. The disk can be re-recorded more than 1 million times without signal degradation; the disks, however, are fairly expensive, costing approximately $1300.

One drawback of this technology is read-write speed. For example, it typically takes 19 to 60 s to write a 3-MB file, and 16 to 33 s to read the same file (depending on model and/or product).[20] This relatively slow speed depends on three factors:

1. Magnetooptical methods require a three-pass procedure to write data: (a) erasure of existing data, (b) writing of new data, and (c) verification of the integrity of the operation.

2. Since laser-based assemblies are expensive, optical drives contain only one assembly, in contrast with hard-disk drives that have multiple read-write assemblies to operate on multiple platters simultaneously.

3. Laser-based assemblies are larger and heavier than hard-drive read-write heads, thus slowing down physical movement.

Techniques used to speed up the process include (1) turning off the verify cycle, (2) using RAM caches, (3) using new split-head optics (a lighter head where only one prism, the laser, and the sensor are on the actual head), and (4) increasing the spindle speed (from 2400 to 3600 rpm, and as high as 5400 rpm). Throughput as high as 2 MBps is being claimed on some units.[20]

TABLE 7.9    Typical Parameters* of Rewritable Magnetooptical
Media

| | |
|---|---|
| Rotation speed | 3000–3600 rpm |
| Average access time | 35–45 ms |
| Data buffer memory | 64–256 kbps |
| Sustained data transfer rate | 600–1000 MBps |
| Maximum data transfer rate | 1.5–2.5 MBps |
| Disk diameter | 90–130 mm ($3\,^1/_2$–$5\,^1/_4$ in) |
| Disk cost | $100–$270 |
| Drive cost | $2500–$5000 |

*Data at press time.

MO disk drives and media are now used in a variety of data-storage
applications, including imaging. They have a burst data rate of 1.25
MBps, sustained rates of 0.5 MBps, and average access time of around
50 ms (including latency); see Table 7.9. They are characterized as providing removability, high capacity, and random-access capabilities.[19]
MOs are being used for "direct-access secondary storage." The drives
have a small footprint and therefore are amenable to desktop applications. The cost is around $0.30 per megabyte. (This compares with $3
per megabyte for primary magnetic storage on fixed disks.) The information transfer rate is similar to those of conventional magnetic disks,
while the access time is still slower than that of a magnetic disk. (This
is driven by the relatively bulky read-write mechanism.)

The density of MO media is expected to increase in the future, while
the access time is expected to decrease. The performance characteristics are a function of the following four factors: (1) optics of drive, (2)
mechanics of drive, (3) electronics of drive, and (4) media substrate configuration. All these factors will see technical improvements in the next
few years. For example, in late 1993 IBM announced a prototype blue-
laser (at 428 nm) optical recording system that can store data on disks
at about 390 million bits per square centimeter; this is about a fivefold
increase in density compared to the current state-of-the-art rewritable
optical disk drives. At this density a $5\,^1/_4$-in optical disk could store 3.25
GB of data. Currently, systems use the infrared range at 780–830 nm.

## 7.6   Optical Jukeboxes

Systems are now being deployed for generic archival, as well as imaging archival, applications that provide relatively rapid access to large
amounts of data stored on removable optical or magnetic media. Many
CD-ROMs and/or WORMs can be housed in a jukebox, as already noted
in Chap. 2. Systems already support 240 CD-ROMs (using multiple drives—disk access time is 8 to 14 s). A CD-ROM jukebox supporting 60
disks can be purchased for about $8000; a CD-ROM jukebox support-

ing 240 disks can be purchased for about $20,000.[21] Practitioners note that 5 1/4-in jukeboxes are not as reliable as the 12-in ones. Large jukeboxes can cost around $150,000.

This type of archiving is accomplished by storing the media on shelves that can be accessed by robotic handlers. When a file needs to be retrieved, the file management system identifies where it can be found within the tape or optical library; the robotic handler exchanges the currently loaded media with the one containing the file in question. The completely automated procedure typically takes a few seconds. High-end systems (e.g., Kodak's Optical Disk System 6800 Automated Disk Library) can support up to one hundred fifty 14-in platters and can therefore store 1000 GB (1 TB); this equates to 3 GB for each side of the 150 platters.

## 7.7 Client-Server Issues

Many users are deploying CD-ROM drives and/or jukeboxes as servers in a client-server environment (particularly with NetWare, at least for BISs), as seen in Chap. 2. In this architecture, the storage and search engine (server) is separated from the user interface running of the user's device (client); the client may have to support a fairly sophisticated graphical interface.

A client-server protocol is required to make this work. Four proposals specifically aimed at CD-ROM servers were under consideration at press time:[22]

- *DSX.* The CD-ROM Database Exchange Standard, proposed by SilverPlatter, Inc.

- *CD-RDX.* CD-ROM Read-Only Data Exchange, proposed by the Information Handling Committee of the U.S. Intelligence Community.

- *SFQL.* Structured full-text query language, proposed by the aerospace industry.

- *Z39.50.* Information retrieval service definition and protocol specifications for library applications, proposed by the library community.

Observers expect resolution of this issue by 1995 or 1996.

## 7.8 Some Practical Issues on Long-term Storage of Images

Some observers are concerned about the long-term retention of image archives given the continual changes in file formats and computer technology. Much of the information collected in the past 30 years is already "stranded on computer tape from primitive or discarded systems—unintelligible or soon to be so."[23]

ANSI standards for photography [e.g., ANSI IT9.1-1988, *Imaging Media (film), Silver-gelatin Type Specifications for Stability*; ANSI PH1.43-1985, *Photography (film), Processed Safety Film-storage*] define archival photographs as "having permanent value when stored under archival conditions"; most observers take the word "permanent" to mean 100 or more years. Techniques have been developed to extend the durability of (traditional) silver halide photographic material; these techniques entail, among other factors, storage in reduced temperature and humidity environments. On the other hand, many fear that achievable life expectancy of electronic media will be less than 100 years. Not only are the media volatile to various degrees, but the media formats and the file formats represent other potential problems. Magnetic tape, CD-ROMs, WORMs, and MOs all are subject to long-term degradation. As discussed in Chap. 4, dozens of file formats are available, including EPS, PCX, PICT, RIFF, and TIFF. Even when the same image compression schemes are used, for example, JPEG, one system's file may not be read on another system. (This, in fact, was the recent motivation for developing the JPEG File Interchange Format, JFIF.) Observers wonder if in 20, 50, or 100 years current PC operating systems such as MS-DOS, Windows, UNIX, and file formats will be around. For example, music in 8-track tape format or video in Beta format may be lost at some point in the near future if the material is available only in those forms. For example, NASA has already lost 225 computerized images of Mars, Venus, Jupiter, and Saturn.[23]

Standards and techniques to assure some level of continuity and permanence are being sought; without these, the twenty-first-century version of the archeologist may well be "digging" computer tapes rather than soil and sea.

## References

1. S. Ranade, *Jukebox and Robotic Libraries for Computer Mass Storage*, Meckler, Westport, CT, 1992.
2. J. P. Roth, *Case Studies of Optical Storage Applications*, Meckler, Westport, CT, 1991.
3. S. Ranade, *Mass Storage Technologies*, Meckler, Westport, CT, 1991.
4. W. Saffady, *Optical Storage Technology 1992—a State of the Art Review*, Meckler, Westport, CT, 1992.
5. T. J. Thiel, "Costs Of CD-ROM Production—What They Are and How to Overcome Them," *CD-ROM Professional*, March 1993, pp. 43 ff.
6. H. Nabil, "CD-ROM Supports Multimedia Applications on the Notebook," *Computer Technology Review*, February 1993, pp. 91 ff.
7. N. K. Herther, "Finding Better Ways to Manage New Media," *CD-ROM Professional*, March 1993, pp. 8 ff.
8. T. Halfhill, "Buying a CD-ROM Drive," *Byte*, February 1993, p. 120.

9. R. H. Katz, "High-Performance Network and Channel Based Storage," *Proceedings of the IEEE,* August 1992, Vol. 80, No. 8, pp. 1238 ff.

10. F. Richardson, "Hierarchical Storage Management: New Model for Network Storage," *Computer Technology Review,* February 1993, pp. 75 ff.

11. O. I. Unna, "Implementing RAID in Cross-Platform Environments," *Computer Technology Review,* February 1993, pp. 43 ff.

12. B. Wiggins, "Document Image Processing—an Overview," *Document Image Automation,* Fall 1992, Vol.12, No. 3.

13. D. Minoli and B. Keinath, *Distributed Multimedia through Broadband Communication Services,* Artech House, Norwood, MA, 1994.

14. L. Payne, "Increased Capacities and Speeds Spur Growth of 3.5-in Optical," *Computer Technology Review,* February 1993, pp. 97 ff.

15. *MACWEEK,* March 1, 1993, p. 7.

16. Dataware Technologies Inc., "CD-R: The Next Stage in CD-ROM Evolution," *CD-ROM Professional,* March 1993, pp. 79 ff.

17. B. A. McFalls, "SCSI-2 Command Sets Address New Device Type Requirements," *Computer Technology Review,* February 1993, pp. 67 ff.

18. J. Udell, "Start the Presses," *Byte,* February 1993, pp. 116 ff.

19. A. Anderson, "Rewritable Magneto-Optical Disk Technology: The Best is Yet to Come," *Document Image Automation,* September–October 1991, pp. 281 ff.

20. C. Piller, "Optical Update," *MacWorld,* November 1992, pp. 124 ff.

21. A. Streeter, "Kubik Jukebox Spins up 240 CDs on Four Drives," *MACWEEK,* March 8, 1993, p. 10.

22. K. Clark, "CD-ROM Retrieval Software: The Year 1992 in Review," *CD-ROM Professional,* March 1993, pp. 130 ff.

23. J. Wallace, "Considerations Regarding the Long-Term Storage of Electronic Images," *Journal of Electronic Imaging,* January 1993, pp. 35 ff.

Chapter

# 8

# Local Area Networks: Imaging Platforms

The installation of LANs in corporate America has advanced at a rapid pace during the past decade, and is expected to continue to grow well into the 1990s. LANs provide high-speed, low-cost communication over limited distances, linking terminals, PCs, workstations, and servers in a building, or in a group of closely located buildings. LANs have access to regional, national, and international networks using bridges and routers. As noted in Chap. 2, many of the BISs, DISs, EIS, and SISs now being deployed are LAN-based. The purpose of this chapter is to provide a basic overview of LAN technology. The chapter focuses on a few key LAN concepts, without added reference to the specific imaging implications already given in Chap. 2. We are intentionally brief, referring the reader needing more information to dozens of recent LAN textbooks, including Ref. 1, on which this chapter is based.

LAN technology has encompassed three generations. *First-generation* technology spanned the period covering the mid-1970s to late 1980s. Many corporations have deployed or are still deploying these "legacy" LANs based on coaxial cable or twisted-pair cable media. These LANs can support, among other applications, BISs and EISs. *Second-generation* technology emerged in the late 1980s to early 1990s, and is based on shared fiberoptic cable media. These LANs can support BISs, EISs, and DISs. *Third-generation* LANs are now beginning to become commercially available, and may see major deployment in the mid-1990s to support new high-bandwidth applications such as multimedia, video, and desk-to-desk videoconferencing. These networks will also be able to support BISs, EISs, DISs, and SISs. The transmission speed achievable with LANs varies from 4 to 16 Mbps for first-generation LANs; 100 Mbps for second-generation LANs; and Gbps rates for

third-generation LANs now under development. The need to interconnect collocated and/or remotely located LANs has emerged as a key
need of the 1990s. The trend is toward enterprisewide networking
where all departments of a company are interconnected with a seamless (backbone) network, allowing companywide access of all information and hardware resources.

## 8.1 LAN Technologies

*First-generation* LANs were developed in the early 1970s to provide
what was then considered high-speed local connectivity among user
devices. The contention-based Ethernet LAN technology was brought
to the market by a joint effort among Xerox, Intel, and Digital
Equipment Corporation. Ethernet initially employed coaxial cable
arranged in a logical bus, operating at 10 Mbps; now, thin coaxial and
twisted-pair cables are used. Extensive standardization work has been
done by the Institute of Electrical and Electronic Engineers (IEEE) in
the past 15 years, leading to well-known standards such as the IEEE
802.2, 802.3, 802.4, and 802.5.

In the early 1980s, a token bus and a token ring technology were also
developed, operating at 4 Mbps. (A 16-Mbps system is also available.)
The token medium-sharing discipline is a variant of the polling method
common in traditional data networks; however, instead of centrally
controlled polling, the token is passed from station to station in an
equitable manner. Only the LAN user possessing the token can transmit. Token-based LANs have penetrated some office environments,
such as for access to IBM's mainframes. Token ring systems took the
approach of using (shielded) twisted-pair wires as the underlying
medium, mainly because such a medium is cheaper and simpler to
install than coaxial cable. Unshielded twisted-pair (UTP) is now the
dominant LAN medium for traditional LANs. Over the past decade, the
cost of connecting a user to a LAN decreased from about $1000 to less
than $200. Ethernet cards costing $100 are appearing on the market;
16-Mbps token ring adapter cards range in price from $700 to $900.

Higher network performance is required in order to support the
applications now being put on line by organizations, including imaging
applications. One way of increasing the bandwidth available to applications is to replace the existing network with one based on FDDI.
Efforts on *second-generation* LANs started in the early 1980s; products
began to enter the market in the late 1980s. This token-based back-
bone-campus technology extends LANs' features in terms of the geographic radius, now covering a campus, as well as in the speed, now
reaching 100 Mbps. Implementors initially settled on multimode fiber

as the underlying medium, although support for single-mode fiber was added in the late 1980s.

One factor that has slowed down the deployment of FDDI systems has been the cost of the interface cards. The cost of connecting a user to a FDDI LAN started out at about $8000 and is now around $900 to $1500. Efforts to facilitate the use of twisted-pair copper wires for FDDI have been under way, in order to bring the station access cost down. (Copper-based interfaces cost in the $500–$700 range.) While standards work in this arena has been slow in picking up speed, progress has been made in the recent past. At publication time there were also suggestions for a new 100-Mbps Ethernet technology as a second-generation system.

Starting in 1990, efforts have been underway to develop *third-generation* LANs supporting gigabit-per-second speeds (0.2 to 0.6 Gbps) over UTP or fiber facilities.[2] These efforts are based on ATM principles; the project is known as *Local ATM* and is sponsored by industry vendors under the auspices of the ATM Forum. ATM principles are discussed in the next chapter in the context of wide area networking; the same technology is being applied in the premises networking context using evolving ATM-based hubs and switches. ATM switches to support high-end workstations were already appearing in 1992. Workstation manufacturers are developing interface cards to connect their equipment to ATM switches. Initial costs may be around $4000 per port, but these costs should come down considerably (to $1000) in the next couple of years as chipsets emerge.

Table 8.1 summarizes some of the features of these three generations of LAN technology.[1] Given the preceding discussion, one should not assume that traditional LANs will disappear from the business landscape. There will be a continued need for text-based business functions. However, as companies move to image-based operations using BISs, DISs, and SISs (PACSs in particular), the higher-speed systems will be required.

## 8.2  LAN Basics

### 8.2.1  LAN topologies

There are three major physical LAN topologies: star, ring, and bus. A *star* network is joined at a single point, generally with central control (such as a wiring hub). In a *ring* network the nodes are linked into a continuous circle on a common cable, and signals are passed unidirectionally around the circle from node to node, with signal regeneration at each node. A *bus* network is a single line of cable to which the nodes are connected directly by taps. It is normally employed with distributed

TABLE 8.1     Typical Features of LANs

| Generation | Speed, Mbps | Equipment | Interconnection speed and services | Applications |
|---|---|---|---|---|
| First | 4–16 (Ethernet; token ring) | Terminals; PCs; workstations | 9.6, 56 kbps; T1; frame relay; SMDS | Office automation; decision support business functions as accounting (spreadsheets), project management, etc.; mainframe access; manufacturing; some imaging applications (BISs, EISs, and some DISs) |
| Second | 100 (FDDI) | PCs; high-end workstations; high-end servers (CD-ROM and WORM image servers) | Fractional T1; T1; T3; SMDS | Backbone interconnection of LANs; CAD/CAM graphics; imaging (BISs, EISs, DISs, and SISs) |
| Third | 52–622* | High-end workstations; video equipment; high-end servers (CD-ROMs, WORM jukeboxes) | SONET; B-ISDN/cell relay; SMDS | Multimedia; desk-to-desk multimedia conferencing; multimedia messaging; CAD/CAM; visualization; animation; imaging; LAN-based video training; supercomputer and scientific applications |

*More in the future.

control, but it can also be based on central control. Unlike the ring, however, a bus is passive, which means that the signals are not regenerated and retransmitted at each node.

Other configuration variations are available, particularly when looking at the LAN from a physical perspective: the *star-shaped ring* and the *star-shaped bus*. The first variation represents a wiring methodology to facilitate physical management: at the logical level the network is a ring; at the physical level it is a star centralized at some convenient point. Similarly, the second variation provides a logical bus, but wired in a star configuration using wiring hubs. Table 8.2 summarizes the use of these topologies in the three generations of LANs.

### 8.2.2   Medium-sharing disciplines

As discussed, in traditional LANs there are two common ways of ensuring that nodes gain orderly access to the network, and that no more

TABLE 8.2    LAN Topologies

| LAN | Early | Recent |
|---|---|---|
| 1st generation, broadband | Bus | Bus |
| 1st generation, Ethernet | Bus | Star-shaped bus |
| 1st generation, token ring | Ring | Star-shaped ring |
| 2d generation | Fiber double ring | Star-shaped double ring |
| 3d generation | Star-based access segments | — |

than one node at a time gains control of the shared LAN channel. The first is by the contention method; the second is by the token variant of polling.

The contention method is known as *carrier sense multiple access with collision detection* (CSMA/CD). If a node has a message to send, it checks the shared-medium network until it senses that it is traffic-free, and then it transmits. However, since all the nodes in the network have the right to contend for access, the node keeps monitoring the network to determine if a competing signal has been transmitted simultaneously with its own. If a second node is indeed transmitting, the two signals will collide. Both nodes detect the collision, stop transmitting, and wait for a random time before attempting to regain access.

Token-based LANs avoid the collisions inherent in Ethernet by requiring each node to defer transmission until it receives a token. The token is a control packet that is circulated around the network from node to node, in a preestablished sequence, when no transmission is otherwise taking place. The token signifies exclusive right to transmission, and no node can send data without it. Each node constantly monitors the network to detect any data frame addressed to it. When the token is received by a node, and the node has nothing to send, the node passes it along to the next node in the sequence. If the token is accepted, it is passed on after the node has completed transmitting the data it has in its buffer. The token must be surrendered to the successor node within a specific time, so that no node can monopolize the network resources. Each node knows the address of the predecessor and the successor.

Token technology has been adopted by vendors, such as IBM and Novell, while the Ethernet technology has been brought to the market by DEC and many smaller vendors.

### 8.2.3   Lower-layer LAN protocols

In a LAN environment, layer 1 and 2 functions of the OSI reference model (OSIRM) have been defined by (1) the IEEE 802 standards for first-generation LANs; (2) ANSI X3T9.5 for second-generation LANs;

and (3) industry groups such as the ATM Forum, Exchange Carriers Standards Association T1S1, and ITU-T (the last two bodies having standardized the supporting ATM functions) for third-generation LANs.

Using "internetworking" protocols defined at layer 3 (such as IP—internet protocol) and connection-oriented (this concept is defined in the next subsection) transport layer protocols (such as TCP—transmission control protocol), one can build the LAN protocol suite up to layer 7 in order to support functions like e-mail, file transfer, and directory. The use of TCP/IP has been commercially common for the *upper layers,* particularly for LANs interconnected via the internet.

Because LANs are based on a shared medium, the link layer is split into two sublayers. These sublayers are the medium access control (MAC) and the logical link control (LLC). The LLC sublayer provides a medium-independent interface to higher layers. The MAC procedure is part of the protocol that governs access to the transmission medium. This is done independently of the physical characteristics of the medium, but taking into account the topological aspects of the subnetwork. Different IEEE 802 MAC standards represent different protocols used for sharing the medium. (IEEE 802.3 is the contention-based Ethernet and IEEE 802.5 is the token-based system.) See Table 8.3.

### 8.2.4  Connectionless versus connection-oriented communication

Two basic forms of operation (service) are possible for both LANs and WANs: *connection-oriented mode* and *connectionless mode.*

A connection-oriented service involves a connection establishment phase, an information transfer phase, and a connection termination phase. This implies that a logical connection is set up between end sys-

TABLE 8.3  Functions at Specified Protocol Levels

| | |
|---|---|
| LLC | Reliable transfer of frames |
| | Connection to higher layers |
| MAC | Addressing |
| | Frame construction |
| | Token and collision handling |
| PHY* | Encoding and decoding |
| | Clocking |
| PMD† | Cable parameters (optical and electrical) |
| | Connectors |

*Physical layer protocol—explicit only in more recent standards such as FDDI, SONET, and LATM.

†Physical-medium-dependent—explicit only in more recent standards such as FDDI, SONET, and ATM.

tems prior to exchanging data. These phases define the sequence of events ensuring successful data transmission. Sequencing of data, flow control, and transparent error handling are some of the capabilities inherent with this service mode. One disadvantage of this approach is the delay experienced in setting up the connection. Traditional carrier services, including circuit switching, X.25 packet switching, and early frame relay (discussed in the next chapter) service, are examples of connection-oriented transmission; LLC 2 is also a connection-oriented protocol.

In a connectionless service, each data unit is independently routed to the destination. No connection-establishment tasks are required, since each data unit is independent of the previous or subsequent one. Hence, a connectionless-mode service provides for transfer of data units (cells, frames, or packets) without regard to the establishment or maintenance of connections. The basic MAC/LLC (i.e., LLC 1) transfer mechanism of a LAN is connectionless. In this connectionless-mode transmission delivery is uncertain, because of the possibility of errors. Connectionless communication shifts the responsibility for the integrity to a higher layer, where the integrity check is done only once, instead of being done at (every) lower layer.

### 8.2.5  TCP/IP protocol suite

The basic TCP/IP protocol suite is shown in Table 8.4 for both LAN and WAN environments. There are about 100 protocols in the internet suite. A TCP/IP LAN application involves (1) a user connection over a standard LAN system (IEEE 802.3, .4, .5 over LLC); (2) software in the PC and/or server implementing the IP, TCP, and related protocols, and (3) programs running in the PCs and/or servers to provide the needed

**TABLE 8.4  TCP/IP-based Communication: Key Protocols**

| Layer | LAN environment | WAN environment |
|-------|-----------------|-----------------|
| 7–5 | Application-specific protocols such as TELNET (terminal sessions), FTP and SFTP (file transfer), SMTP (e-mail), SNMP (management), and DNS (directory) | |
| 4 | TCP, UDP, EGP/IGP | TCP, UDP |
| 3 | IP, ICMP, ARP, RARP | IP, ICMP, X.25 PLP |
| 2 | LLC, CSMA/CD, token ring, token bus | LAP-B |
| 1 | IEEE 802.3, .4, .5 (PMD portions) | Physical channels |

*Acronyms:* SFTP = simple file transfer protocol; FTP = file transfer protocol; SMTP = simple mail transfer protocol; SNMP = simple network management protocol; DNS = domain name service; UDP = user datagram protocol; ICMP = internet control message protocol; ARP = address resolution protocol; RARP = reverse address resolution protocol; EGP = external gateway protocol; IGP = internal gateway protocol; PMD = physical-medium-dependent.

application. (The application may use other higher layer protocols for file transfer, network management, and so on.) The most widespread traditional TCP/IP user applications are electronic mail (e-mail), file transfer, and access to hosts on remote networks.

**IP protocol.**  In a TCP/IP environment, IP provides the underlying mechanism to move data from one end system on one LAN to another end system on the same or different LAN. IP makes the underlying network transparent to the upper layers, TCP in particular. It is a connectionless packet delivery protocol, where each IP packet is treated independently. (In this context, packets are also called *datagrams.*) IP provides two basic services: addressing and fragmentation/reassembly of long packets. IP adds no guarantees of delivery, reliability, flow control, or error recovery to the underlying network other than the data link layer mechanism already provides. IP expects the higher layers to handle such functions. IP may lose packets, deliver them out of order, or duplicate them; IP defers these contingencies to the higher layers (TCP, in particular). Another way of saying this is that IP delivers on a "best-effort basis." There are no connections, physical or virtual, maintained by IP. To provide its services, IP employs four key packet header fields (among others):

- *Type of service*—parameters set by the end station specifying, for example, expected delay characteristics or expected reliability of path

- *Time to live*—parameter used to determine the packet's lifetime in the interconnected system

- *Options*—parameters to specify security, time stamps, and special routing

- *Header checksum*—a two-octet field used by IP to determine packet integrity

**Transmission control protocol.**  Since IP is an "unreliable," best-effort connectionless network layer protocol, TCP (a transport layer protocol) must provide reliability, flow control, and error recovery. TCP is a connection-oriented, end-to-end reliable protocol providing logical connections between pairs of processes. Some TCP features are:

- *Data transfer.*  From the applications viewpoint, TCP transfers a contiguous stream of octets through the interconnected network. The application does not have to segment the data into blocks or packets since TCP does this by grouping the octets in *TCP segments,* which are then passed to IP for transmission to the destination. TCP determines how to segment the data, and it forwards the data at its own convenience.

- *Reliability.* TCP assigns a sequence number to each TCP segment transmitted, and expects a positive acknowledgment (ACK) from the receiving peer TCP.* If the ACK is not received within a specified timeout interval, the segment is retransmitted. The receiving TCP uses the sequence numbers to rearrange the segments if they arrive out of order, and to discard duplicate segments.

- *Flow control.* The receiving TCP signals to the sender the number of octets it can receive beyond the last received TCP segment, without causing an overflow in its internal buffers. This indication is sent in the ACK in the form of the highest sequence number it can receive without problems. (This approach is also known as a *window mechanism.*)

- *Logical connections.* In order to achieve reliability and flow control, TCP must maintain certain status information for each "data stream." The combination of this status, including sockets, sequence numbers, and window sizes, is called a *logical connection* (also known as *virtual circuit*).

- *Multiplexing.* This is achieved through the use of a ports mechanism.

- *Duplex communication.* TCP provides for concurrent data streams in both directions.

## 8.3  Supporting Hardware

This section surveys some of the hardware supporting LANs.

**Cables.**  Considerations in selecting the type of cable include (1) the medium type (coaxial, twisted-pair, fiber, etc.), (2) physical characteristics (typically with respect to local and national fire codes, plenum vs. nonplenum, etc.), and (3) the medium's electrical and optical characteristics. In a twisted-pair (10Base-T) LAN, now common, stations, servers, bridges, routers, and gateways are attached to wiring hubs using *two pairs* of twisted-pair cable. Devices are connected in a star configuration to a hub that is usually located in a wiring closet. A hub (also known as *wiring concentrator*) can support from eight to a few hundred stations. Several hubs may be used to support a large population of users. In turn, the hubs are connected with each other, using any LAN medium (coaxial, twisted-pair, or fiberoptic cable).

---

*In actuality, sequence numbers are assigned to each octet in the stream, but only the sequence number of the first octet in the stream is transmitted remotely.

**Network interface cards.**  PCs and workstations obtain physical access to a LAN with the use of a network interface card (NIC). A NIC is a "board" that is placed in the PC to support medium-sharing and timing functions. These cards typically implement the IEEE standards like 802.2 and 802.3, 802.4, or 802.5. Newer PCs and workstations come with integrated network interfaces.

**Wiring hubs.**  As indicated, wiring hubs provide a control point for end-user device wiring. They provide the network administrator with a central cabling location to facilitate performance and fault monitoring, moves, and growth. They also serve to link a LAN area (a group of offices, a floor, or perhaps even an entire building) into a larger backbone network. There have been four generations of hubs. Hubs are now being targeted by some vendors for upgrade to ATM by 1993 or 1994. The trend is toward putting more functions, such as routing, into the hub; this results in space savings and simplifies manageability and control by reducing the number of separate devices required. The term *managed hub* is employed to identify these new sophisticated hubs. Wiring hubs now also support the function of application servers. At a macro level, hubs can be categorized as (1) Ethernet hubs, fixed configuration; (2) Ethernet hubs, modular or multislot configuration; and (3) multifunction and/or mixed-LAN hubs.

**Repeaters, bridges, routers, and gateways.**  There is an increased need for LAN interconnection, both locally and remotely. LAN connectivity can be extended using (1) repeaters, (2) bridges, (3) routers, and (4) gateways. These devices support the connection function in a different manner and at distinct layers of the protocol hierarchy.[3]

**Repeaters.**  Repeaters are devices that amplify the signals in order to increase the physical range of the LAN. A repeater usually extends a single segment of a LAN to accommodate additional users, although some repeaters are capable of extending two LANs simultaneously. The two segments can conceivably use two different media or physical topologies, although this is not a frequent occurrence. Three limitations of repeaters are (1) the amplification of noise, along with the signal; (2) the limited nature of the extension; and (3) the fact that the network remains a single network at the logical level, thereby keeping the number of users that can be supported bounded by medium-sharing considerations.

**Bridges.**  Bridges connect two or more LANs at the MAC layer. A bridge receiving packets (frames) of information will pass the packets to the interconnected LAN based on some forwarding algorithm selected by the manufacturer (explicit route, dynamic address filtering, static address filtering, etc.). The receiving LAN must typically run the same MAC protocol as the transmitting LAN in order to read the frame (although translating bridges are also available—some administrators use routers instead for this function). As networks become complex with the addition of multiple departments and additional servers that share a common backbone, bridges provide the network administrator with the ability to divide the network into smaller logical segments to make them more manageable. Unlike repeaters, bridges regenerate the signals, so that noise is not propagated.

There are several network design possibilities for local bridges. Segment-to-segment bridging is relatively straightforward. Multiple cascaded segments are possible; however, the traffic destined for a "far" node must pass through several bridges, causing a possible degradation in quality of service (delay and frame loss). Multiple LANs use backbone bridging to avoid local traffic congestion, although a first- or second-generation backbone may eventually become a bottleneck. Multiport bridging allows several LANs to share the bridge. Devices communicate with each other through the bridge's internal bus.

"Transparent" bridges utilized in Ethernet (i.e., bridges that do not require the user to specify the path to the destination) need to maintain address tables. Until the early 1990s, these tables were able to store 2000 to 5000 entries; newer bridges can store up to 60,000 entries. In contrast, "source routing" bridges used in token ring LANs require that the sending user station (i.e., the source) supply instructions as to how to reach the destination. Frame filtering-forwarding rates vary from a few thousand per second at the low end, to a few tens of thousands at the midrange, to a few hundreds of thousands at the high end (as high as 200,000). Rates in the 10,000-to-20,000 range are common.

**Routers.** Routers connect at a higher protocol layer than bridges (at the network layer). Routers provide flow control for the incoming LAN frames, thereby increasing the reliability of the interconnection, and allow the use of a variety of interconnection subnetworks. Different frames can, in principle, be routed over different networks, for example, for security or least-cost-routing reasons. Routers operate with a particular WAN protocol or with a number of protocols. If multiple protocols are being used to interconnect LANs, a manager can either select a separate router for each protocol, or have a router that is capable of retaining multiple protocols in one chassis. Disadvantages of routers, relative to bridges, include reduction of frame filtering speed and increased cost (however, low-cost routers—$3500 range—are beginning to emerge). Chapter 9 discusses communication services that are used by these routers to achieve wide area connectivity.

**Gateways.**   Gateways are used to interconnect LANs that employ completely different protocols at all communication layers. The complete translation of incoming data units associated with completely different protocols affects transmission speed.

**Servers.**   A *server* is a LAN-attached device that provides functions such as file storage, printing, or communications services to other entities on the LAN. As networks grow and start to support higher-level applications (such as imaging), the server performance becomes critical to overall performance.

There are three basic functions supporting computing: (1) data management, (2) processing, and (3) presentation (to user). Client-server systems allow the distribution of these functions among appropriate devices. A client-server LAN architecture is a computing approach in which software applications are distributed among entities on the LAN. The clients request information from one or more LAN "servers" that store software applications, data, and network operating system modules. The network operating system allows the clients to share the data and applications that are stored in the server, and to share peripherals on the LAN.

Any system in the network can be a client or a server. The *client* is the entity requesting that work be done; a server is the entity performing a set of tasks on behalf of the client. The user's processor controls the user interface and issues commands to direct the activity of the server across the LAN. This is done through the use of remote procedure calls (RPCs). RPCs are software programs with distributed capabilities. Applications that are implemented on the LAN can "call" these procedures by ordering messages, translating different codes, and maintaining the integrity of the protocol. Not all applications in a client-server architecture are stored on a server; clients are capable of storing applications and data locally. When clients possess individual operating systems the network is referred to as *loosely* coupled.

In a client-server environment, the file server has the capability to perform database management. This means that the server (also known as *back-end* or *database engine*) can run a (relational) database management system using a multitasking operating system (e.g., OS/2 or UNIX). In the client-server environment, the workstation (also known as *front-end processor*) is responsible for "presentation" functions (i.e., display of data according to specified user interfaces, editing and validating data, and managing the keyboard and mouse).

## 8.4   Support of System Network Architecture

Many corporate mission-critical networks installed during the past 25 years were of the centralized kind. In a centralized environment, one node controls the communication actions of all nodes in the network. Many used IBM's Systems Network Architecture (SNA) and supporting hardware and software. For transaction-based processing, where users enter simple records (orders, inventory, employee data, claims, sales figures, etc.) from "dumb" terminals for processing and storage at a mainframe, centralized networks have proved adequate. Business applications and requirements, however, are now changing: (1) PCs and intelligent workstations populate the network; (2) files of all types, including image data, need to be exchanged; (3) a lot of the computing is done locally or in a distributed fashion; and (4) users have an increasing need to exchange information between each other, rather than simply updating some remote database.

Network managers, in turn, have deployed systems that can handle this diversity quickly and efficiently. During the past few years, many organizations have installed LANs that allow devices to be easily added or moved through "self-discovery" mechanisms. An SNA host, on the other hand, necessitated the predefinition of every node in the network in large tables maintained in the mainframe and in the front-end processor. Also, every route had to be predefined, making the network slow to adapt to device addition, deletion, and moves. At the very least, a network manager wants to be able to just add a new node, and without much preconfiguration, have it immediately start accessing the mainframe or other resources connected to the network.

As centralized networks begin the transition to a distributed architecture, the issue is how one can accommodate them within the context of the larger end-user computing network of interconnected LANs. Since some of the BISs are mainframe-based, a short discussion of this topic is in order.

Both the manager of a distributed set of end-user LANs needing to connect to an SNA mainframe and the SNA manager trying to bring a distributed set of LANs not currently communicating with the mainframe into one cohesive network are interested in the options that are available. Two particular methods are described below. Although both methods would work if the network were pure SNA, the advantages of one approach over the other take on a different dimension where the user has deployed multiple platforms.[4]

**Two approaches to distributed SNA.**   Beginning in 1985, SNA has evolved in an effort to meet the new networking demands for distributed computing; however, it was only with the publication of IBM's *Networking Blueprint* (March 1992) that a more aggressive posture has been taken. The *Networking Blueprint* identifies the Advanced Peer-to-Peer Networking (APPN), a proprietary IBM transport layer protocol announced in 1985, as the means by which distributed access will be fully supported.

Although already 7 years in the making at press time, APPN has only been deployed in a small number of platforms, notably in IBM's AS/400 and a few other systems. The proprietary nature of APPN has raised concerns, particularly in the TCP/IP vendor community that is accustomed to open standards, about the viability of the APPN strategy in today's multivendor, multiprotocol corporate computing environment. To encourage vendors to incorporate APPN in their products, IBM has licensed the APPN source code. This move has heated up the debate as to whether APPN should be the backbone protocol to achieve distributed computing in a corporate enterprisewide environment consisting of multiple networks including SNA, or whether a TCP/IP-based protocol is the more flexible and open way to achieve the same goal. In particular, Cisco Systems has proposed an open alternative for support of APPN nodes in a multiprotocol network called *Advanced Peer-to-Peer Internetworking* (APPI).* A short discussion of these two methods follows.

**IBM's Advanced Peer-to-Peer Networking.** APPN is a decentralized peer-based protocol used to connect different SNA nodes into a generally nonhierarchical topology. APPN permits autonomous control using dynamic definition of network resources via an intrinsic node-to-node dialogue that is transparent to the user. The APPN network is based in a two-tiered architecture as shown in Fig. 8.1.

APPN network nodes (NNs) are "backbone" nodes within the APPN network that maintain knowledge of the topology of the overall network and that can perform intermediate routing. NNs can be either full SNA host nodes supporting user applications (e.g., an AS/400) or can simply be a routing node (e.g., a 3174). The NN contains a software module, known as *control point* (CP), that provides the directory for logical units' (LUs—e.g., terminals, printers) names, coordinates LU searches with other APPN nodes, facilitates session setup among LUs, maintains and exchanges topology information with other NN nodes, and selects routes on behalf of the users they serve. Put more formally, they support the following functions at the peer level with other NN nodes: (1) dynamic registration of SNA resources, (2) dynamic discovery of SNA resources, (3) automatic selection of route, and (4) dynamic updates to changes in topology. IBM has indicated that it will license the APPN NN source code to other vendors.

APPN end nodes (ENs) are pendent nodes attached to the NNs that do not maintain knowledge of the network's topology. ENs are SNA nodes that provide services to end-user applications. ENs rely exclu-

---

*In late 1993, faced with patent and technical problems, Cisco Systems announced that it was abandoning its effort to build the APPI alternative to APPN.

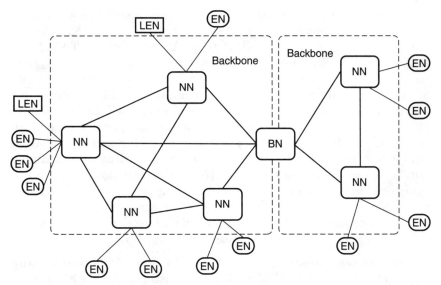

**Figure 8.1**   APPN architecture. NN = network node; EN = end node; BN = border node; LEN = low-entry networking node.

sively on the NNs to which they are physically attached for APPN services. This NN provides the following three services to the ENs connected to it: (1) dynamic registration of SNA resources, (2) dynamic discovery of SNA resources, and (3) automatic selection of route. The first two functions are implemented in a "shared mode" between the EN and the parent NN, while the last function is implemented entirely by the network of NNs and the appropriate information is communicated as needed to the EN.

A special EN known as a *low-entry networking* (LEN) node also can connect to the NN, but it requires static definition of network resources. LENs are SNA end systems similar to ENs; however, although they are also directly attached to NNs, they must contain static definitions of all SNA destinations that they need to access. All these destinations appear to the LEN to be in the NN; in turn, the NN assumes responsibility for transmitting the data to the correct node. Similarly, all the resources in the LEN node that are accessible from the backbone network must be statically defined in the parent NN.

In addition to not being "open," APPN has a number of other limitations. For example, it does not support dynamic alternate routing in case the physical link on which the route has been established suddenly fails. It does not support load sharing over parallel links. Also, once a route has been selected, it remains in place even when intermediary nodes become congested.

At the commercial level, APPN has been implemented on a variety of IBM platforms; some of these IBM systems can be configured to be any one of the nodes described above (e.g., AS/400, OS/2, VTAM/NCP, RS/6000), while other implementations are limited to only one type of node (e.g., 3174 as NN, OS/2 as EN). In terms of the vendor community at large, there are a number of implementations of LEN nodes; some NN implementation and/or support are expected by late 1993 to late 1994. Given the availability of licensed source code, one can expect an increased number of vendors incorporating NN functionality in their equipment. By incorporating NN software, a third party can supply non-IBM-based hardware for the NN routing function (i.e., can sell equipment in that highly defined SNA/routing market). In addition, the third party may (although does not have to) include gatewaying capabilities to enable internetworking between that vendor's subnetwork (or some other vendor's subnetwork) and the APPN/SNA network.

**Advanced Peer-to-Peer Internetworking.** In lieu of the networking approach advocated by IBM with the licensing of APPN NN source code, Cisco Systems has advocated an open architecture that accommodates APPN nodes within the context of a multivendor network. The proposed architecture is called *Advanced Peer-to-Peer Internetworking* (APPI). APPI enables users to take advantage of the benefits that APPN has over traditional SNA environments but to do so within the context of an open backbone. In addition, rather that using predeveloped NN code, third-party vendors can develop code optimized to their own router platforms.

The basic characteristic of APPI is that while the edge nodes of an APPN network, ENs and LENs, are accommodated in native APPN fashion, the core of the (backbone) network is based on open protocol principles. Another way of looking at this would be to say that some vendors seem to want to provide NN routing (and other services) in their boxes, in addition to their existing protocol support, without having to spend money to license NN software.

As seen above, NNs provide two services to the ENs and LENs: (1) intermediate routing through knowledge gained about network topology and (2) distributed directory services. The primary function of APPI is to provide APPN NN services to ENs while retaining the flexibility of an open multiprotocol backbone network (namely, the flexibility to run multiple protocols on the same box—an alternative approach for a router vendor would be simply to view APPN as another protocol they choose to support, and install NN software in their equipment).

To APPN pendent nodes, ENs and LENs, the architecture of an APPI-based network looks identical to straight APPN, but in reality it takes on the characteristics of an open and dynamic network at the backbone tier. The isolation between the APPN network on the fringes and the open network in the backbone tier is established through a facility on a multiprotocol router that provides a protocol wall between the two networks. A router that provides this isolation is called an open network node (ONN) in the APPI architecture. An ONN device communicates with ENs and LENs using IBM protocols but communicates with the multiprotocol network (including other ONNs) using TCP/IP protocols. It uses IP services as the transport vehicle to move SNA session data over the backbone. The APPN routing protocol (i.e., backbone-based exchanges to obtain topology information) no longer exists and does not have to be supported. Thus, ONN is basically a router running specialized software that provides APPN-like services to the APPN ENs. ONNs encapsulate the APPN traffic in TCP/IP Protocol Data Units (PDUs) over an IP-only backbone.

Figure 8.2 shows that, since ONNs support the NN-to-EN protocol, existing user systems and subnetworks (e.g., LEN) remain completely unaffected by the introduction of the APPI backbone. Although an ONN does have to implement an SNA protocol stack, it does not need all the complexity of an full APPN NN. Instead, its functionality is at the LEN level of complexity; such complexity is relatively minor when compared to the complexity of APPN NN implementation.

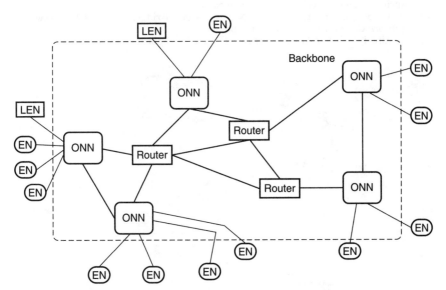

**Figure 8.2**   APPI architecture. ONN = open network node; EN = end node; BN = border node; LEN = low-entry networking node.

APPI directory services can be centralized, distributed, or hybrid. The goal is to minimize name searches using a full-broadcast mechanism. For example, when employing a hybrid directory service, a client ONN first attempts to locate a name in its cache memory, and if it is not found, it directs the request to the central server rather than broadcasting to all the ONNs on the backbone network.

APPI was slated to be implemented in two stages before it was abandoned, as noted earlier. The first stage, APPI/1, scheduled for 1993, saw the deployment of ONNs as peer-to-peer routers based on IP networking principles. The second APPI stage, APPI/2, scheduled for 1994, was to enhance the ONNs to include SNA intermediate routing functions. In APPI/2 ONNs will act not only as access routers but also as intermediate routers for transporting SNA peer-to-peer traffic, recognizing particular SNA sessions rather than simply using IP to pass them through the backbone network. By providing visibility of SNA sessions, intermediate ONNs allow for improved SNA-level congestion and flow control. APPI and APPN will be interoperable in the sense that users can connect both types of nodes in an arbitrary manner, with full communications capabilities.

### References

1. D. Minoli, *1st, 2nd, and Next Generation LANs,* McGraw-Hill, New York, 1994.
2. D. Minoli, "Third Generation LANs," *Proceedings of TEXPO 1993,* San Francisco, April 6–8, 1993, Pacific Bell, San Francisco.
3. D. Minoli, "Internetworking LANs: Repeaters, Bridges, Routers & Gateways," *Network Computing,* October 1990, pp. 96 ff.
4. D. Minoli, "APPI or APPN?" *Network Computing,* February 1993.

# Wide Area Networking Services and Technologies for Imaging Systems

This chapter provides a survey of wide area networking services and technologies that can be used to support distributed imaging applications. Since many premises systems in general, and imaging systems in particular, are now LAN-based, as noted in the previous chapters, this WAN discussion focuses on LAN-interconnection solutions. At first, LANs were islands unto themselves, but now corporations are putting in place enterprisewide networks connecting many if not all departments of the organization. Imaging applications can take advantage of these corporate connectivity trends.

Figure 9.1, based on discussion from Chap. 4, depicts typical bandwidth requirements for image communication. A variety of communication options are available to meet specific users' needs. Just a few years ago, one tended to employ low-speed dedicated communication channels between routers or for other data communication needs. Now there are communication solutions suited to a variety of throughput requirements, traffic burstiness, and amount of daily utilization. Below, we survey some of the communications services that can be employed to achieve distributed data processing in support of imaging. Wide area dedicated high-speed digital services and switched services (frame relay, ATM/cell relay, and SMDS) are discussed. These services are used to support bridge-to-bridge and router-to-router communication.[1-4] See also Ref. 5, or other books, for additional information.

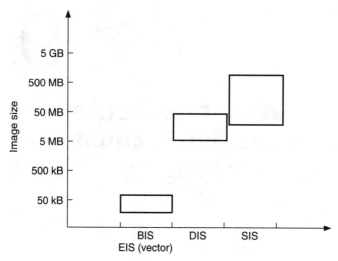

**Figure 9.1**  Typical image size that need to be supported.

## 9.1  Communications Options to Support Interconnection

The computing environment has evolved from standalone PCs during the 1980s, to locally networked PCs on site- or campus-based LANs in the late 1980s, to interconnected enterprisewide systems in the early to mid-1990s. As noted in Chap. 2, high-speed digital services can be classified as *dedicated services,* such as fractional T1 links, T1 links, and T3 links, and *switched services,* such as ISDN H0, ISDN H11, switched T1, frame relay service (public or private), SMDS, and ATM/cell relay. ISDN H0, ISDN H11, and switched T1 are traditional circuit-switched services (i.e., after call setup, the bandwidth is reserved for that user whether that bandwidth is needed by the user or not). Frame relay service, SMDS, and ATM/cell relay service are packet-switched services (i.e., the bandwidth is—in theory—allocated to the user only when the user needs it) (see Fig. 9.2).

## 9.2  Interconnecting LANs over a Wide Area: Nonswitched Services

In the 1980s, corporate networking in general, and LAN interconnection in particular, utilized dedicated carrier facilities, which have also been known as *private lines.*[6] Various user's networks were unintegrated, so that different departmental data applications used separate

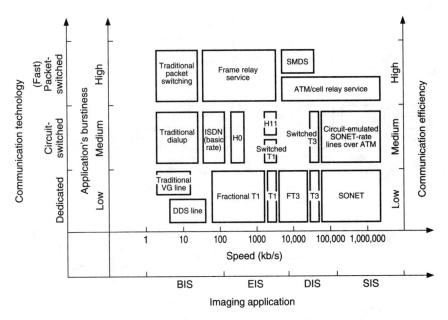

**Figure 9.2**    Spectrum of communications services in support of imaging.

networks. LAN connectivity, if at all, used its own transmission facilities. Not only was this solution expensive because of the duplicate transmission costs; it was also difficult to manage and grow. This approach evolved with the introduction of T1 multiplexers in the mid-1980s. The data applications were now aggregated over a common backbone network, improving network management, simplifying the topology, and reducing the communications costs. One shortcoming of this approach, however, was the fact that the LAN traffic usually remained separate, giving rise to two overlay networks; LAN interconnection continued to be outside the "mainstream" data communication–data processing infrastructure.

More recently, T1 multiplexers have been used to support the LAN interconnection traffic, by statically allocating some of the bandwidth to the router-to-router traffic over the private enterprise network. In same cases, the routers need the entire T1/DS1 bandwidth (1.544 Mbps), so that the T1 multiplexer is not used. Figure 9.3 depicts a LAN interconnection example using dedicated lines. Notice that remote imaging clients access the information stored in the server over the wide area network.

Interconnection of LANs using dedicated facilities can be expensive when the number of sites becomes large. Networks based on dedicated

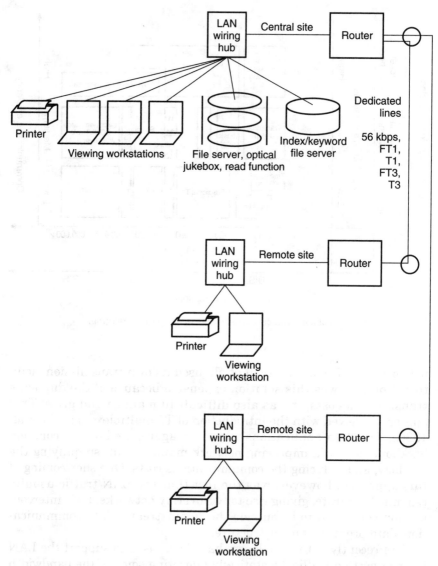

**Figure 9.3** Interconnection of LANs supporting imaging.

services may require as many as $n(n-1)/2$ links, where $n$ is the number of sites.[7] This is the reason why LANs internetworking is now transitioning to switched services such as frame relay, cell relay, and SMDS. This section focuses on dedicated services, while Sec. 9.3 looks at switched services.

### 9.2.1  Analog private lines

The classical interconnection method employed by network designers for the past quarter-century has been to use analog private lines. This approach involves a permanently installed voice-grade (VG) line (3000 Hz) between two points. These channels are adapted from voice communication to data communication through the use of a modem. The modem transforms data into an analog signal suitable for transmission over the traditional telephone network. While digital backbones are now becoming popular, a large portion of today's data communications is still carried by voiceband modems over the analog telephone network, particularly for terminal-to-mainframe applications. This approach, although relatively inexpensive (approximately $80 + $0.75/mi per month), supports a bandwidth in only the 9.6-to-19.2-kbps range. (Modems with compression may support speeds of up to 38.4 or 57.6 kbps; however, this rate may not be sustained for the entire transfer session and may not be achievable with images already compressed.) Some BIS applications could use this approach, but such a configuration is very limited.

### 9.2.2  Fractional T1, T1, T3 and SONET private lines

Dedicated "private line" digital services provide transparent bandwidth at the specified speed ($N \times 64$ kbps for FT1, 1.544 Mbps for T1, and 44.736 Mbps for T3), and are suitable for point-to-point interconnection of low-burstiness (i.e., steady) traffic. Data submitted at one end is "sure" to get to the other end (except for unexpected failures of the link and other low-occurrence errors). T3 (also known as *DS3*) facilities are increasingly available in many parts of the country, although they are still fairly expensive. If one needs more than 6 to 10 (depending on distance) T1 circuits between two points, then it is cheaper to use a T3 link. In addition, a number of carriers have started to offer a fractional T3 service that allows the user to specify the desired number multiple of T1s.

A digital hierarchy suited for high-bandwidth fiber-based signals was developed in the late 1980s. The standard is known in the United States as *synchronous optical network* (SONET). Telephone operating companies and interexchange carriers are now deploying network equipment meeting the new SONET standards. SONET's hierarchy of rates and formats starts at a 51.840-Mbps rate. The SONET hierarchy addresses transmission of up to 2.5 Gbps and is extensible, if necessary, to more than 13 Gbps. The basic building block is a 51.840-Mbps signal known as a synchronous transport signal—level 1 (STS-1). SONET defines the basic STS-1 signal and an associated byte-interleaved multiplex structure that creates a group of standard rates at $N$ times the STS-1 rate. $N$ takes selected integer values from 1 to 255; currently, the following values are defined: $N$ = 1, 3, 9, 12, 18, 24, 36, and 48 (corresponding rates are 51.840, 155.250, 466.560,...Mbps). One can expect to see commercial availability of SONET facilities for end-user applications in the 1993–1995 time frame. (Deployment internal to the network will occur sooner.) At that time one will be able to order point-to-point lines operating at multiples of 51 Mbps. These high-end facilities clearly would be used only where the traffic across the LANs is very high, for example, in high-resolution imaging (e.g., DISs and SISs) and multimedia applications.

Figure 9.3 depicts the networking configuration under discussion. This approach can be effective in supporting imaging between fixed user sites, particularly when there is a small number of large sites (e.g., sites with many users).

### 9.2.3 Image transmission time

Figure 9.4 depicts the approximate transmission time (i.e., not including protocol overhead) for various imaging systems, predicated on the image sizes of Fig. 9.1. As can be noted, BISs can do reasonably well on a number of low- and medium-speed WAN communication services. DISs and SISs (including PACSs) may be better off with higher-speed services.

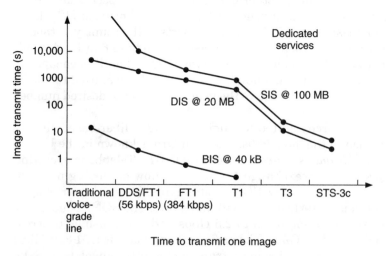

**Figure 9.4**  Approximate time to transmit a single image.

## 9.3   Interconnecting LANs over a Wide Area: Switched Services

Seamless distribution of imaging information requires the existence of a communication infrastructure to connect distributed users, servers, databases, LANs, and other subnetworks. In Sec. 9.2 we discussed some communications services that are suited to connect a few islands of users who have high cross-network traffic requirements. In fact, this has been the traditional LAN interconnection approach until recently. This section examines other techniques that are suited to interconnect LANs when one or more of the following conditions hold:

1. The number of user islands is relatively large.

2. The traffic per site (user) is relatively low.

3. A small delay (2 to 5 s) in setting up a connection between two islands is acceptable for the low-end solutions (this delay is not present in the high-end solutions such as SMDS).

4. The cost of the connection is important.

### 9.3.1   Dial-up link between LAN routers

This approach involves the use of modems connected to the LAN server (bridge or router), to utilize the analog public telephone network. Circuit switching implies that the communications channel is not dedicated 24 h per day, but must be brought on line when needed (via a process called *call setup*), and then taken down when no longer needed. Traditional modems have operated at speeds up to 19.2 kbps; however, until recently, 9.6 kbps has been more common. This implies that the throughput across this type of LAN-to-LAN link is fairly small. Consequently, only a small number of users and/or short inquiry/response-like transactions can be supported. Since the link between the two servers is not available on a dedicated basis, the bridge or router would have to dial up the remote device, as needed; this implies that a delay of approximately 2 to 5 s would be incurred.

The advantage of this approach is, however, that this type of connectivity is fairly inexpensive, and would be ideal for an environment where there are dozens (or even hundreds) of remote LANs, with only an occasional need to exchange data. Long-distance telephone service can be obtained for 10 to 25 cents per minute depending on distance, time of day, and carrier. If there is sufficient calling volume, bulk rates are available from carriers. A 9.6-kbps full-duplex operation modem for dial-up lines can now be purchased for as little as $300. High-speed modems can now achieve up to 38.4 kbps on dial-up lines using error correction and data compression; these modems be purchased for approximately $900 or less. Modems with high-end compression may support speeds of up to 57.6 kbps; however, this rate may not be sustained for the entire transfer session and may not be achievable with images already compressed.

Imaging applications that use fax servers, as illustrated in Chap. 2, do in fact use dial-up facilities (Group 3 fax). One can also *encode* the image using Group 4 fax techniques, but send it out at 9.6 kbps (rather than at 56 or 64 kbps as would be usual with Group 4 facsimile machines).

### 9.3.2 Integrated services digital network (ISDN) connectivity between LAN routers

This interconnection approach involves the use of switched *digital* facilities between the LAN routers. ISDN provides end-to-end digital connectivity with access to voice and data services over the same digital transmission and switching facilities. It provides a range of services using a limited set of connection types and multipurpose user-network interface arrangements. ISDN provides three channels types: B channels, D channels, and H channels. The *B channel* is a 64-kbps access channel that carries customer information, such as voice calls, circuit-switched data, or packet-switched data. The *D channel* is an access channel carrying control or signaling information and, optionally, packetized customer information; the D channel has a capacity of 16 or 64 kbps. The *H channel* is a 384-kbps, 1.536-Mbps, or 1.920-Mbps (Europe) channel that carries customer information, such as videoteleconferencing, high-speed data, high-quality audio or sound programs, and imaging information.

ISDN defines *physical user–network interfaces.* The more well known of these interfaces are as follows:

2B + D      Two switched 64-kbps channels, plus a 16-kbps packet and signaling channel (144 kbps total)

23B + D     Twenty-three switched 64-kbps channels, plus a 64-kbps packet and signaling channel (1.536 Mbps total)

H0 + D      Switched aggregated 384-kbps links

H10 + D     Switched aggregated 1.544-Mbps links

As can be seen, ISDN provides considerably more bandwidth on a circuit-switched connection than is possible with standard analog circuits. ISDN is now available in most major markets, and is expected to be increasingly available in other areas. Figure 9.5 depicts one example of how ISDN would actually be used.

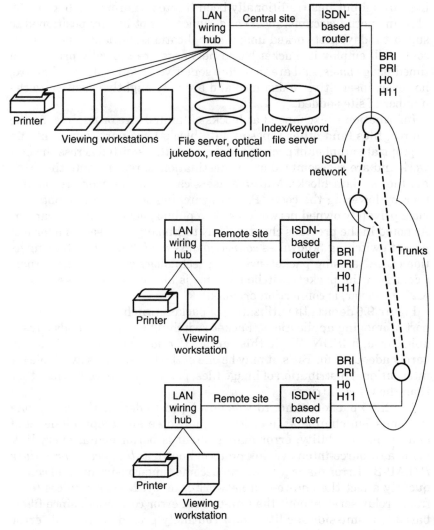

**Figure 9.5**   Using ISDN to connect LANs supporting imaging.

### 9.3.3  Packet-switching service to connect routers

Packet switching, a technology that first arose in the mid-1960s, affords statistical allocation of bandwidth. Packet switching has been standardized according to the ITU-T Recommendation X.25, first published in 1976. (The recommendation was significantly revised in both 1980 and 1984; minor revisions have taken place since.) Packet-switching throughput has traditionally been limited to around 9.6 kbps (56 kbps in special circumstances) and, hence, is not ideally positioned to support today's networked imaging applications, although some users could still employ it. Packet-based networks are typically priced on a timed-usage basis, and are therefore sensitive to data volume; they are, however, insensitive to distance and are only slightly sensitive to the number of sites added.

Information is exchanged as blocks of limited size or *packets*. At the source, files (and other types of data blocks) are partitioned into an appropriate number of packets; packets are transmitted across the network and are reassembled at the destination to reconstitute the original file (or data block). Multiple users can share network resources, thereby lowering the costs. Packet-switching service can be obtained via a privately owned network, or via a public packet-switched carrier. As noted in the previous chapter, LAN technology is based on a form of packet switching (known as *connectionless mode*); hence, interconnection of LANs using packet-switching technology can be efficient (particularly if the packet-switched service is also connectionless mode—X.25, however, is connection-oriented).

Figure 9.6 depicts the utilization of packet-switching services in support of imaging applications. Packet-switching services are also available through ISDN. While this service is relatively slow and, hence, barely adequate for BISs, it may be one of the few services available for international distribution of image files, particularly to countries other than the G7 countries.

The X.25 packet standard was developed to deal with error-prone transmission channels. In order to guarantee an acceptable level of end-to-end reliability, error management is performed at every link using a resource-intensive link protocol known as *link access procedure B* (LAP-B). Error management can become time-consuming and consequently affect the end-to-end network latency. Newer services (e.g., frame relay service) omit the link-by-link error correction, since fiber-based transmission facilities now routinely provide a $10^{-9}$-bit error rate; such streamlining reduces latency. The amount of bandwidth required by users has increased in the recent past; for example, image transmission needs more bandwidth than does text-based e-mail. These new conditions are opening up the door for frame relay, SMDS, and cell relay. (These services, which eliminate the performance restrictions of X.25, are discussed below.)

X.25 is a standard interface protocol between packet-switched user equipment and a packet switch, covering the lower three layers of the OSIRM. The *physical layer,* or layer 1, is concerned with physical connectivity to the network. The next layer, the *link layer,* or layer 2, deals with error control and flow between two adjacent points. Layer 3, or the

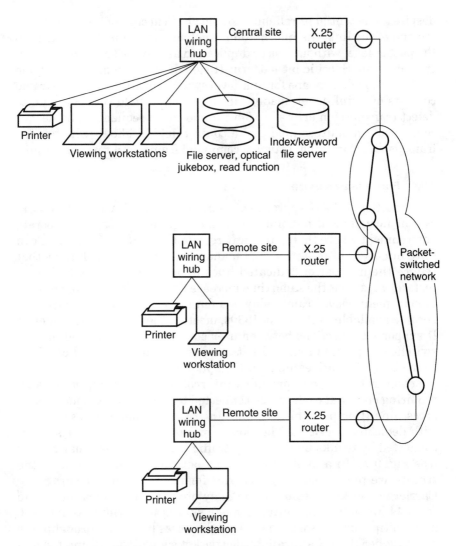

**Figure 9.6**  Imaging distribution over packet-switching services.

*network layer,* deals with end-to-end networking aspects, including routing.

The physical level deals with the representation of data bits, timing aspects, and the physical interface between terminal and modem. These functions are handled by the X.21, X.21bis, X.20, and X.20bis specifications. The link level provides the functions of link initialization, flow control, and error control. LAP-B provides an error-free data channel despite the potential unreliability of the physical channel. At the receiving end of the link, the information is delivered in units (or packets) to the packet level without loss or duplication and in the same sequence of transmission. Specific bit patterns (flags) delimit the data link frame and also provide a means for link-level synchronization. A LAP-B frame consists of a link-level header, an information field (if any), and, to detect transmission errors, a 16-bit frame check sequence. The header consists of an address field and a control field; it shows whether the frame is an information frame, a command frame, or a response frame.

### 9.3.4  Frame relay service

The traditional WAN approach of connecting a few LANs with routers over dedicated point-to-point lines is no longer adequate in a corporate environment where there are many remote LANs. (Some networks can have hundreds of routers.) LAN managers have sought solutions that reduce the number of dedicated lines in order to keep transmission costs down, and at the same time increase flexibility and make network management easy. Frame relay is a data communication service that became available in the early 1990s, meeting these user requirements. It supports connections between user equipment (routers and private switches in particular), and between user equipment and carriers' frame relay network equipment (i.e., public switches).

Frame relay service provides interconnection among $n$ sites by requiring only that each site be connected to the "network cloud" via an access line. (Compare this with the $n(n - 1)/2$ end-to-end lines required with dedicated services.) The cloud consists of switching nodes interconnected by trunks used to carry traffic aggregated from many users (see Fig. 9.7). In a public frame relay network the switches and the trunks are put in place by a carrier for use by many corporations. Carrier networks based on frame relay provide communications at up to 1.544 Mbps (in the United States), shared bandwidth on demand, and multiple user sessions over a single access line. The throughput is much higher than that available for packet switching, making the service attractive for imaging applications. In a private frame relay network, the switches and trunks are put in place (typically) by the corporate communications department of the company in question.[7] Each approach has advantages and disadvantages within the framework of a corporate network.

The frame relay protocol supports data transmission over a connection-oriented path; it enables the transmission of variable-length data units, typically up to 4096 octets (in some cases as high as 8192), over an assigned virtual connection. As is the case in X.25, frame relay standards specify the user interface to a device or network supporting

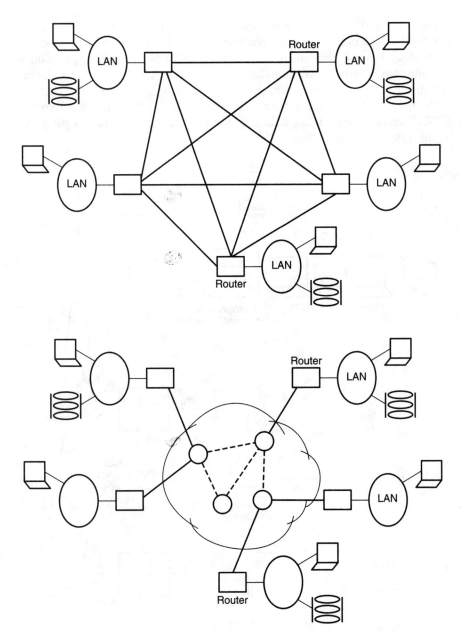

**Figure 9.7**   Interconnection of imaging LANs using dedicated lines (top) and switched services (bottom).

the service. This interface is called *frame relay interface* (FRI). A FRI, whether to a public or to a private network, supports access speeds of 56 kbps, $N \times 64$ kbps, and 1.544 Mbps (2.048 Mbps in Europe). Some vendors are attempting to extend the speed to 45 Mbps. Over a dozen U.S. carriers now offer the service, including the Bell Operating Companies, and the number is likely to grow.[6–10] Figure 9.8 depicts WAN connectivity using public frame relay service for LANs supporting imaging applications.

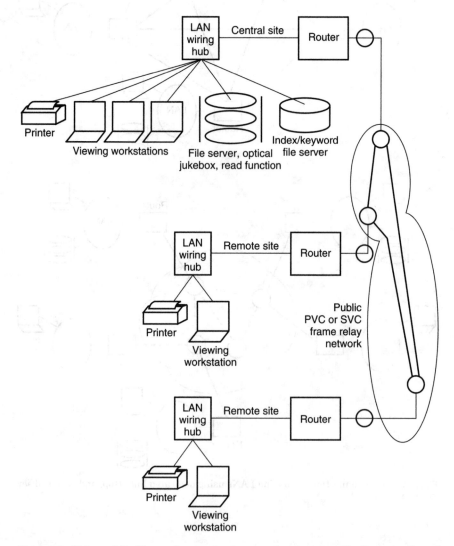

**Figure 9.8** Using public frame relay service to support enterprisewide dissemination of images.

Frame relay service can be deployed (1) utilizing a point-to-point link between two routers, (2) using customer-owned frame relay processors (basically, frame relay switches, but, typically, using cell relay trunking—discussed in Sec. 9.3.6), and (3) utilizing a carrier-provided service. In order to achieve savings, frame relay networks rely on the statistical variation of the traffic input from the pool of users to provide nominal combined input exceeding the actual throughput of the trunks in the backbone network. This is the reason why frame relay networks work best for bursty traffic applications. Because of the statistical nature of the network, carriers typically tariff a "committed" information rate (CIR), which, supposedly, the network can support from a specified source or sources. In actuality, the network may become congested and data submitted to the network, at the CIR or even below, *may or may not be delivered.*

In a frame relay environment the user needs a device (such as a router) to run the frame relay protocol. Some networks provide conversion for non-frame-relay devices. The network forwards frames submitted by the origination device and to the destination device. The transit delay through the network is about an order of magnitude lower than that experienced in packet switching because the frame relay protocol is simpler. Frame relay provides error detection but not correction (that was provided by X.25); the correction must be supported by the user equipment. A frame relay network can cost as little as a third as much as a fully interconnected network of private lines (one-half of a fully interconnected network, when also considering the cost of the required switches, if the network is private). A carrier can multiplex the traffic of one user with that of other users, and can, therefore, pass back to the users the economic advantages of bandwidth sharing. The financial advantage of a frame relay network becomes more substantial when the number of routers is high (half a dozen to a dozen, or more), and when the distances between routers is considerable [hundreds or thousands of miles—if the routers are all located within a small geographic area, like a city, a county, or a LATA (local access and transport area), the economic advantage of eliminating lines is less conspicuous].

Another way to benefit from frame relay is to use it in conjunction with customer-deployed "fast packet switch(es)." Using these frame relay processors can, in many instances, be cost-effective, since the user can obtain from the backbone bandwidth-on-demand, rather than on a preallocated (and inefficient) basis. The "saved" bandwidth is then available to other corporate users of the same backbone, in theory minimizing the amount of new raw bandwidth the corporation needs to acquire from a carrier in the form of additional T1 or fractional T1 links. These devices typically implement the frame relay protocol on the user's side and cell relay in the trunk side since cell relay principles facilitate dynamic bandwidth allocation. In the private network application, the user leases from a carrier private lines between the remote devices and the frame relay processors, and between the frame relay processors. The user employs frame relay to statistically multiplex traffic, in a standardized way, in order to achieve better utilization of the (wide area) backbone transmission resources. The frame relay processors must be housed in selected user locations. About a dozen vendors now manufacture frame relay processors.

Standards work for frame relay started in 1986; work accelerated in 1989, after the publication of the original ITU-T frame relay standards. Frame relay standards were published in final form in 1991. Three key ANSI standards are T1.606-1990, T1.617-1991, and T1.618-1991. T1.606-1990 specifies a framework for frame relay service in terms of user-network interface requirements and internetworking requirements. T1.617-1991, Annex D specifies critical network management functions, particularly useful in the public frame relay service context. The protocol needed to support frame relay is defined in T1.618-1991 (LAP-F Core); the protocol operates at the lowest sublayer of the data link layer and is based on the core subset of T1.602 (LAP-D). The frame relay data transfer protocol defined in T1.618/LAP-F Core is intended to support multiple simultaneous end-user protocols within a single physical channel. This protocol provides transparent transfer of user data and does not restrict the contents, format, or coding of the information, or interpret the structure.[6-10]

Frame relay technology as currently implemented commercially supports a "connection-oriented" permanent virtual circuit (PVC) service; in the future it may also support a switched virtual circuit (SVC) service. Switched implementations use the ITU-T Q.933 protocol for call setup. The PVC does not require call setup and call termination, but it obviously is not as efficient in resource utilization as SVC. All public network services at press time were PVC-based; user-owned frame relay processors also only support a PVC implementation. SVC frame relay service is expected to become available in 1994.

Three basic ways of using frame relay to connect LANs in general and imaging systems in particular are as follows:

1. Deploy a private frame relay network using frame relay processor(s). Instead of physical point-to-point links, this approach requires connecting the routers to the frame relay processor(s) with only a single physical link. Connection between various routers is accomplished with PVCs that are set up by the LAN administrator.

2. Utilize a PVC-based carrier-provided frame relay network. Instead of many physical point-to-point links, this approach requires connecting the routers to the carrier's switch with only a single physi-

cal link. Connection between various routers is accomplished with PVCs that are established at service subscription with the carrier.

3. Utilize a SVC-based carrier-provided frame relay network. Connection between various routers is accomplished as needed by establishing a real-time SVC that is in existence only for the duration of the session.

### 9.3.5  Switched multimegabit data service

SMDS is similar in some respects to frame relay service in that it provides, from the user's point of view, a "cloud" of switches and trunks, eliminating the need for dedicated point-to-point links. However, there are some substantial differences as follows:[10,11]

1. SMDS operates at 1.544 Mbps (1.17 Mbps actual) and 44.736 Mbps (34 Mbps actual); hence, it is better suited for the evolving LAN applications in general and imaging in particular. (There is also work under way for access at $n \times 64$ kbps.[12]) It is a connectionless service, while frame relay is connection-oriented.

2. The user needs a device (such as a router) to run the SMDS interface protocol (SIP), as contrasted to the FRI for frame relay.

3. The transit delay is smaller than that experienced in a frame relay network (guaranteed to 20 ms 95 percent of the time with DS3/T3 access) and is tightly controlled by the network, as are other grade-of-service parameters (lost cells, misrouted cells, etc.); this is far from being the case in a frame relay network.

4. SMDS is a robust carrier-grade service. Sophisticated management and operations features are built into SMDS to facilitate its administration and monitor service quality. Security is also guaranteed.

5. Traffic can be input at the T1 or T3 rate (as well as other rates in between). SMDS may support SONET rates in the future.

6. SMDS is a "connectionless" service; that is, no call setup or teardown is needed, making it faster.

There are several documented applications of SMDS in support of imaging applications. Figure 9.9 depicts the use of SMDS for BIS, DIS, EIS, and SIS (PACS) applications. SMDS is starting to become widely available from the Bell Operating Companies in a 1993 time frame.

### 9.3.6  Cell relay service

Asynchronous transfer mode, as the term is used in the common parlance, refers to a high-bandwidth, low-delay switching and multiplexing technology now becoming available for both public and private net-

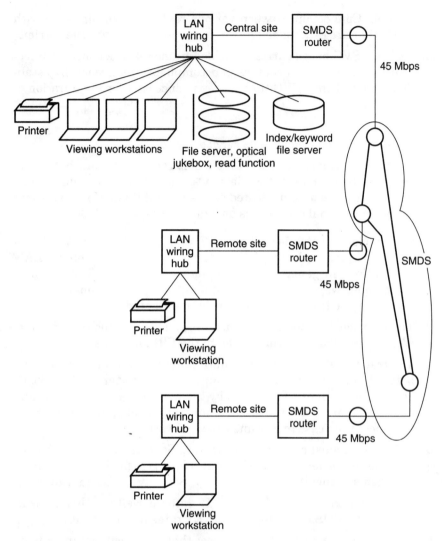

**Figure 9.9** Use of SMDS to support BIS, DIS, and SIS applications.

works. While ATM in the strict sense is simply a (data link layer) protocol, ATM principles and ATM-based platforms form the foundation for a variety of high-speed digital communication services aimed at corporate users for high-speed data, LAN interconnection, imaging, and multimedia applications. Residential applications, such as video distribution, videotelephony, and other information-based services, are also planned. ATM is the technology of choice for evolving broadband integrated services digital network (B-ISDN) public networks, for next-generation LANs, and for high-speed seamless interconnection of

LANs and WANs. ATM supports transmission speeds of 155 and 622 Mbps now, and can go as high as 13 Gbps in the future. As an option, ATM will operate at DS3 (45 Mbps); some are also looking at operating at DS1 (1.544 Mbps).

Cell relay service (CRS) is one of the key services enabled by ATM. Cell relay service* can be utilized for enterprise networks that use completely private communication facilities, completely public communication facilities, or that are hybrid. Cell relay service supports a variety of evolving applications such as desk-to-desk videoconferencing, multimedia conferencing, multimedia messaging, distance-learning, imaging tasks (including CAD/CAM), animation, and cooperative-work (e.g., joint-document editing). Cell relay is one of three "fast packet" technologies that have entered the scene recently (the other two are frame relay service and SMDS). A generic ATM platform can support cell relay service, frame relay service, SMDS, and circuit emulation.

The year 1993 saw the culmination of 9 years of ATM standard-making efforts. Work started in 1984 and experienced an acceleration in the late 1980s and early 1990s. With the ITU-T standards and the ATM Forum implementers' agreements, both sets of which emerged in 1993, the technology is ready for introduction in the corporate environment. A variety of vendors are now readying end-user products for 1994 market introduction; some prototype products have already been on the market for a couple of years. A number of carriers either already provide services or are poised to do so in the immediate future.

The main aspect of B-ISDN is the support of a wide range of data, video, and voice applications in the same public network. A key element of service integration is the provision of a range of services using a limited number of connection types and multipurpose user-network interfaces. ATM support both switched (SVC) and nonswitched (PVC) connections. ATM supports services requiring both circuit-mode and packet-mode information transfer capabilities. ATM can be used to support both connection-oriented and connectionless services (e.g., SMDS).[13]

**ATM protocol model, an overview.**  As noted, ATM's functionality corresponds to the physical layer and *part* of the data link layer of the OSIRM. This protocol functionality needs to be implemented in appropriate user equipment (e.g., routers) and in appropriate network elements (e.g., switches and service multiplexers). A *cell* is a block of information of short fixed length (53 octets) that comprises an overhead section and a payload section (5 of the 53 octets are for "overhead" and

---

*The term *cell relay* is used synonymously with *cell relay service*. The term *ATM* used by itself refers to the underlying technology, platform, and principles. *B-ISDN* refers to the overall blueprint for the evolution of public networks.

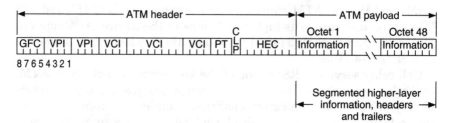

Figure 9.10   ATM cell.

48 are for user information), as shown in Fig. 9.10. Effectively, the cell corresponds with the data link layer frame that is taken as the atomic building block of this service. The term *cell relay* is used since ATM transports user cells reliably and expeditiously across the network interface to the destination. *ATM* is a transfer mode in which the information is organized into cells; it is asynchronous in the sense that the recurrence of cells containing information from an individual user is not necessarily periodic.

The ATM architecture utilizes a logical protocol model to describe the functionality it supports. The ATM logical model is composed of a user plane, a control plane, and a management plane. The *user plane,* with its layered structure, provides for user information transfer. Above the physical layer, the ATM layer provides information transfer for all applications the user may want to have; the ATM adaptation layer (AAL) provides service-dependent functions to the layer above the AAL. In approximate terms the AAL supplies the balance of the data link layer not included in the ATM layer. It supports error checking, multiplexing, segmentation, and reassembly. The *control plane* also has a layered architecture and performs the call control and connection functions. Specifically, the layer above the AAL in the control plane provides call control and connection control. It deals with the signaling necessary to set up, supervise, and release connections. The *management plane* provides network supervision functions. It provides two types of functions: layer management and plane management. Plane management performs management functions related to a system as a whole and provides coordination among all planes; layer management performs management functions relating to resources and parameters residing in its protocol entities (see Fig. 9.11).

As noted, four "user plane" protocol layers are needed to undertake communication, for example, in support of imaging:

1. A layer below the ATM layer, corresponding to the physical layer. The function of the physical layer is to manage the actual medium-dependent transmission. SONET is the technology of choice for speeds greater than 45 Mbps.

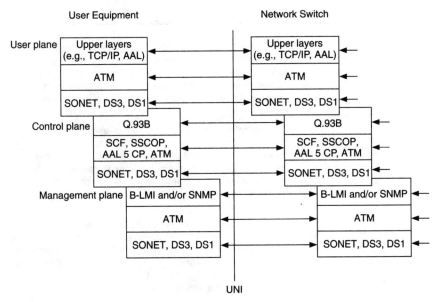

User Equipment                                    Network Switch

**Figure 9.11**   Planes constituting the ATM protocol model. UNI = user-network interface.

2. The ATM layer (equating approximately to the upper part of a LAN's MAC layer), which has been found to meet the stated objectives of throughput, scalability, interworking, and consistency with international standards. The function of the ATM layer is to provide efficient multiplexing and switching, using cell relay mechanisms.

3. The layer above the ATM layer, that is, the AAL. The function of the AAL is insulate the upper layers of the user's application protocols (e.g., TCP/IP) from the details of the ATM mechanism.

4. Upper layers, as needed. These include TCP/IP, IBM APPN, and OSI TP.

SVC service needs both an information transfer protocol stack and a companion signaling protocol stack. Early PVC service users do not need the signaling stack. This situation is analogous to the early PVC frame relay environment; SVC frame relay service planned by some carriers for the future would also require the signaling stack.

**ATM applications.**   Two main service categories have been identified (from the network point of view): (1) interactive broadband services and (2) distributive broadband services (see Table 9.1).[14] Figure 9.12 depicts the use of a cell relay in support of LAN interconnection for distributed imaging applications.

**TABLE 9.1    Broadband Services Supported by ATM/Cell Relay**

| Interactive services | *Conversational services*—provide the means for bidirectional communication with real-time, end-to-end information transfer between users or between users and servers. Information flow may be bidirectional symmetric or bidirectional asymmetric. Examples: high-speed data transmission, image transmission, videotelephony, and videoconferencing. |
|---|---|
| | *Messaging services*—provide user-to-user communication between individual users via storage units with store-and-forward, mailbox, and/or message handling (e.g., information editing, processing, and conversion) functions. Examples: message handling services, and mail services for moving pictures (films), store-and-forward images, and audio information. |
| | *Retrieval services*—allow users to retrieve information stored in information repositories (information is sent to the user on demand only). The time at which an information sequence is to start is under the control of the user. Examples: film, high-resolution images, information on CD-ROMs, and audio information. |
| Distributive services | *Distribution services without user individual presentation control*—these broadcast services provide a continuous flow of information that is distributed from a central source to an unlimited number of authorized receivers connected to the network. User can access this flow of information without the need to determine at which instant the distribution of a string of information will be started. User cannot control the start and order of the presentation of the broadcast information, so that depending on the point of time of the user's access, the information will not be presented from its beginning. Examples: broadcast of television and audio programs. |
| | *Distribution services with user individual presentation control*—provide information distribution from a central source to a large number of users. Information is rendered as a sequence of information entities with cyclical repetition. The user has the ability of individual access to the cyclically distributed information, and can control the start and order of presentation. Example: broadcast videography. |

**Equipment availability.**   As with any other service, there is at least a triumvirate at play to make this technology a commercial reality (if any other of these three parties fails to support the service, it will not see any measurable deployment): (1) carriers must deploy the service, (2) equipment manufacturers must bring products to the market, and (3) users must be willing to incorporate the service in their networks.

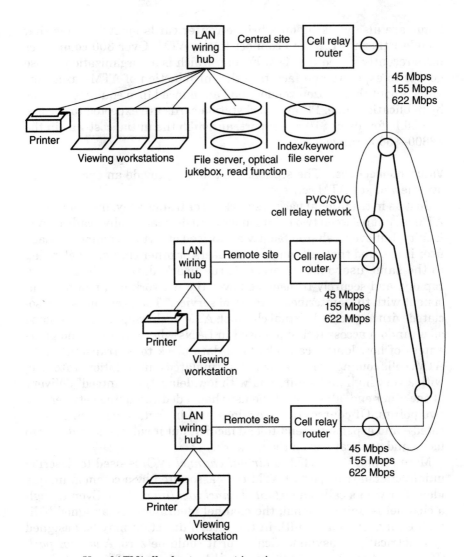

**Figure 9.12** Use of ATM/cell relay to support imaging.

[Some observers add two more forces: (1) agencies supporting R&D and standardization and (2) trade press to "educate" the end users.]

It is likely that, by the end of 1994, there will be a dozen ATM hub vendors and a dozen ATM workstation vendors. Some equipment vendors are building standalone switches; others are adding switching capabilities to their hubs and at the same time are developing ATM adapter cards for workstations to allow them to connect to the hub.

Some are also working on a bridge-router cards for ATM hubs that enable Ethernet LANs to connect to the ATM. Over 300 companies have recently joined the ATM Forum, which is an organization whose goal is to expedite and facilitate the introduction of ATM-based services. About three dozen vendors had announced firm equipment plans by publication time. PC and workstation cards are expected to become available for about $1000 per port, although the initial cost was in the $2800–$5000 range.

**Virtual connections.**    The sections that follow provide an encapsulated overview of key ATM concepts.

Just as in traditional packet switching or frame relay, information in ATM is sent between two points, not over a dedicated, physically owned facility, but over a shared facility comprised of virtual channels.* Each user is assured that, although other users or other channels belonging to the same user may be present, the user's data can be reliably, rapidly, and securely transmitted over the network in a manner consistent with the subscribed "quality of service." The user's data is associated with a specified virtual channel. ATM's "sharing" is not the same as a random access technique used in LANs where there are no guarantees of how long it can take for a data block to be transmitted. In ATM, cells coming from the user at a stipulated (subscription) rate, are, with a very high probability and with low delay, "guaranteed" delivery at the other end, almost as if the user had a dedicated line between the two points. Of course, the user does not, in fact, have such a dedicated—and expensive—end-to-end facility, but it will seem that way to users and applications on the network.

More formally, in ATM, a *virtual channel* (VC) is used to describe unidirectional transport of ATM cells associated by a common unique identifier value, called a *virtual channel identifier* (VCI). Even though a channel is unidirectional, the channel identifiers are assigned bidirectionally. The bandwidth in the return direction may be assigned symmetrically or asymmetrically, or it could be zero. A *virtual path* (VP) is used to describe unidirectional transport of ATM cells belonging to virtual channels that are associated by a common identifier value, called a *virtual path identifier* (VPI). See Fig. 9.13. VPIs are viewed by some as a mechanism for hierarchical addressing. The VPI/VCI address space allows in theory up to 16 million virtual connections over a single interface; however, most vendors are building equipment supporting (a minimum of) 4096 channels on the user's interface. Note that these labels are only locally significant (at a given

---

*The access lines are "owned" by the user, but the WAN facilities are shared.

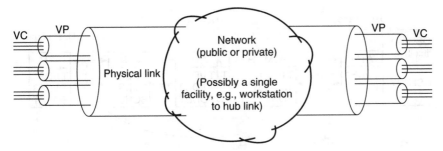

**Figure 9.13**   Relationship of VCs and VPs.

interface). They may undergo remapping in the network; however, there is an end-to-end identification of the user's stream so that data can flow reliably. Also note that on the network trunk side more than 4096 channels per interface are supported.

Cells are identified and switched by means of the label in the header, as seen in Fig. 9.10. Cell relay service allows for a dynamic transfer rate, specified on a per-call basis. Transfer capacity is assigned by negotiation and is based on the source requirements and the available network capacity. Cell sequence integrity on a virtual channel connection is preserved by ATM.

**ATM protocols overview.**   Figure 9.14 depicts the cell relay protocol environment, which is a particularization of the more general B-ISDN protocol model described earlier.

**Physical layer functions.**   The physical layer consists of two *logical* sublayers: the *physical-medium-dependent* (PMD) sublayer and the *transmission convergence* sublayer. PMD includes only physical-medium-dependent functions. It provides bit transmission capability, including bit transfer, bit alignment, line coding, and electrical-to-optical conversion. Transmission convergence performs functions required to transform a flow of cells into a flow of information (i.e., bits) that can be transmitted and received over a physical medium. Transmission convergence functions include (1) transmission frame generation and recovery, (2) transmission frame adaptation, (3) cell delineation, (4) header error control (HEC) sequence generation and cell header verification, and (5) cell rate decoupling.

The transmission frame adaptation function performs the actions that are necessary to structure the cell flow according to the payload structure of the transmission frame (transmit direction) and to extract this cell flow out of the transmission frame (receive direction). The transmis-

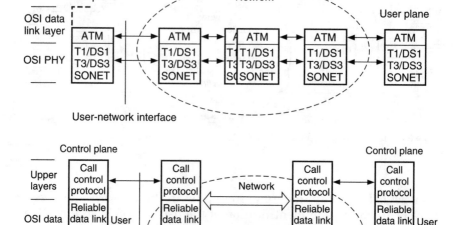

**Figure 9.14** CRS environment. Top: user plane (information flow). Bottom: control plane (signaling).

sion frame requires (in the United States) SONET envelopes. Cell delineation prepares the cell flow in order to enable the receiving side to recover cell boundaries. In the transmit direction, the ATM cell stream is scrambled. In the receive direction, cell boundaries are identified and confirmed and the cell flow is descrambled. The HEC mechanism covers the entire cell header, which is available to this layer by the time the cell is passed down to it. The code used for this function is capable of either single-bit correction or multiple-bit error detection. The transmitting side computes the HEC field value. Cell rate decoupling includes insertion and suppression of idle cells, in order to adapt the rate of valid ATM cells to the payload capacity of the transmission system.

The service data units crossing the boundary between the ATM layer and the physical layer constitute a flow of valid cells. The ATM layer is unique, that is, independent of the underlying physical layer. The data flow inserted in the transmission system payload is physical-medium-independent and is self-supported; the physical layer merges the ATM cell flow with the appropriate information for cell delineation, according to the cell delineation mechanism.

In ATM, the transfer capacity at the user-network interface (UNI) is 155.52 Mbps, with a payload capacity of 149.76 Mbps. Since the ATM cell has 5 octets of overhead, the 48-octet information field equates to a maximum of 135.631 Mbps of actual user information. A second UNI interface is defined at 622.08 Mbps, with the service bit rate of approximately 600 Mbps. Access at these rates requires a fiber-based loop. Other UNIs are also being contemplated in the United States at the DS1 and DS3 rate. The DS1 UNI is discussed in the context of an electrical interface (T1); so is the DS3 UNI.

**ATM layer functions.** Connection identifiers are assigned to each link of a connection when required and are released when no longer needed. The label in each ATM cell is used to explicitly identify the VC to which the cells belong. The label consists of two parts: the VCI and the VPI. A VCI identifies a particular VC link for a given virtual path connection. A specific value of VCI is assigned each time a VC is switched in the network. With this in mind, one can define a VC as a unidirectional capability for the transport of ATM cells between two consecutive ATM entities where the VCI value is translated. A VC link is originated or terminated by the assignment or removal of the VCI value. ATM offers a flexible transfer capability common to all services, including connectionless services (if these are provided). The transport functions of the ATM layer are independent of the physical layer implementation.

The functions of ATM include

*Cell multiplexing and demultiplexing.* In the transmit direction, the cell multiplexing function combines cells from individual VPs and VCs into a noncontinuous composite cell flow. In the receive direction, the cell demultiplexing function directs individual cells from a noncontinuous composite cell flow to the appropriate VP or VC.

*Virtual path identifier and virtual channel identifier translation.* This function occurs at ATM switching points and/or cross-connect nodes. The value of the VPI and/or VCI fields of each incoming ATM cell is mapped into a new VPI and/or VCI value. (This mapping function could be null.)

*Cell header generation and extraction.* These functions apply at points where the ATM layer is terminated. The header error control field is used for error management of the header. In the transmit direction, the cell header generation function receives cell payload information from a higher layer and generates an appropriate ATM cell header except for the HEC sequence. In the receive direction, the cell header extraction function removes the ATM cell header and passes the cell information field to a higher layer.

For the UNI, as can be seen in Fig. 9.10, 24 bits are available for routing: 8 bits for the VPI and 16 bits for the VCI. Three bits are available for payload-type identification; this is used to indicate whether the cell payload contains user information or network information. In user information cells the payload consists of user information and service adaptation function information. In network information cells the payload does not form part of the user's information transfer. If the cell loss priority (CLP) is set (CLP value is 1), the cell is subject to discard, depending on the network conditions. If the CLP is not set (CLP value is 0), the cell has higher priority. The header error control field consists of 8 bits.

**ATM adaptation layer.** Additional functionality on top of the ATM layer (i.e., in the ATM adaptation layer) must be provided to accommodate various services. The ATM adaptation layer enhances the services provided by the ATM layer to support the functions required by the next-higher layer. The AAL function is typically implemented in the user's equipment.

Connections in an ATM network support both circuit mode and packet mode (connection-oriented and connectionless) services of a single medium and/or mixed media and multimedia. ATM supports two types of traffic: constant bit rate (CBR) and variable bit rate (VBR). CBR transfer rate parameters for on-demand services are negotiated at call setup time. (Changes to traffic rates during the call may eventually be negotiated through the signaling mechanism; however, initial deployments will not support renegotiation of bit rates.) CBR transfer rate parameters for permanent services are agreed with the carrier from which the user obtains service. This service would be used, for example, to transmit real-time video. VBR services are described by a number of traffic-related parameters (minimum capacity, maximum capacity, etc.). They support packet-like traffic (e.g., variable-rate video). The AAL protocols are used to support these different connection types. Image transfer may employ either CBR or VBR services.

The AAL performs functions required by the user, control, and management planes and supports the mapping between the ATM layer and the next-higher layer. Note that a different instance of the AAL functionality is required in each plane. The AAL supports multiple protocols to fit the needs of the different users; hence, the AAL is service-dependent (namely, the functions performed in the AAL depend on the higher-layer requirements). The AAL isolates the higher layers from the specific characteristics of the ATM layer by mapping the higher-layer protocol data units into the information field of the ATM cell and vice versa. The AAL entities exchange information with the peer AAL entities to support the AAL functions.

The AAL functions are organized in two logical sublayers: the convergence sublayer (CS) and the segmentation and reassembly sublayer (SAR). The function of CS is to provide the AAL service at the AAL-service access point; this sublayer is service-dependent. The functions of SAR are (1) segmentation of higher-layer information into a size suitable for the information field of an ATM cell and (2) reassembly of the contents of ATM cell information fields into higher-layer information.

In order to minimize the number of AAL protocols, a service classification is defined based on the following three parameters: (1) timing relation between source and destination (required or not required), (2) bit rate (constant or variable), and (3) connection mode (connection-oriented or connectionless). Other parameters such as assurance of the communication are treated as quality-of-service parameters, and therefore do not lead to different service classes for the AAL. The five classes of application are as follows:

*Class A*—timing required, bit rate constant, connection-oriented

*Class B*—timing required, bit rate variable, connection-oriented

*Class C*—timing not required, bit rate variable, connection-oriented

*Class D*—timing not required, bit rate variable, connectionless

*Class X*—unrestricted (bit rate variable, connection-oriented or connectionless)

Three AAL protocols have been defined in support of these applications: AAL Type 1, AAL Type 3/4, and AAL Type 5. Type 1 supports Class A; Type 3/4 supports Class D; Type 5 supports Class X. It appears that the computer communication community (building LAN and multiplexing equipment) will use AAL Type 5. Additionally, the ATM service likely to be available first (and the one supported by evolving computer equipment) is the one related to Class X, known as *broadband connection-oriented bearer service*—Class X (i.e., cell relay service).

Note that two stacks must be implemented in the user's equipment in order to obtain VCs on demand (i.e., SVC service) from the network. With this capability, the user can set up and take down multiple connections at will. Initially only PVC service will be available. In this mode, the control plane stack is not required, and the desired connections are established at service initiation time and remain active for the duration of the service contract. Also note that AAL functions (SAR and CS) must be provided by the user equipment (except in the case where the network provides interworking functions). Also, the user equipment must be able to assemble and disassemble cells (i.e., run the ATM protocol).

### 9.3.7    Multiprotocol routers

In some LAN interconnection cases it may be desirable to utilize multiple WAN services, based on a variety of considerations (availability, cost, bandwidth, etc.). In this case the user would employ a multiprotocol router, as shown in Fig. 9.15.

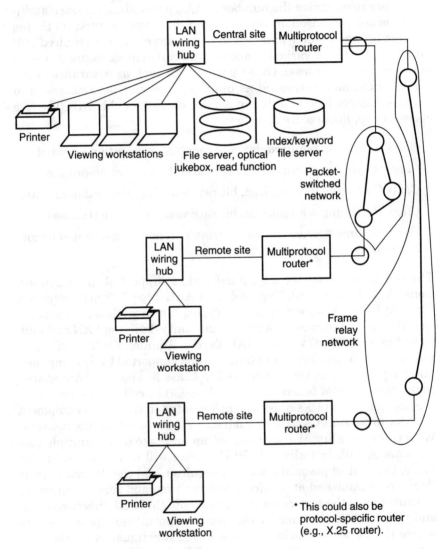

**Figure 9.15**  Use of multiprotocol routers.

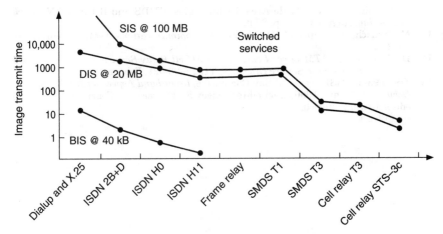

**Figure 9.16**  Transmission time for images when using switched WAN services.

### 9.3.8  Image transmission time

Figure 9.16 depicts the approximate transmission time when utilizing switched services (i.e., not including protocol overhead) for various imaging systems, predicated on the image sizes of Fig. 9.1. As can be noted, BISs can do reasonably well on a number of low- and medium-speed switched WAN communication services. DISs and SISs (including PACSs) may be better off with higher-speed services, particularly cell relay service/ATM.

### References

1. D. Minoli, "Internetworking LANs: Repeaters, Bridges, Routers & Gateways," *Network Computing,* October 1990, pp. 96 ff.
2. D. Minoli, "Connecting LANs to WANs, Low Speed, Non-Switched Solutions," *Network Computing,* November 1990, pp. 86 ff.
3. D. Minoli, "Interconnecting LANS over a Wide Area: High Speed, Non-Switched Solutions," *Network Computing,* December 1990, pp. 82 ff.
4. D. Minoli, "Interconnecting LANS over a Wide Area: Switched Solutions," *Network Computing,* February 1991, pp. 81 ff.
5. D. Minoli, *1st, 2nd, and Next Generation LANs,* McGraw-Hill, New York, 1994.
6. A. Tumolillo, *Frame Relay vs. SMDS vs. T1, The Best Technology/Service Fit for Networked Applications,* Probe Research, Cedar Knolls, NJ, 1992.
7. AT&T Network Systems, *The Frame Relay Alternative, A Network Manager's Guide to Understanding, Evaluating, and Implementing a Private Frame Relay Network,* Document 55-300-915.
8. D. Minoli, *Technology Overview: Frame Relay,* Datapro Report CA09-020-501, January 1991.
9. D. Minoli, "The New Wide Area Networking Technologies: Frame Relay," *Network Computing,* May 1991, pp. 102 ff.
10. D. Minoli, *Enterprise Networking, Fractional T1 to SONET, Frame Relay to B-ISDN,* Artech House, Norwood, MA, 1993.

11. D. Minoli, "The New Wide Area Technologies: SMDS and B-ISDN," *Network Computing*, August 1991, pp. 88 ff.
12. M. Strizich, "Low Speed SMDS in Focus," *Communications Week*, November 30, 1992.
13. D. Minoli et al., *ATM Layer Bearer Service/Cell Relay Service Extended Stage 1 Description for Public Service Offerings*, T1S1.5/93-021, February 1993.
14. T1S1.5/93-52, T1S1 Technical Sub-Committee, *Broadband Aspects of ISDN Baseline Document*, August 1990, chief editor Rajeev Sinha; reissued February 1993, chief editor Erwin Fandrich.

# Additional Reading

The present text aims at a pragmatic review of this field, from the perspective of a corporate planner. Readers wishing additional details, perspectives, or analytical machinery may consult any of the following texts. No individual should expect to learn a technical topic from a single book.

## Textbooks

Avedon, D. M., *Introduction to Electronic Imaging,* Avedon Associates, Potomac, MD, 1992.

Avedon, D. M., and J. R. Levy, *Electronic Imaging Systems,* McGraw-Hill, New York, 1993.

Chellappa, R., *Digital Image Processing,* IEEE Computer Society Press, Los Alamitos, CA, 1992.

CIE, *Colorimetry,* 2d ed., Publication No. 15.2, Central Bureau of the Commision Internationale de L'Eclairage, A-1033 Vienna, P.O. Box 169, Austria, 1986.

Clarke, R. J., *Transform Coding of Images,* Academic Press, London, 1985.

Daily, F. E., Jr., *Implementing Image Technology for the 1990s,* Computer Technology Research, 1993.

Dove, B., *Printing Technologies for Images, Gray Scale and Color,* SPIE (International Society of Optical Engineering), Vol. 1458, SPIE Optical Engineering Press, Bellingham, WA, 1991.

Durrett, J., *Color and the Computer,* Academic Press, San Diego, 1987.

Gersho, A., and R. Gray, *Vector Quantization and Signal Compression,* Kluwer Academic, Norwell, MA, 1992.

Gonzalez, R. C., and P. Wintz, *Digital Image Processing,* 2d ed., Addison-Wesley, Reading, MA, 1987.

Hsing, T. R., and A. G. Tescher, *Selected Papers on Visual Communications: Technology and Applications,* SPIE Milestone Series, Vol. MS13, SPIE Press, Bellingham, WA, 1990.

Jain, A. K., *Fundamentals of Digital Image Processing,* Prentice-Hall, Englewood Cliffs, NJ, 1989.

Jensen, J. R., *Introductory Digital Image Processing—a Remote Sensing Perspective,* Prentice-Hall, Englewood Cliffs, NJ, 1986.

Kasturi, R., and M. M. Trivedi, *Image Analysis Applications,* Marcel Dekker, New York, 1990.

Lim, J. S., *Two-Dimensional Signal and Image Processing,* Prentice-Hall, Englewood Cliffs, NJ, 1990.

Muller, N. J., *Computerized Document Imaging Systems: Technology and Applications,* Artech House, Norwood, MA, 1993.

Netravali, A. N., and B. G. Haskell, *Digital Pictures: Representation and Compression,* Plenum Press, New York, 1988.

Nickblack, W., *An Introduction to Digital Image Processing,* Prentice-Hall, Englewood Cliffs, NJ, 1985.

Nier, M., *Standards for Electronic Imaging Systems,* SPIE Milestone Series, Vol. MS13, SPIE Press, Bellingham, WA, 1991.

Pearson, D., *Image Processing,* McGraw-Hill, New York, 1992.

Pratt, W. K., *Digital Image Processing,* 2d ed., Wiley-Interscience, New York, 1991.

Rabbani, M., *Image Coding and Compression,* SPIE Optical Engineering Press, Bellingham, WA, 1992.

Rabbani, M., and P. W. Jones, *Digital Image Compression Techniques,* SPIE Optical Engineering Press, Bellingham, WA, 1992.

Ranade, S., *Jukebox and Robotic Libraries for Computer Mass Storage,* Meckler, Westport, CT, 1992.

Ranade, S., *Mass Storage Technologies,* Meckler, Westport, CT, 1991.

Rao, K. R., and P. Yip, *Discrete Cosine Transform: Algorithms, Advantages, Applications,* Academic Press, San Diego, 1990.

Roth, J. P., *Case Studies of Optical Storage Applications,* Meckler, Westport, CT, 1991.

Russ, J. C., *The Image Processing Handbook,* CRC Press, Boca Raton, FL, 1992.

Saffady, W., *Electronic Imaging Systems: Design, Evaluation and Implementation,* Meckler, Westport, CT, 1992.

Saffady, W., *Optical Storage Technology 1992—a State of the Art Review,* Meckler, Westport, CT, 1992.

Schreiber, W. F., *Fundamentals of Electronic Imaging Systems,* Springer-Verlag, New York, 1986.

Sincerbox, G. T., and J. M. Zavislan, *Optical Storage,* SPIE Optical Engineering Press, Bellingham, WA, 1992.

Storer, J. A., *Image and Text Compression,* Kluwer Academic Publishers, Boston, 1992.

Tapper, C., and K. Tombs, *The Legal Admissibility of Document Imaging Systems,* Meckler, Westport, CT, 1992.

## Papers and Journals

(*Note:* Several thousand papers have been published in the past 10 years; this short list is based partially on M. Rabbani, *Selected Papers on Image Coding and Compression,* SPIE Milestone Series, Vol. MS 48, Bellingham, WA.)

### Special issues

Special Issue on Digital Image Processing and Applications, *IEEE Trans. Circuits Syst.,* November 1987.

Special Issue on Low-Bit-Rate Coding of Moving Images, *IEEE J. Select. Areas Commun.,* August 1987.

Special Issue on Visual Communication Systems, *Proc. IEEE,* April 1985.

Special Issues on Visual Communications and Image Processing, *Opt. Eng.,* July 1987, July 1989, July 1991.

### Articles

Anastassious, D., et al., "Gray-scale Image Coding for Freeze-Frame Videoconferencing," *IEEE Trans. Commun.* **COM-34**(4), 382–394 (April 1986).

Chou, P. A., T. Lookabaugh, and R. M. Gray, "Entropy-Constrained Vector Quantization," *IEEE Trans. Acoust., Speech, Signal Process.* **37**(1), 31–42 (Jan. 1989).

Chou, P. A., T. Lookabaugh, and R. M. Gray, "Optimal Pruning with Applications to Tree-structured Source Coding and Modeling," *IEEE Trans. Inform. Theory* **35**(2), 299–315 (March 1989).

Cox, J. R., Jr., et al., "Optimization of Trade-offs in Error-free Image Transmission," *Medical Imaging III, Proc. SPIE* **1091**, 19–30 (Feb. 1989).

Darragh, J. C., and R. L. Baker, "Fixed Distortion Subband Coding of Images for Packet-Switching Networks," *IEEE J. Select. Areas Commun.* **7**(5), 789–800 (June 1989).

Daugman, J., "Complete Discrete 2-D Gabor Transforms by Neural for Image Analysis and Compression," *IEEE Trans. Acoust., Speech, Signal Process.* **36**(7), 1169–1179 (July 1988).

Equitz, W. H., "A New Vector Quantization Clustering Algorithm," *IEEE Trans. Acoust., Speech, Signal Process.* **ASSP-37**(10), 1568–1575 (Oct. 1989).

Kanefski, M., and C. Fong, "Predictive Source Coding Techniques Using Maximum Likelihood Prediction for Compression of Digitized Images," *IEEE Trans. Inform. Theory* **IT-30** (5), 722–727 (Sept. 1984).

Langdon, G. G., "An Introduction to Arithmetic Coding," *IBM J. Res. Dev.* **28**(2), 135–149 (1984).

Le Gall, D., and A. Tabatabai, "Sub-band Coding of Digital Image Using Symmetric Kernel Filters and Arithmetic Coding Techniques," *Proc. ICASSP*, 764 (April 1988).

Lema, M. D., and O. R. Mitchell, "Absolute Moment Block Truncation Coding and Its Application to Color Images," *IEEE Trans. Commun.* **COM-32**(10), 1148–1157 (Oct. 1984).

Lempel, A., and J. Ziv, "Compression of Two-dimensional Data," *IEEE Trans. Inform. Theory* **IT-32**(1), 2–8 (Jan. 1986).

Limb, J. O., and C. B. Rubinstein, "On the Design of Quantizers for DPCM Coders: A Functional Relationship Between Visibility, Probability, and Masking," *IEEE Trans. Commun.* **COM-26**(5), 573–578 (May 1978).

Mallat, S. G., "Multifrequency Channel Decompositions of Images and Wavelet Models," *IEEE Trans. Acoust., Speech, Signal Process.* **37**(12), 209–211 (Dec. 1989).

Martens, J. B., "Application of Scale to Image Coding," *IEEE Trans. Commun.* **38**(9), 1585–1591 (Sept. 1990).

Ramabadran, T. V., and K. Chen, "Efficient Compression of Medical Images through Arithmetic Coding," *Medical Imaging IV, Proc. SPIE* **1234**, 761–776 (1990).

Rioul, O., and M. Vetterli, "Wavelets and Signal Processing," *IEEE Spectrum Magazine,* October 1991, pp. 14–38.

Rissanen, J., and K. M. Mohiuddin, "A Multiplication-free Multialphabet Arithmetic Code," *IEEE Trans. Commun.* **37**(2), 93–98 (1989).

Smith, M. J., and S. L. Eddins, "Analysis/synthesis Techniques for Subband Image Coding," *IEEE Trans. Acoust., Speech, Signal Process.* **38**(8), 1446–1456 (Aug. 1990).

Tood, S., et al., "Parameter Reduction and Context Selection for Compression of Grayscale Images," *IBM J. Res. Dev.* **29**(2), 188–193 (March 1985).

Vitter, J. S., "Design and Analysis of Huffaman Codes," *J. ACM* **34**(4), 825–845 (Oct. 1987).

Ziv, J., and A. Lempel, "A Universal Algorithm for Sequential Data Compression," *IEEE Trans. Inform. Theory* **IT-23**(3), 337–343 (May 1977).

# Acronyms

| | |
|---|---|
| AAL | ATM adaptation layer |
| ABIC | Adaptive bi-level image compression |
| AIMS | advanced image management system |
| AN/HP | Alphanumeric handprint recognition |
| APPI | Advanced Peer-to-Peer Internetworking (Cisco) |
| APPN | Advanced Peer-to-Peer Networking (IBM) |
| ATM | Asynchronous transfer mode |
| B-ISDN | Broadband integrated services digital network |
| BCR | Bar code recognition |
| BIS | Business imaging system |
| CAD/CAM | Computer-aided design/computer-aided manufacturing |
| CAT | Computer-aided tomography |
| CBR | Constant bit rate |
| CCD | Charge-coupled device |
| CD-DA | Compact Disk Digital Audio (Philips-Sony) |
| CD-I | Compact Disk Interactive (Philips-Sony-Microware) |
| CD-R | CD-recordable |
| CD-RDX | CD-ROM read-only data exchange |
| CD-ROM | Compact disk read-only memory |
| CGA | Color graphics adapter |
| *CMYK* | Cyan, magenta, yellow, and black |
| CRS | Cell relay service |
| CSMA/CD | Carrier sense multiple access with collision detection |
| DAT | Digital audio tape |
| DCA | Document Content Architecture (IBM) |
| DCT | Discrete cosine transform |
| DIP | Document image processing |
| DIS | Desktop imaging system |
| DSX | CD-ROM Database Exchange Standard |

| | |
|---|---|
| DTP | Desktop publishing |
| EGA | Enhanced graphics adapter |
| EIS | Engineering imaging system |
| EPS | Encapsulated PostScript (Adobe Systems) |
| FDCT | Forward DCT |
| FDDI | Fiber distributed data interface |
| FRI | frame relay interface |
| GIF | Graphic Interchange Format (CompuServe Inc.) |
| GUI | Graphical User Interface (Microsoft) |
| HDTV | High-definition television |
| ICR | Intelligent character recognition |
| IDCT | Inverse DCT |
| IEEE | Institute of Electrical and Electronic Engineers |
| IGES | Initial graphics exchange specification |
| IOCA | Image Object Content Architecture (IBM) |
| ISDN | Integrated services digital network |
| ITU-T | International Telecommunications Union— Telecommunications (formerly, CCITT) |
| JBIG | Joint Bi-level Image Expert Group (ITU-T/ISO) |
| JPEG | Joint Photographic Expert Group (ITU-T/ISO compression standard) |
| LAN | Local area network |
| LATM | Local ATM |
| LCD | Liquid-crystal display |
| LLC | Logical link control |
| LSR | Light signature recognition |
| MAC | Medium access control |
| MFLOPS | Million floating-point operations per second |
| MICR | Magnetic ink character recognition |
| MO | Magnetooptical |
| MRI | Magnetic resonance imaging |
| NHP | Numeric handprint recognition |
| NIC | Network interface card |
| OCR | Optical character recognition |
| ODA | Office Document Architecture (ISO) |
| ODIT | Optical digital imaging text |
| OMS | Optical mark sense |
| OSIRM | Open system interconnection reference model |
| PACS | Picture archival and communication system |

| | |
|---|---|
| PAD | Packet assembler/disassembler |
| PAL | Phase-alternation line |
| PDL | Page description language |
| PET | Positron emission tomography |
| PVC | Permanent virtual circuit |
| RAID | Redundant array of inexpensive disks |
| RAM | Random-access memory |
| *RGB* | Red, green, and blue |
| RISC | Reduced instruction set computer |
| RPC | Remote procedure calls |
| SCSI | Small computer system interface |
| SFQL | Structured full-text query language |
| SIS | Scientific imaging system |
| SMDS | Switched multimegabit data |
| SNA | Systems Network Architecture (IBM) |
| SONET | Synchronous optical network |
| SQL | Structured query language |
| STS-1 | Synchronous transport signal—level 1 |
| SVC | Switched virtual circuit |
| TCP/IP | Transmission control protocol/internet protocol |
| TIFF | Tagged image file format |
| UTP | Unshielded twisted pair |
| VBR | Variable bit rate |
| VCI | Virtual channel identifier |
| VGA | Video graphics adapter |
| VPI | Virtual path identifier |
| WAN | Wide area network |
| WIIS | Wang Integrated Imaging System |
| WORM | Write once read many |

# Index

## ABOUT THE AUTHOR

Daniel Minoli is an expert in the data communications and telecommunications fields with recent experience in multimedia and imaging. He has spent the past eight years at Bell Communications Research as a strategic data communications planner, with research aimed at supporting the internal data communications needs of the Bell Operating Companies, identifying data services that can be provided in the public network, designing large end-user networks, and working on cell relay/ATM signaling standards. He serves on DataPro's advisory board for broadband networking, speaks frequently at conferences, and is an adjunct associate professor at New York University's Information Technology Institute. Mr. Minoli has published approximately 200 technical and trade articles, is a contributing editor for *Network Computing*, and is the author of *1st, 2nd, and Next Generation LANs*, published by McGraw-Hill. Forthcoming from Mr. Minoli for McGraw-Hill are *Outsourcing IS and Communications Functions* and *ATM and Cell Relay Service for Corporate Environments*.